AND I SAW A RIVER

A History of the Catholic Church in Pointe Coupée, St. Mary of False River, & St. Francis Chapel

AND I SAW A RIVER:
A History of the Catholic Church in Pointe Coupée, St. Mary of False River, & St. Francis Chapel
Copyright © 2023 Brian J. Costello
All rights reserved by the author and publisher

Hardcover: ISBN-13: 978-1-950782-54-3
Paperback: ISBN-13: 978-1-950782-53-6
Holy Water Books. First Edition 2023.
Revised and expanded from the original.

HOLYWATERBOOKS

please check out our
other titles online at
www.holywaterbooks.com

Cover design by Holy Water Books

DEDICATION

To the greater glory of God and His Holy Name; and in memory of all those who have gone before us: our ancestors, whether they came to Pointe Coupée voluntarily or involuntarily, who colonized this community and instilled in us the Faith; and to the priests, religious and instructors who gave their lives in nurturing that Faith in us, that we might pass to future generations our most precious heritage.

EPIGRAPH

AND I SAW A RIVER
over which every soul must pass
to reach the Kingdom of Heaven,
and the name of that river was Suffering,
and then I saw a boat which carried souls across the river,
and the name of that boat was Love

– Saint John of the Cross

"And I saw a River," which has been taken as the title of this volume, is relevant not just to the eschatological nature of the Church from St. John's poem above, but is also appropriate to the Iberville travel account of exiting the portage and re-entering the Mississippi River at present-day Pointe Coupée.

"The old church of Sainte Marie is at one end, the big red courthouse with its deep-set porch at the other, and thus between the law and the prophets the town thrives....

Between me and the water there loomed a great cross – tall and black and heavy as the one once carried to the height of Calvary. It stood on the green before the church just as I have seen one like it in far-off Brittany, or in the olive hills of Tuscany. Its shadow leaned out and fell across the still waters, where stars seemed to enamel all its length. It almost reached the Island across the waterway. Somehow from no part of the village was that cross or its soft admonishing shadow invisible."

– Catherine Cole,
nom de plume of Martha R. Field
"Pointe Coupée Parish,"
New Orleans *Daily Picayune*,
Sunday, 29 November 1891

TABLE OF CONTENTS

TABLE OF IMAGES

Catholic History of Pointe Coupée Timeline

The following timeline and photographic feature, among several such photographic features included in this volume, was originally published in the St. Mary of False River Sunday Mass bulletin in anticipation of the Bicentennial Celebration of 2023.

St. Mary of False River Bicentennial Year 2023

Historical Highlights by Brian J. Costello

The year 2023, in addition to being designated The Year of the Eucharist, has special meaning for the local community, as it marks the bicentennial of the establishment of St. Mary of False River, as the first mission of historic St. Francis, "Mother Church of Pointe Coupee," in 1823.

In observance of the bicentennial, a 260-odd page, 8 ¼" by 11" format, illustrated volume, entitled *And I Saw a River: A History of the Catholic Church in Pointe Coupée, St. Mary of False River, & St. Francis Chapel*, is being produced by St. Mary parishioners Brian J. Costello and Scott L. Smith, Jr. Authored by Costello, it is his 29th book in Louisiana, European, and spiritual studies, and will be the latest title published by Smith through his company, Holy Water Books.

Though St. Mary's history proper began in 1823, the story of the Faith in Pointe Coupee Parish is one of the oldest in the Mississippi River Valley, and may be started to begin with Holy Mass celebrated for the Iberville expeditionary part in 1699. A timeline gleaned from the text of *And I Saw a River* will appear in the St. Mary Parish Bulletin in logical sections between this issue and the time of the chief bicentennial jubilee liturgy to be celebrated at St. Mary on 13 August 2023.

1699 – 1823

1699: First known celebration of the Holy Mass in what is now Pointe Coupee Parish, during return trip of Iberville party down Mississippi River.

1720: First European settlers, from Hainaut (in present-day Belgium), arrive in Pointe Coupee area.

1722-1723: First known missionary efforts begun at Pointe Coupee, by Franciscan Capuchin Fathers.

1727: Pointe Coupee is served by Jesuit missionaries from France, including Rev. Paul du Poisson, who performs the first recorded baptisms in the community, those of siblings Jean Louis and Marie Marguerite Homard.

1728: Maximin de Thionville, a Capuchin, is named first pastor of Pointe Coupee.

1738: The first St. Francis Church of Pointe Coupee is dedicated, likely just above the later site of Waterloo, Louisiana, with Rev. Anselm de Langres, Capuchin, as pastor. The church parish is designated in Latin as *Retusia* and the congregation as *Retusiani Retusianorum*.

St. Mary of False River founder, Lyon native Rev. Antoine Blanc, subsequently Fourth Bishop and First Archbishop of New Orleans.

St. Francis Chapel
1760 - 1892

1760: The first St. Francis Church, asserted to have been destroyed by a storm, is replaced by the second St. Francis Church, which stood until being dismantled in 1892 when its site, just northwest of the New Roads-Bayou Sara ferry crossing, crumbled into the Mississippi River.

1764: The St. Francis Cemetery is blessed and, like the church, survives until the site caves into the Mississippi River in the 1890s.

1776: Approximate date that Spanish authorities open a *Camino Real* (Royal Road) linking the Mississippi River to the north with False River to the south. The French call the thoroughfare the *Chemin Neuf* (New Road), from which the town of New Roads would adopt its name.

1798: The exiled Duc d'Orleans (future King Louise Philippe of France) and brothers, the Duc de Montpensier and the Comte de Beaujolais, are said to have visited the St. Francis *presbytere* (rectory) during their travel along the Mississippi Rivers.

1814: Corporation of the Roman Catholic Church of St. Francis of Pointe Coupee is recognized by the Louisiana legislature. The corporation is directed by a fabrique (board) of marguilliers (vestrymen) who conduct its civil affairs, often contrary to wishes of the pastors, until after the Civil War.

1822: Catherine Depau, nicknamed *La Fille Gougis* (Gougis' Daughter), a free woman of color, established a six-block, 20-lot subdivision at the front of her False River plantation: the genesis of the town of New Roads.

1823: Widow Marie Pourciau Robillard Olinde donates a lot immediately west of the Gougis subdivision at New Roads, upon which St. Francis of Pointe Coupee pastor Rev. Antoine Blanc has the first St. Mary of False River church built. Mass is first celebrated on All Saints' Day. St. Mary is a mission of St. Francis Church from 1823 until being elevated to parish status in 1865. The first church of St. Mary stood at the northwest corner of West Main and St. Mary Streets until demolition in 1907, when the present church was completed.

Marie Pourciau died in 1833, and was interred beneath the original St. Mary Church. Her remains were transferred to a brick subterranean vault below the Sacred Heart altar in the present church during its 1904-1907 construction. A merci (thanksgiving plaque) honoring her memory and benevolence is located nearby.

"Merci" plaque honoring Marie Pourciau located in the northwestern corner of St. Mary Church

St. Mary of False River's
Bicentennial Year 2023

1823 – 1896

Rev. Joseph Philibert Gutton
Pastor of St. Mary: 1865 - 1896

1823: The first recorded marriage at St. Mary of False River is that of Joseph Chustz and Melanie St. Cyr

1835: Rev. Antoine Blanc, former pastor of St. Francis-St. Mary, is named fourth Bishop of New Orleans. In 1851, he is elevated to first Archbishop of New Orleans

1841: A large cross is erected on the bank of False River, opposite St. Mary Church and a trans-False River ferry landing established there in 1847. This lot, marked by a large cross well into the 1890s, is called *Place de la Croix* (Square of the Cross)

1857: Immaculate Conception mission is established at Chenal on the Island of False River as a mission of St. Francis Church. By 1861 a church building is completed and Immaculate Conception is elevated to independent parish status that year

1865: Federal troops encamp on the Place de la Croix during a mission to capture Confederate soldiers in the New Roads area

1865: St. Mary of False River is elevated to independent parish status, with Rev. Joseph Philibert Gutton, native of Lyon, as first pastor. The church parish is designated in Latin as *Sancta Maria Interrupto Flumine*.

1865: St. Mary Cemetery is established on the New Road but, owing to two years of Mississippi River floods, the first burial – that of Amelina Olinde – was held in 1866

1869: After four years of abandonment due to storm damage, Mississippi River floods and legal issues, St. Mary Church is restored, enlarged and reopened for services by Father Gutton

1870: A chapel is established at New Texas Landing, Raccourci as a mission of St. Francis Church. In 1872, the New Texas mission is elevated to independent parish status, under the name Our Lady of Seven Dolors

1876: A bell, cast by Meneely & Kimberly foundry of Troy, New York and shipped down the Mississippi River via steamer *Robert E. Lee*, installed in old St. Mary Church; christened "Maria Seraphina" after its sponsors, Mrs. Seraphine Gosserand Richy and Mr. Jean Clair Cazayoux, is transferred to present St. Mary Church upon completion in 1907

1882: St. Mary Church properties suffer flood damage with four feet of water on Main Street and five feet of water in cemetery due to Mississippi River levee failures

1888-1892: Due to caving of the Mississippi river bank, several burials and markers are transferred from St. Francis to St. Mary Cemetery

1890: St. Mary Cemetery is flooded for seventh time since 1865 due to Mississippi River levee failures

Archbishop Napoleon Perche with clergy at St. Mary Bell Ceremony, 1876

First St. Mary Church,
photographed circa 1880s

1890: St. Francis, "Mother Church of Pointe Coupee," becomes a mission of Our Lady of Seven Dolors, parish of Raccourci; dating from 1760, dismantled in 1892; many furnishings and fixtures retained and moved into the 3rd (present) St. Francis church, completed in 1895 as a mission of Seven Dolors parish, on property donated by Jules Labatut, 4 miles upriver from 1760 church

1893: St. Mary associate pastor Rev. Auguste Rochard establishes a Catholic school for African-American children adjacent to the church. Enrollment is reported at 20 in 1895, but there is no further mention of the school after 1904

1895: Corporation of the Congregation of St. Mary Roman Catholic Church chartered, by which act the Archdiocese of New Orleans transfers all of St. Mary's property to congregation

1896: Beloved pastor Father Gutton dies and his funeral services and burial are reportedly the greatest-attended of all time in Pointe Coupee Parish, with an estimated 3,000 persons attending the Mass or lining the route of the cortege from the church to the cemetery.

1898 – 1958

1898: Old St. Mary Church, long regarded as inadequate in size for the growing population of New Roads, is enlarged by incorporation of its lateral, exterior galleries.

1904: Sisters of St. Joseph arrive in New Roads to establish St. Joseph Convent and School on Richy Street, the genesis of the present Catholic Interparochial School System of Pointe Coupee.

1904: Cornerstone for present St. Mary Church laid on December 4, under pastorate of Father Laroche.

1906: Town of New Roads builds water, and subsequently electric plant on foot of St. Mary Street and St. Mary's riverbank property, for which Town allows church free utilities, periodically renewed until being abrogated in early 21st century.

1907: Present St. Mary Church of Gothic Revival design by German-born New Orleans architect Theodore Brune, completed and dedicated on March 16, though the bell tower remains incomplete until 1929.

Above: Cornerstone as still seen in the western front of St. Mary
Right: New & Old St. Mary Churches, photographed together circa 1905

1915: Framed oil on canvas Stations of the Cross, copied from Old World originals, are installed in the church
1915: St. Mary Church Park developed as children's playground east of St. Mary
1917: Rev. John Hoes, pastor of St. Mary, and Mother (now Saint) Katherine Drexel correspond
1919: New Roads Council Knights of Columbus founded, and chartered in 1926 as Council No. 1998
1921: Munich stained glass windows by F.X. Zettler of Chicago, Illinois and representing the Glorious Mysteries of the Rosary installed in the Sanctuary

FIGURE 1: ST. MARY'S SANCTUARY, BEFORE AND AFTER
THE SECOND VATICAN COUNCIL

1922: Sanctuary vault above Main Altar stenciled in sky and angel motif, said painting covered during the 1950s

1922: Rev. Edward Hartnett, a Josephite Father, establishes St. Augustine Church in New Roads. St. Augustine church, school, cemetery, and Sisters of the Holy Ghost Convent all built on land donated by St. Mary Parish

1923: Catholic Daughters of the Americas "Court Maria Theresa" established at St. Mary

1924: Present St. Mary Rectory completed

1925: Interior lateral galleries and raised pulpit removed from St. Mary

1929: Crowning pinnacles and balustrade atop church bell tower, designed by Theodore Brune, with façade tympanum panels, executed by Italian cast stone artist Angelo Lachin, completed

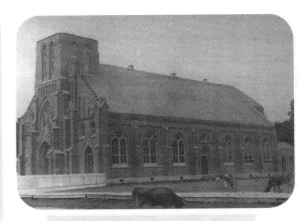

St. Mary of False River,
prior to construction of spires

St. Mary Rectory,
photographed in 1929

1931: Present organ, a 1917 model 433-pipe instrument by Hinners Organ Co. of Pekin, Ill. is installed

1936: Holy Name Society chartered at St. Mary

1936: Natural gas heaters installed in the church

1937: Nave and aisle vaults stenciled in garland and cartouche motif by artist A. Schnyder, said paintings covered during the 1950s

1937-1940: Munich stained glass windows by Emil Frei of St. Louis, Missouri and representing the Joyful and Sorrowful Mysteries of the Rosary, two of Christ's miracles and symbols of the Virgin Mary and the Church are installed in lateral walls of the church

1958: Air conditioning installed in the church

1961 - 2023

1961: St. Mary Church Parish is included in new Diocese of Baton Rouge, created from northernmost section of Archdiocese of New Orleans.

1962: Fr. A. J. LeBlanc, first American-born pastor of St. Mary, native of Lockport, La., assumes pastorate.

1962: St. Francis Chapel, dating from 1895 and formerly a mission of Our Lady of Seven Dolors and subsequently St. Ann Church Parish of Morganza, becomes a mission of St. Mary of False River.

1977-1979: Extensive restoration of church undertaken; altars reworked and tabernacle moved to side altar

1979: St. Mary Church is solemnly re-consecrated following completion of restoration project and 75th anniversary of laying of cornerstone of present church, arrival of the Sisters of St. Joseph and foundation of the present Catholic Interparochial School System are commemorated.

Fr. Frank Uter at dedication of St. Mary following restoration, December 9, 1979

Original Eucharistic Adoration Chapel

1979: St. Francis Chapel restored and listed on the National Register of Historic Places
1980: St. Mary Parish Hall, designed by parishioners A. Major Hebert and Glenn Morgan, is completed
1983: A large cross is re-erected on the Place de la Croix opposite the church for the first time in nearly a century
1992: Outward facing stained glass windows designed by parishioner Glenn Morgan and produced by Laukhuff Stained Glass Co. of Memphis, Tennessee and Mitchell-Marionneaux of Maringouin, Louisiana are installed in face of the church
1992: St. Joseph Center designed by Hebert & Morgan completed
1992: Perpetual Adoration of the Eucharist is begun in a small building adjacent to the Rectory
1997: Native Pointe Coupeean, St. Mary parishioner and St. Joseph Academy alumnus, former U.S. Congresswoman Corinne "Lindy" Claiborne Boggs is named U.S. Ambassador to the Holy See
2003: Portion of substantial bequest of late Murphy Porche to St. Mary-St. Francis church parish is employed in construction of Parish Office building and new Perpetual Adoration Chapel

2004: Celebration held to commemorate the 100th anniversary of the laying of the cornerstone of the present St. Mary church and to dedicate new Parish Office and Perpetual Adoration Chapel
2010: Marble Merci (thanksgiving) plaque in memory of St. Mary benefactress Marie Pourciau is installed near Blessed Sacrament Altar, beneath which is the subterranean crypt containing her remains
2016: $1.5 million renovation of St. Mary completed
2022: Tabernacle resumes place of honor on main altar reredos. Catholic Daughters of the Americas and Holy Name Society reactivated, and Guild of St. Stephen for altar servers established
2023: Bicentennial celebration for St. Mary of False River to be held on August 13, 2023

St. Mary of False River, photographed during 2016 renovations

A Eucharistic Community Since 1699

How fitting, and a sublime blessing, that the bicentennial of St. Mary of False River church of New Roads, Louisiana, occurred in the year 2023, that had been declared by His Holiness Pope Francis (born Mario Bergoglio): "The Year of the Eucharist."

New Roads, and Pointe Coupée Parish, Louisiana, of which it is governmental seat and center of the Faith, is center of one of the first Roman Catholic settlements in the Mississippi River Valley. From the celebration of the area's first known liturgy during the Iberville exploration of 1699, through the elaborate Corpus Christi processions of beloved *Pére* Joseph Philibert Gutton during the 19th century, and the establishment of Perpetual Adoration at St. Mary by Rev. Miles Walsh in 1992, until the present day, the faithful of Pointe Coupée have had a profound reverence, indeed for many, a foundation, in the Eucharistic Presence of Jesus Christ.

As a moving and timeless expression of the Faith and the honor accorded the Divine Prisoner of Love in the Blessed Sacrament, the following account of St. Mary's *Fete-Dieu* or Corpus Christi procession of 1885, during the pastorate of Pére Gutton, and published in the 13 June 1885 *Pointe Coupée Banner,* is reverently offered:

> The great solemnity of Corpus Christi (the French *Fete-Dieu*) was celebrated at St. Mary's Church, New Roads, with all the pomp and grandeur usually displayed by the Catholic Church on these occasions.
>
> Immediately after Vespers, the procession formed in line, headed by the banner of the Benevolent Society of St. Vincent de Paul and its members in full dress and regalia.
>
> A concourse of people seldom witnessed here, followed; then came the banner of the Holy Virgin, which had had to be borne for that day by a stout young man, escorted by the young ladies.
>
> The New Roads Brass Band came next, and by their skilled performances during the whole of the ceremony contributed largely to its *éclat.*
>
> In front of the canopy, under which Father [Pierre] Berthet, ever ready to assist his colleagues, held the Holy Sacrament, a group of young boys and little girls had been properly trained to execute various figures and changes, such as front rank by file, in semi-circle, a cross, and at each summons of the master of ceremonies a cloud of incense and flowers saluted the slowly advancing Sacrament.
>
> The procession moved first to the station or *réposoir* erected in Mr. Joseph Richy's front yard, in front of the newly finished [fire] engine house our village owes to his generosity — a temporary altar, adorned by the ladies with the good taste which distinguishes our Créoles.

After the first blessing, the column moved again without confusion, so had the marshal, Mr. W. [William] Morel, and his assistant, Mr. Charles H. LeBeau, taken their measures.

The canopy, which had hitherto been borne by the Catholic Knights of America, was then taken charge of by the Society of St. Vincent, and triumphantly carried amid the alternate songs of the choir and the lively strains of music of the band to the house of Mr. O.O. Provosty, where had been erected the second station.

Anyone who knows this beautiful residence [former Michel Olinde home] can imagine the scenery which presented itself when the priest, from the foot of the really splendid altar erected on the high front gallery, gave his blessing to the kneeling multitude in the yard.

The return to the church, and the third and last benediction by Father Berthet, closed the religious exercises of that Sunday, which will leave in our minds and hearts long and pleasant recollections.

"Long and pleasant recollections" is an apt term for most of the history of the Catholic faith in Pointe Coupée Parish and, in particular, that of mother church St. Francis of Assisi and its daughter parish and successor, St. Mary of False River.

The following chronicle traces the journey of the faithful of New Roads and Pointe Coupée Parish through centuries checkered by floods, hurricanes, epidemics, wartime occupation, crop failures, and socio-economic oppression. The community has been sustained throughout the vicissitudes of time and trial by its deep and childlike faith, ever hopeful, and shared in charity.

FIRST CAME THE FAITH

The Catholic faith journey in Pointe Coupée Parish is as old as the story of Louisiana itself, for the earliest European explorers – Spanish and French – who travelled the Mississippi River through that region of forest and lowland which would become known as Pointe Coupée, brought with them the Catholic religion. Centuries later, the Faith survives as the community's oldest institution.

While ascending the river in Lent of 1699, on 18 March, the Canadian explorers under Pierre LeMoyne, Sieur d'Iberville encountered a 22-mile-long horseshoe bend embracing a narrow portage.

The account of the expedition relates that Bayougoula Native American guides accompanying the Canadians convinced Iberville and his crew to save time on their journey by crossing the portage via a small channel, 350 feet long by six feet wide.

They did so, entered the main channel again, and camped on the riverbank where Iberville's younger brother, Jean Baptiste LeMoyne, Sieur de Bienville, cooked a meal, and the party spent the night, on what is now Pointe Coupée Parish soil.

Traveling further upriver the next day, they spent the night of the 19th again on the west bank of the Mississippi, just upriver of present-day Morganza, and on the 20th, reached their destination: the village of the Houma, on the east bank of the river, near present-day Angola, Louisiana.

FIGURE 2: SHIP'S BELL, DATED 1719, IS THE OLDEST KNOWN IN POINTE COUPEE PARISH

Careful analysis of the dates and distances recorded in Iberville's 1699 travel account suggests that the Holy Sacrifice of the Mass was offered on their return trip downriver, on the west bank somewhere between Morganza and the former New Roads-St. Francisville Ferry crossing. This is the first-known record of Holy Mass being offered in the region, and specifically in present-day Pointe Coupée Parish.

By 1722, periodic flooding caused the Mississippi River, in a natural geological process, to cut a new channel across the portage through which the explorers had paddled, leaving behind an oxbow lake. The early French settlers named the area *Pointe Coupée* (Cut Point), the oxbow lake left behind as *Fausse Riviere* (False River), and the point thus cut, surrounded by the old and new channels as *l'Ise de la Fausse Riviere* (The Island of False River).

The Mississippi continued flowing through the False River bend at times of high water, until the lower mouth of the oxbow was dammed in line with the Mississippi River levee near what was subsequently known as Hermitage, Louisiana by Joseph Leblanc de Villeneuve in 1835, and the same done to the upper mouth at Waterloo in 1842 by the State of Louisiana, using convict labor.

Pointe Coupée ranks as one of the oldest settlements in the Mississippi River valley. French *coureurs des bois* or woods runners from the Illinois area are said to have come through Pointe Coupée as early as 1708, this statement having come down through oral history of the LeBeau family, who had lived at Kaskaskia in Missouri before moving downriver to Pointe Coupée in the early Spanish period.

The first European families of record to settle permanently at Pointe Coupée included natives of the Hainaut province in what is now Belgium who arrived in 1720 as *engagés* or indentured laborers at Ste. Reyne Concession on the east bank of the Mississippi. Conflict with the hostile Natchez Native Americans and the financial collapse of the concession system of settlement resulted in these pioneers moving to the west bank of the Mississippi.

The 1727 census is the first to identify settlement on the west bank of the Mississippi River, in present-day Pointe Coupée Parish. Their surnames included Decuir, Decoux and Haussy from the original colonists, and additional ones such as LePorche (subsequently Porche) and Allain. They left countless descendants in Pointe Coupée and surrounding parishes, as have the Pourciau and Lacour families, who, had also arrived in the Louisiana colony aboard *La Loire*, in 1720.

From 1733 comes the first mention of a military redoubt or *poste* at Pointe Coupée, an institution which provided a sense of stability in this remote region of French Louisiana. The 30 April 1891 New Orleans *Daily Picayune* told of traces of trenches on what was then the plantation of Jean Arthur Porche, a mile up the Mississippi River from the Pointe Coupée

FIGURE 3: CYPRESS STATUE OF ST. FRANCIS OF ASSISI, REPUTEDLY CARVED BY TUNICA FAITHFUL CA. 18TH CENTURY

Parish port community of Waterloo. This same account claims that the military *poste* was moved from there to a point approximately five miles upriver, and a second St. Francis Church subsequently built adjacent to it.

CAPUCHIN AND JESUIT MISSIONARY WORK

The first recorded religious activity at Pointe Coupée comes from 1722-1723 when a Franciscan Capuchin Father from Metz named Philibert de Vianden included Pointe Coupée on his missionary tour up the Mississippi River.

Later, in 1727, Jesuit missionaries from France visited the area, and the earliest-known sacramental records of Pointe Coupée date from that year, attesting to the baptism of two children of pioneers Jean Baptiste and Marguerite Motel Homard by Fr. Paul DuPoisson: four-month-old Marie Marguerite Homard on 7 August and two-year-old Jean Baptiste Homard II on 21 August.

Late St. Mary parishioners, brothers Bernard Curet, a longtime editor and columnist of the *Pointe Coupée Banner*, and Louis D. Curet, a Baton Rouge attorney, were adamant in speech and writing that they were "descended from the first white child born in Pointe Coupée," a Marie Charlotte Gosserand, for whom they gave a birth date of 1 April 1728.

When informed that the sacramental records of Pointe Coupée did not indicate such, Louis Curet ascribed the date to "Mr. Alcée Fortier," who supposedly wrote that the record testifying to such had been "lost." Marie Charlotte Gosserand does appear in sacramental records, as a sister of the Curets' direct ancestor Antoine Gosserand, but born 28 October 1735 and baptized 1 April 1736 at Pointe Coupée.

While the Franciscan Capuchins ministered mainly to the French colonists, the Jesuits tended to concentrate their efforts toward the evangelization of the various Native Americans in the regions. Alas, Fr. Paul DuPoisson was among the colonists killed by the Natchez at present-day Natchez, Mississippi, in 1729.

Another missionary of the order, Pierre Vitry, S.J., occasionally visited during 1728-1735 and in 1737. He administered baptisms and performed marriages, making record of these sacramental acts on *feuilles volantes* ("flying," i.e. loose, sheets of paper). Nearly two decades later, in 1755, these sheets were inserted into a permanent register by Pierre de Luxembourg, O.F.M.Cap.

The church of Pointe Coupée is popularly said to date from 1728 for it was in that year that a Capuchin named Maximin de Thionville was named by the Capuchin Superior in New Orleans as pastor of the settlement.

Enslaved persons from Africa are first mentioned at Pointe Coupée in 1731. The earliest recorded baptism of a native African in the community was Louis, slave of Jean Baptiste Homard, on 28 August 1735. Sacramental records also indicated that group baptisms of slaves were made on Holy Saturdays and on Pentecost during the period around 1740.

The Africans at Pointe Coupée had diverse origins, including Senegal, Biafra, Benin, Angola and the Congo. Similarly, the French settlers were of different provinces of France, each area having its own dialect. The Pointe Coupée Créole language, which has an archaic French vocabulary and African sentence structure, as in French Caribbean communities, likely arose as a common language all could understand.

Speakers of more standard French, who practiced that language in Pointe Coupée Parish well into the 20th century, logically had to have a basic knowledge of Créole, in order to converse and do business with the majority of the population, both French and African-American, who understood only Créole.

In addition to the French colonists and the Africans, the names of Native Americans are frequent in the colonial sacramental records of Pointe Coupée, mainly of the Houma, Tunica, Biloxi, Ofo, and Tensas peoples. The Tunica in particular embraced Catholicism, as they were ministered to by the Capuchin fathers at the Tunica, former Houma, main village near present-day Angola, West Feliciana Parish.

The first baptism of Native Americans in the Pointe Coupée records appears to be of Jean Louis and Marie, of an unidentified nation, slaves of Jean Rondot, on 28 March 1739. Many of the Tunica had been baptized by the venerable Fr. Antoine Davion, O.F.M.Cap., in their former village, in present-day Southwestern Mississippi, when the prelate arrived as part of the LaSalle expedition in 1682.

Touching is the record of baptism of 27 Tunica children at the Tunica village by Fr. Anselm de Langres, O.F.M.Cap., then pastor of St. Francis of Pointe Coupée, in 1740. The entry states that the parents of the children had been baptized years before by Fr. Davion, and they requested the same sacrament be administered to their offspring.

Pious legend has it that the cypress statue of St. Francis of Assisi which was located in the church of that name of 1760 and in the present chapel since its construction in 1895 was carved by Tunica faithful. It is one of the earliest surviving artforms in Louisiana.

The sacramental records of Pointe Coupée Parish, beginning with the Homard baptism in 1727, are a priceless resource in genealogical research, as well as a testimony to the faith of the Native American, European, and Africans who built and sustained the community. Before the mandated institution of Louisiana State Death Records (and then, only if a testifying physician was present at time of death), and the institution of the federal Social Security system years later, sacramental records of birth, baptism and burial were the chief source of vital records, and only if the parties were Catholic. Substantial lacunas spot the Pointe Coupée records, but the situation is similar in other early Catholic communities.

Names given to children at baptism ignored, apparently with the consent of priest administering the sacrament, the Church's dictate that mythological, pagan or fantastic names are not acceptable, hence the gamut of names from Adonis and Artémise to Zephyr and even Zoroaster. Having exhausted the plethora of such names, some parents named their children for local physicians, like Claiborne, Provosty and Singletary or international figures, ranging from Henry Clay, James Buchanan and George Washington to Juarez, Maceo and Santa Ana. The Civil War era witnessed the baptism of children named Albert Sydney, Beauregard and Davisia (for Jefferson Davis). The trove of German, Polish and Jewish names was appreciated as well, attested by children baptized Gustav, Leopold and Wilhelm; Lodoiska, Nogolka and Stanislas; and Esther, Ismael and Israel.

Generally names such as the above were the middle, and commonly-used names. Christian and Biblical names, with Marie and Joseph overwhelmingly predominating, were normally the first name, and in some families only one, Christian or Biblical name was given. The latter was the custom of Italian families, with the added penchant for naming the eldest son and daughter for the paternal grandparents, the second son and daughter for the maternal grandparents, and succeeding children named for parents, grandparents, aunts and uncles, or baptismal sponsors. This makes for particularly tedious genealogical research, as numerous persons of the same name, all named for a grandparent, lived and appeared in the records at any given time.

Besides first names of the archangels, saints or scriptural figures, some of the Christian names reflected Church feasts and seasons, such as Noel, Octave and Rogatien. "Saint" was often given as part of the name, as in St. Elia, St. Luc, and St. Theresa, and the especially revered name "Marie" was borne by boys as well as girls, the former being given names such as Marie Joseph, Marie Leopold, and Marie Olivier.

The above stated, most of the Créole population, white, African American or of blended ethnicity, were commonly known by their *ti nom* (little name, or nickname). In at least one case, a prospective bridegroom was apparently ignorant of his fiancée's *bon* (good, or given) *nom*, and identified her to the Clerk of Court when applying for the marriage license in 1917 as "Tiboute." The primary sources of baptism and the marriage record itself indicate her given name as Hélena.

The staff of the Baton Rouge Diocesan Archives, the repository for most sacramental records 50 years or older, have done a remarkable job of abstracting the sacramental entries of the various churches, through the periods when Pointe Coupée was, successively, part of the Diocese of Quebec, Diocese of Cuba, and the Diocese, eventually Archdiocese of New Orleans. Despite some significant lacunae, particularly during the 1810s-1830s, the collection is an invaluable record, for historical and genealogical purposes, as well as sacramental documentation.

These Diocese of Baton Rouge has abstracted sacramental entries are available in volume form in regional libraries and for purchase from the Diocese, and in early 2023 comprised the period 1727 through 1905. The former represents the Homard baptism at Pointe Coupée in 1727, the earliest known in the present Diocese of Baton Rouge.

St. Francis: Mother Church of Pointe Coupée

Though the need for a church at Pointe Coupée was expressed as early as 1725, by Fr. Raphael, then Superior of the Capuchins from New Orleans, 12 years elapsed before funds were available and a sense of tranquility existed for the work to proceed.

The first church dedicated to St. Francis of Assisi at Pointe Coupée is believed through oral tradition and surmised by early historians to have been located on the Mississippi River, just above what would be the town of Waterloo, east of New Roads. The fact that trenches, supposed to be of an early fort of Pointe Coupée were visible at that location as late as 1840, bolstered the surmise that church and fort would have existed side by side, as they were to do some two decades later, at another location upriver.

The church was blessed and placed under the patronage of St. Francis of Assisi on 16 March 1738 by Fr. Mathias, O.F.M.Cap. Superior, who came up from New Orleans. That same day, the pastor, Fr. Anselm de Langres, O.F.M. Cap., and officials of the Pointe Coupée post, signed a declaration of the blessing, adding that Pointe Coupée was designated *Retusia Retusia* and its people *Retusiani Retusianorum*, "which will be observed in the Latin extracts."

Soon after, on Holy Saturday, 5 April of that year, two small bells were consecrated for service. Church bells were traditionally sponsored by leading members of communities, and in St. Francis' case the "godfathers" and "godmothers" of these bells Pierre Haussy, Pierre Germain, Albert Decuir, Jean Baptiste Decuir, Anne Gilan, Marie Augustine Haussy, and Marie Decoux. In 1741, a third bell was blessed, the godmother again being Augustine Haussy. This bell was the gift of one of the settlement's wealthiest members, Claude Trénonay de Chanfret.

A *presbytere* (presbytery or rectory) was likewise built in 1738, and from there the pastors ministered at the adjacent church and set off on ministry throughout the settlement. The construction of the presbytere was financed through fines imposed by civil authorities upon lawbreakers. In subsequent decades, this presbytery, or more likely a successor which stood as late as 1891, hosted a number of distinguished visitors. These were identified in a 30 April New Orleans *Daily Picayune* feature on St. Francis Church and Cemetery as (names corrected by this author):

Giovanni / Jean de Gradenigo, a descendant of three Doges of Venice and a pioneer settler of the Opelousas area; the Marquis de Maison Route, *en route* in the Spanish period to claim a vast land grant in the Ouachita territory of present-day North Louisiana; the exiled royal brothers Louis Philippe, Duc d'Orleans (future King Louis Phillippe), the Duc de Montpensier, and the Duc de Beaujolais; and, finally, in the early American period, naturalist and chronicler Herzog (Duke) Paul Wilhelm of Wurttemberg. The latter included extensive observations of Pointe Coupée in his subsequently published *Travels in North America, 1822-1824* (University of Oklahoma Press, 1973).

Despite increasing population and a military presence, Pointe Coupée continued to be a frontier outpost during the French colonial period, and subject to attack by hostile Native Americans, who are recorded as kidnapping enslaved persons and stealing cattle from the community.

In 1740, on the feast of *Fete Dieu* (Corpus Christi) some 50 to 60 settlers are said to have passed in procession "a pistol shot away" from seven of the Chickasaw nation hiding on the Ricard habitation. The latter seized and fled with a white boy and three enslaved African girls. The colonists pursued them, but in vain. The boy was believed to have been killed, and the three girls sold to English settlers beyond the Mississippi River.

St. Francis Church of Pointe Coupée received its first substantial donation in 1742, when Philippe Hainaux willed the church of Pointe Coupée the sum of 1,000 *livres*. The inventory of Hainaux' movable goods include "a red Capuchin handkerchief," though it is unclear as to exactly what was intended, e.g., perhaps a red pall for altar service.

According to a circa 1892 unpublished manuscript by Rev. Joseph Philibert Gutton, then pastor of St. Mary of False River, who may have relied on oral tradition, the first St. Francis Church was "destroyed by storm." Regardless of its actual location and fate, the location of its successor is definitely known, and a number of images of exterior and interior survive into the 21st century.

This successor, what is referred to in documentation and oral history as "Old St. Francis Church," was built in 1760 immediately west of the subsequent New Roads-St. Francisville ferry crossing, but at a site long within the bed of the river owing to its steady encroachment during the late 19th century.

ST. FRANCIS CHURCH OF 1760

The second St. Francis Church was a frame structure, surrounded by galleries, and similar in appearance to French colonial residential architecture such as the LaCour House, of circa 1765 construction and relocated in the late 20th century by Mr. and Mrs. Jack Holden at Chenal, Louisiana. It is recorded that the 1760 St. Francis was constructed under the direction of colonial surgeon Henri Pierre Gérard.

The church was blessed and the first offering of Holy Mass held therein on 4 October 1760. In his official record of the ceremonies, Fr. Irenée, O.F.M.Cap., pastor, stated that the church had been constructed in part by donations of inhabitants of the parish and others, and in part by a tax upon each enslaved person.

The above was approved in an "assembly of the community by Mr. [Vincent de] Rochemore, Administrator of this said province [Louisiana] and Mr. [Claude] Trénonay, subdelegate in this matter." The donations and taxes collected were said to be in equal amounts, and the tax was collected through the church council, notably Dr. Gérard, who in addition to coordinating the construction, was head of the council and community syndic.

FIGURE 4: SECOND ST. FRANCIS OF POINTE COUPÉE, DEMOLISHED IN 1892. AT FRONT IS TOMB OF THE
TERNANT FAMILY WHICH WAS MOVED TO NEW ROADS DURING THE ABANDONMENT OF THIS CHURCH
CEMETERY.

FIGURE 5: REAR VIEW OF SECOND ST. FRANCIS CHURCH
SHOWS GRAVES OF POINTE COUPÉE PIONEERS

FIGURE 6: SECOND ST. FRANCIS OF POINTE COUPÉE

On Passion Sunday, 8 April 1764, Fr. Irenée blessed the cemetery. Through the years this hallowed ground came to surround the church on all four sides, as generations of Pointe Coupéeans and visitors and travelers who died in the community were therein interred or entombed.

Pointe Coupée, like the rest of Louisiana, was officially transferred from French to Spanish colonial rule in 1769, and the males of the community were obligated to sign an oath of allegiance to the new government. The Spanish immediately noted the lack of missionaries serving the vast colony.

It is significant that in 1770 only eight ecclesiastical parishes were functioning in the whole of the vast Louisiana colony: New Orleans, Les Allemands (German Coast), Pointe Coupée, Attakapas (St. Martinville), Les Appalages (Rapides), Natchitoches, and two in the Illinois country.

Though the Spanish authorities forbade the Acadian exiles from settling at Pointe Coupée upon their arrival in Louisiana, Acadian marriage entries are found in the records of St. Francis Church. This was due to the temporary settlement of Acadian families in the Feliciana territory, across the Mississippi River from Pointe Coupée, who were en route to settle areas of Southwest Louisiana. Interestingly, the Acadians were accompanied on their journey by Spanish soldiers, and a number of the latter chose brides from among the young Acadian maidens.

The flow of settlers into Pointe Coupée throughout the 18th and early 19th centuries came preponderantly from mainland France, Quebec, Alsace-Lorraine, and Switzerland. Only a few known Spanish and *Isleneo* (Canary Island) made their homes in the community, namely Aguiar (subsequently Gallicized to Aguillard), Ortis and Pamias.

Marriages between French and Anglo-Saxon parties at Pointe Coupée began in the early Spanish period, according to the sacramental records of St. Francis. Growth in the Anglo-Saxon population, who hailed principally from Mississippi and the Atlantic coast was predominantly Protestant, and increased after Louisiana was admitted into the union of the United States in 1812. Many of the Protestants married Catholics, and their children usually baptized and reared in the Catholic faith.

By the late 1700s the Pointe Coupée settlement had greatly expanded in size, stretching for more than 20 miles along the *Cote de la Pointe Coupée*, or Pointe Coupée Coast, along Mississippi River, from the mouth of the Lower Chenal of False River at the Mississippi on the south to the *Raccourci* (short cut) bend above present-day Morganza.

Historically an agricultural community, Pointe Coupée came to comprise large plantations on the Mississippi River, and subsequently along False River, with smaller holdings interspersed throughout. Tobacco and indigo were the first "cash" crops, i.e. grown for sale, in Pointe Coupée, but shortly after 1800 cotton and, eventually sugar cane, succeeded as the principal crops of the area and basis of its economy.

The importation of enslaved persons had been banned in colonial times, and their growth occurred mainly through natural increase, and introduction of enslaved persons from elsewhere in the American South. By the time of the Civil War, the African population outnumbered that of the Europeans by more than three to one.

Franco-African and to a lesser extent, Native American unions were first evident in the French colonial time and increased through the decades. Their progeny, the *Créoles de couleur*, or Creoles of color, were free from birth if born to a free mother or subsequently emancipated, and the wealthiest of their number came to form a significant and influential part of the population.

FIGURE 7: SECOND ST. FRANCIS CHURCH OF POINTE COUPÉE STOOD 1760-1892

Louisiana was transferred from Spain back to France in 1800, and purchased by the United States in 1803. It was admitted to the Union as a state in 1812. The civil parish of Pointe Coupée was created to correspond with the ecclesiastical boundaries of St. Francis Church Parish. During this period, the Capuchins closed their ministry at Pointe Coupée, and the parish was sporadically served by secular clergy until the arrival of Rev. Antoine Blanc in 1820.

CORPORATION OF ST. FRANCIS CHURCH

In order for the Catholic Church to be recognized and function as a legal authority in the eyes of the American government, Corporations of individual church parishes were formed. The Corporation of the Roman Catholic Church of St. Francis of Pointe Coupée was organized through an act passed by both houses of the Louisiana Legislature in 1814. The temporal business of the Corporation was directed by a *fabrique* (board) of *marguilliers* (wardens or vestrymen), elected civilly by the free white male population.

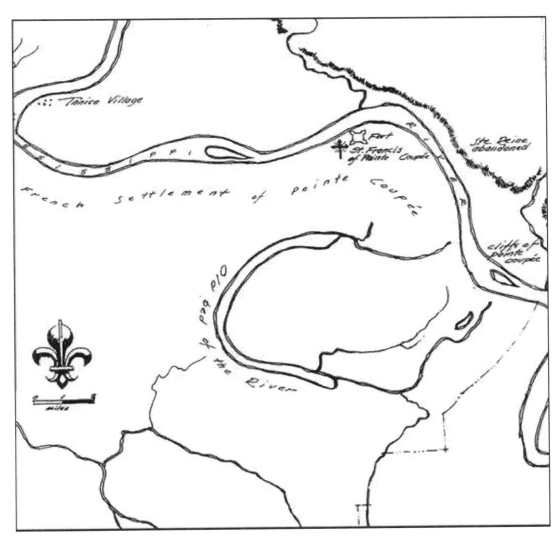

FIGURE 8: IN THE BEGINNING ... POINTE COUPÉE DURING COLONIAL AND EARLY AMERICAN PERIODS.

The seats were normally held by influential men of Pointe Coupée civil parish, and early marguilliers included Julien Poydras, Arnaud Beauvais, Joseph Decuir, Joseph Gremillion, and Pierre L'Hermite. The last-named, a native of France, was a surveyor whose remarkable ink and water color survey of various tracts in the parish survived into the 21st century, in bound form, by the Pointe Coupée Parish Clerk of Court in New Roads. L'Hermite was also responsible for recopying for posterity many of the old and fragile sacramental records of the Church in Pointe Coupée.

Two years after he formation of the Corporation, on 29 March 1816, an inventory was made of the sacred items and fixtures in St. Francis Church and entered into the book of Minutes. Included in the itemization were: four copper crucifixes, a copper cross "with image of the Virgin," eight large copper candlesticks, two small candlesticks, two medium sized silver-plated copper candlesticks, two small copper bells, a copper lamp, an iron "host maker" (i.e., mold), a decorated "bell glass," altar frontals and cloths, and vestments. Of especial interest were six robes, two sashes, and three veils for (the statue of) the Holy Virgin, and some "ornaments" for the Infant Jesus (statue).

In the same year, 1816, the Minutes of the Corporation state that the Congregation had received from Francois Chéssé a valuable donation in the form of a tract of land measuring 10 arpents' front on the Mississippi River by a depth of 40 arpents, at *L'Anse* (The Bend), just above present-day Morganza. It was held until sold for a handsome sum a quarter-century later.

Following Fr. Juan Brady, the next priest to serve the parish was a Rev. DeCrugy, "Vicar General," who was named administrator of St. Francis of Pointe Coupée by Bishop Louis Guillaume DuBourg. Despite his prominent role in diocesan and local affairs, DeCrugy remains enigmatic, and futile thus far has been the search for his given name.

Moreover, though Bishop DuBourg spelled the surname "DeCrugy," two other contemporary Sulpician Fathers offered different ones: Rev. Jean Tessier as "de Groachi," and Rev. Simon Guillaume Gabriel Bruté as "de Grushi." Of the scanty record found of DeCrugy, he did accompany DuBourg from Lyon, via Bordeaux to Annapolis, Maryland and thence to South Louisiana, suggesting that he was a Sulpician Father as well, alas he might have returned to France, as no one named DeCrugy, de Groachi or de Grushi, or any other similar spelling is indicated in the Necrology of the Society of Saint Sulpice, Province of the United States.

Shortly after the Minutes of the Corporation dated 1 November 1818, there appears in the volume a letter without date or recipient's name, but as it states, "Hardly, had you arrived in your diocese than you thought of giving us a pastor, and Mr. DeCrugy, your worthy vicar, informed us of your intentions on this subject," it is obvious that the marguilliers were writing to Bishop DuBourg in New Orleans.

The effusive epistle, signed by A. (Dr. Auguste) Provosty, president, on behalf of the Corporation, includes the following:

We know that your sole ambition is to promote our welfare. In fact, who could calculate the happy results of the re-establishment of religion in our parish? They are innumerable. Since they have been delayed, have we not seen the flaunting of and conduct, broken promises, failures in manners, chicanery, and bad faith dictate contracts: In a word crime honored and virtue an object of contempt?

It is certain that those who calculate on our miseries, or see their fortune grow with our demoralization will oppose our instruction. To fight them advantageously a young priest would not have enough power or feel enough confidence; an old man would let himself be dominated; all our intellectual faculties weaken in old age; but a pastor of mature age, of an engaging and respectable appearance, of sweet and affable ways, of agreeable and instructive conversation, endowed with the talents of the pulpit, merciful and charitable, winning hearts by his openness, commanding esteem and respect by his virtues, reversing all the fallacies of the century, pious, eloquent, yes, there is the person we need.

To that enumeration Monsignor will believe we need himself. It is true that no one more than you is so eminently gifted with these beautiful qualities; but we do not set our sights so high, and we would be too happy to have your worthy vicar and representative Mr. DeCrugy.

Another interesting item in the Minutes of the Corporation comes from 1820, when Arnaud Beauvais, then president of the fabrique and subsequently acting governor of Louisiana, was authorized by the fabrique to purchase from a Mr. Ernest "a picture representing Christ," presumably for the interior of St. Francis Church.

Though the history of the above image is unknown, neither is the origin of two fine oil paintings, a copy of Murillo's *Madonna and Child* and *The Holy Family* which have graced the church for generations, and have been ascribed to an Alberto Pasini. The known painter of that name was an Italian artist of the 19th century specializing in Orientalist works.

In the following year, 1821, the fabrique authorized the installation of pews along the lateral walls of the church, for the accommodation of free people of color.

Infrequent but important visitations were made in the antebellum period by the bishops of New Orleans. One noted in the Minutes of the Corporation occurred in 1833, when Bishop Leo Raymond de Néckére was received by the population and visited St. Francis and St. Mary churches. Shortly after returning to New Orleans, Bishop de Néckére was dead, aged 33, and a victim of one of the city's most fatal yellow fever epidemics.

TOMB ROBBERY IN OLD ST. FRANCIS CEMETERY

The growth in the community and increased number of burials over the years resulted in the St. Francis Cemetery if 1764, which existed on all four sides of the church, reaching capacity. The marguilliers in 1834 authorized the moving of the rear fence of the church and cemetery an *arpent* (192 feet) further back and the lateral fences extended to meet it, thus providing more burial space.

On the night of 17 January 1843, a ghoulish felony was committed in St. Francis Cemetery, which resulted in lengthy litigation and subsequently entered into Pointe Coupée Parish legend. The "low brick tomb" of Dorothée Legros, first wife of prominent False River planter Vincent Ternant II, was broken into and robbed of the diamond and gold jewels – necklaces, rings, earrings and buckle - with which she had been buried nearly eight years prior. These were collectively valued at $2,000, and a diamond necklace and other items overlooked by the grave robbers were estimated at an additional $1,000.

The culprits were apprehended in New Orleans, attempting to sell the treasure, and identified as brothers Adolph and L. Connor, residents of the Waterloo area. Upon arraignment, Adolph and Connor pleaded guilty to larceny and sentenced to four month's imprisonment. Evariste Boudreau, only child of Dorothée Legros (through her first marriage to Pierre Hébert *dit* Boudreau), kept the items left in the tomb, and claimed possession of those which had been retrieved from the robbers in New Orleans.

Virginie Ternant, half-niece and ward of the late Dorothée Legros, had married after the latter's death her widower, Vincent Ternant. Ternant having also died, in 1842, Virginie sued Evariste Boudreau for possession of the jewels, claiming them for her and Vincent's children. Her reasoning was that when Boudreau had sold all of his rights of inheritance from his mother, Dorothée, to his step-father, Ternant, in 1835, it included all that the inheritance might accrue in the future.

The local court ruled in Boudreau's favor, ruling that items from a grave were *hors du commerce*, sacred goods that could neither be bought nor sold. Virginie appealed to the Louisiana Supreme Court, which in 1844 overturned the ruling of the lower court, and assigned to her the jewels.

During the local court proceedings, it was advised that Dorothée Legros' remains be transferred from her violated tomb. Accordingly, she was placed in the lavish mausoleum built after the death of Vincent Ternant II in 1842, which was subsequently dismantled, moved to, and re-erected in St. Mary Cemetery in New Roads in 1888.

The 1830s through the 1850s were marked by disputes concerning authority in the churches of Louisiana, with the fabriques of marguilliers on one side and the pastors on the other, and the parishioners divided into two camps. Pointe Coupée's situation was one of the most volatile, and is detailed in a subsequent chapter of this work.

Rev. Antoine Blanc, and St. Mary, at the New Road, on False River

Rev. Antoine Blanc, a native of Sury, France, was assigned in 1820 by New Orleans Bishop Louis Guillaume DuBourg to reorganize the old but neglected church parish of Pointe Coupée. Much of the information on Father Blanc's ministry in Louisiana comes from his personal correspondence as well as the archives of the *Propagation de la Foi* (Propagation of the Faith). This apostolate was founded in Lyon in 1822 by Blessed Pauline-Marie Jaricot, an ardent devotee of St. Philomena, Virgin and Martyr, the latter of whom attracted a devoted following in Pointe Coupée.

While undertaking the herculean task of resurrecting the neglected parish of St. Francis, Rev. Blanc simultaneously administered to the Catholics living across the Mississippi River in the Felicianas, on the Plains, and at Baton Rouge. Antoine Blanc was assisted in his ministry by his brother, Jean Baptiste Blanc, who was said by church historian Roger Baudier, K.S.G. to have been one of the first priests ordained in Louisiana.

French and African settlement had spread from the *Cote de la Pointe Coupée*, or Pointe Coupée Coast along the Mississippi River, onto the former horseshoe bend of the great river, now an oxbow lake called *la Fausse Riviere* (False River).

Plantations and smaller agricultural enterprises commenced and population increased along False River, alas the new settlement was about five miles distant, at its closest point from the fort of Pointe Coupée and St. Francis Church and Cemetery.

Spanish authorities, therefore, opened a *camino real* or royal road between the Mississippi River on the north and False River on the south circa 1776. As relative few Spanish speakers settled in the parish, the numerically preponderant French and African populations referred to the new thoroughfare as the *Chemin Neuf*, or New Road. The upper and lower stretches of the New Road were adjusted from time to time, and in 1805 the lower part was

ANT: BLANC.

FIGURE 9: ARCHBISHOP ANTOINE BLANC

shifted from what is now St. Mary Street to present-day New Roads Street in the City of New Roads.

Despite the short cut offered by the new roads, plural, the residents of False River continued to increase in number. In 1822, a free woman of color named Marie Catherine Depau, but commonly known in speech and official records as *La Fille Gougis*, ostensibly because she was the natural daughter of Ste. Domingue *emigré* Dr. Louis Gougis, opened a six-block, 20-lot subdivision of her property, located at the terminus of the New Road at False River.

Surveyor and longtime St. Francis Church *marguillier* (warden) Pierre L'Hermite, surveyed the property, set boundaries, and filed a plat of the development in the official records of Pointe Coupée Parish. Residences and stores were built on the lots, and this was the genesis of the City of New Roads.

Running parallel to False River, from south to north, the streets were named *Rue de Commerce* (Commercial Street, present-day West Main), *Rue du Jackson* (Jackson Street, for hero of the Battle of New Orleans and subsequent United States President Andrew Jackson), and *Rue de la Promenade* (or Walking Street). From east to west, perpendicular to False River were *Rue du Pont Neuf* (New Bridge Street, in actuality the southern stretch of the New Road but

FIGURE 10: COAT OF ARMS, ARCHBISHOP ANTOINE BLANC

named for the bridge in the *cypriere* or cypress swamp in the lowland midway False River and the Mississippi to the north; present-day New Roads Street), *Rue de l'Independence* (Independence Street, subsequently Richy), and *Rue du Marché* (Market Street, now St. Mary Street).

Pioneer journalist Martha R. Field, of the New Orleans *Daily Picayune*, writing under the *nom de plume* of Catherine Cole, viewed this L'Hermite survey during her visit to the old Pointe Coupée Parish Courthouse. In her Sunday, 29 November 1891 feature "Pointe Coupée Parish," she stated:

> Like line engravings were the maps of the river and bayous, and nothing was ever better in the way of India ink than the plan of New Roads, drawn up ages ago, when some good woman gave the land for a town that should grow like children about the wooden skirts of Sainte Marie.

FIRST ST. MARY, A MISSION OF ST. FRANCIS

With the establishment of a town on False River, Rev. Blanc was determined to open a chapel to serve the population along the lake and in its inner bend, *l'Isle de la Fausse Riviere* (the Island of False River), to which population had spread shortly after 1800.

The marguilliers were in favor, and on 28 July 1822, they agreed to purchase from Marie Pourciau, widow of first marriage to Charles Robillard and in second marriage to Barthelemi Olinde, a plot of land measuring 180 feet on present-day West Main Street by a depth of 210 feet to the north, and bordered on the east by Saint Mary Street.

FIGURE 11: ST. MARY CHURCH SEAL

Included in the transfer was the corresponding river bank between West Main Street and False River. According to the Minutes of the Corporation and subsequent correspondence, the Widow Olinde ultimately decided to donate the property to the Corporation, and Rev. Blanc honored her request by allowing her use of a pew, rent-free, in the new church, for life.

On 18 November 1822, the marguilliers contracted with one John Vondorff for the building of the new church for the sum of $2,500, and agreed to borrow no more than $1,000 to defray the expense of construction. The balance of the cost was paid by subscriptions from the residents of False River and the Island.

The church at False River was named *Sainte Marie de la Fausse Riviere*, or St. Mary of False River, in honor of the Blessed Mother. It was dedicated on 19 October 1823, in the presence of "a majority of the population of False River and the Isle," according to the act of dedication which was inserted in the sacramental records of Pointe Coupée.

FIGURE 12: FIRST ST. MARY'S CHURCH AT NEW ROADS STOOD 1823-1907

The frame building was flanked by exterior galleries on east and west sides, had a semicircular entrance portico, and was surmounted by an octagonal belfry. The structure measured 33 wide by 80 feet deep, and was likely the inspiration for the church of St. Augustine on Isle Brevelle, Natchitoches Parish, which was soon after commissioned by Fr. Jean Baptiste Blanc upon his assignment there.

The presence of the galleries on either side of the original St. Mary Church allowed for the accommodation of enslaved worshippers and vehicles from the elements.

Holy Mass was first offered in St. Mary on All Saints' Day, 1 November 1823. The first marriage recorded there, celebrated on 23 December of 1823, united Joseph Chustz, son of George Chustz and Pélagie Lejeune, and Mélanie St. Cyr, daughter of Joseph St. Cyr and Modeste Saizan, all of False River.

The first marriage of "colored" parishioners on record was that of George *dit* Robert, son of Lucie *dite* Robert, and Marguerite Bonnefoi, daughter of Marie Louise Viard, all free persons of color, on 3 May 1825.

As the Pointe Coupée sacramental records of baptisms from 1816-1834 have not survived to present, it is, therefore, quite impossible to determine who were the first children baptized at St. Mary.

Owing, no doubt, to the limited size of the St. Mary property, no cemetery was established there, and burials continued to be made at old St. Francis Church on the Mississippi River until, and in some cases after, the establishment of St. Mary Cemetery on New Roads Street in 1865.

In 1825, substantial gifts were presented to St. Mary's congregation: Jean Baptiste Désormes, a marguillier, donated a monstrance; Revs. J. and L. Boué of the Diocese of Lyon, France gave the congregation a bell; Madeleine Olivo, widow of Simon Porche and owner of the Olivo plantation on False River, presented a silver cross; and Rev. Blanc gave a flag.

Mme. Porche, who resided in an early Créole residence with distinctive double-hipped roof which stood on the river bank at the mouth of Bayou Corne de Chevreuil (Buckhorn), was one of Pointe Coupée's most remarkable figures and a sounding voice for the emancipation of enslaved persons.

THE ISSUE OF ENSLAVEMENT

The arrival and rapid rise of *Américain* (Anglo-Saxon newcomers) land and slave holdings in Pointe Coupée in the wake of the Louisiana Purchase of 1803 introduced an alternate, more severe, outlook on interracial relations and plantation operation. Owing likely to the genealogical and spiritual ties in Pointe Coupée, and the Catholic Church's respect of African Americans as people with souls and deserving ministry, mutual respect was stronger in the prevailing Créole environment than in the remainder of the predominantly Protestant South.

Contrasting modes of the plantation system were evident, through written record and oral history. The native Créole "plan" or manner obliged enslaved persons to work but part of the time for their holders and allowed the remainder of the work week to cultivate crops and raise livestock for their own consumption and profit. Through sales of the latter, often to their holders, many enslaved persons were able to accumulate funds by which they were able to purchase their and loved ones' freedom. Striking in its difference, the American "plan" forced enslaved persons to devote all of their labor to their holders and, thereby, receiving little opportunity for emancipating themselves.

In addition to being a strong supporter of Rev. Antoine Blanc and his successors' ministries, including hosting periodic group baptisms on her plantation, Madeleine Olivo, widow of Simon Porche was "notorious" as being an especially indulgent mistress. Testimony was plentiful that she allowed her labor force to make larger crops for themselves than for her. Moreover, one of her laborers prospered enough to purchase a carriage for himself, and he loaned it to the Widow Porche when she needed transportation, as she had no vehicle of her own.

FIGURE 13: OLIVO HOUSE, HOME OF WIDOW MADELEINE OLIVO PORCHE, ADVOCATE OF EMANCIPATION; LATER ST. CATHERINE CHAPEL OF JOSEPHITE FATHERS; NOW SITE OF CAROLYN "CAPI" BERGERON MERRICK HOME, WHERE FR. ANDREW MERRICK GREW UP

Likely a testament to her own conscience, and inspired by the papal bull *In Supremo Apostolatus* issued in 1839 by Pope Gregory XVI (born Bartolomeo Alberto Cappellari), the Widow Porche repeatedly told her friend and attorney, Alphonse Robin, of her desire to emancipate all of her labor force, who numbered nearly 100 men, woman and children. Robin regretfully replied that the Pointe Coupée Parish Police Jury, who alone could authorize emancipations, would not countenance the liberation of so many people. Mme. Porche responded by allowing a native Mexican named Gaitan Nietto to operate a "camp" in the woods at the rear of her plantation to provide a station for enslaved persons fleeing the False River area.

Mme. Porche was especially protective of the Olivo family *de couleur*, who were the natural children and grandchildren of her predeceased brother George Olivo II. Soon after her death in 1850, her legal heirs had the Olivos *de couleur* abducted and trans-ported for sale in the slave markets of New Orleans and Mobile.

Through the efforts of St. Mary congregants - attorney Henry Beatty and men of the LeBeau, Bergeron, Gremillion and LeMay families, the latter being the natural fathers and godfathers of those abducted – a lengthy trial of the kidnappers resulted in the releasing of Olivo family.

The familiar Olivo – Porche house served as St. Catherine Chapel, a mission of the Josephite Fathers of St. Augustine Church of New Roads, during 1938-1952, and a number of area white children attended catechism and made their First Communion there along with the African Americans for whom the chapel had been established. After its demolition in 1977, the site of the 200-year-old landmark was occupied by the new residence of the family of Edward "Sandy" and Carolyn "Capi" Bergeron Merrick, whose son Rev. Andrew Merrick was the community's latest ordained native son.

With the stabilization of the church parish of Pointe Coupée, Rev. Antoine Blanc was transferred to other ministries in the diocese in 1826. In 1835 he was named fourth Bishop of New Orleans, and when the see was elevated to archdiocese status in 1851, he was named first Archbishop.

Archbishop Blanc referred often in writing of his affection for Pointe Coupée and chose as part of his coat of arms *la croix de la Pointe Coupée,* or "the cross of Pointe Coupée." It is trefoil in design, but exactly what was the cross of Pointe Coupée – an interior or exterior cross or depicted on an image at either St. Francis or St. Mary – remains unknown.

One of the most spiritual and productive prelates in Louisiana history, Archbishop Antoine Blanc died in New Orleans in 1860, and was the first archbishop to be buried in the new St. Louis Cathedral in that city.

FIGURE 14: OLIVO HOUSE WHEN SERVING AS ST. CATHERINE CHAPEL, CA. LATE 1930s

GROWTH OF THE TOWN OF NEW ROADS

The community around St. Mary of False River church developed into the commercial center of Pointe Coupée Parish, and it was referred to in legal documents and correspondence alternately as *Chemin Neuf* (New Roads) or the Village of St. Mary, in honor of the church. In 1847, after the courthouse at the former fort site adjacent to St. Francis Church on the Mississippi River was destroyed by fire, the seat of parish government was moved from the Pointe Coupée coast to New Road.

A post office was established in 1858 as "False River, Louisiana" but it closed in 1861. The community was first incorporated in 1875 as the Town of New Roads, but when the post office reopened in 1878 it was named "St. Mary's, Louisiana" for the church. In the following year, 1879, the name of the post office was changed to "New Roads," alas when the original corporation lapsed and the town was incorporated again in 1894, it was as New Rhodes (sic), Louisiana. The post office refused to change the spelling of its name, and the Town changed the spelling of its name to New Roads in consistency with the post office in 1900.

The earliest families in New Roads area bore surnames including: Langlois, Pourciau, Patin, Fabre, Olinde, Samson, Chenevert, Lejeune, Villiers, Labbé, Bondy, Boudreau, Kleborn, Gebhart, Graugnard, Demouy, Fernandez, Knaps, Richy, Saizan, Dispau de Savarie, and Mars.

Families further south on False River who were active members of old St. Mary's included Bergeron, Chustz, Robillard, Saizan, Didier, St. Cyr, Gosserand, Janis, St. Amant, Ladmirault and LeBeau.

Those faithful of the Island who frequented St. Mary in its early years included the following families: Gremillion, Major, Jewell, Bouanchaud, Sicard, Picard, Chustz, Delage, Bergeron, Saizan and Lejeune. The white community continued to be predominantly French in population, with some from the German and Italian states arriving in the late antebellum period. Jewish individuals and families settled in and around New Roads as well, alas never established a synagogue or cemetery.

Holy Mass was celebrated at St. Mary by the pastors from St. Francis at least two Sundays each month. Though regular church attendance in those days of primitive transportation was mainly limited to those within the town of New Roads itself, those attending divine services went however they could, whether by road or water.

The Minutes of the Corporation of the Church of Pointe Coupée in 1843 document the erection of a large cross, surrounded by a fence of lattice work, and both painted, as built across the street from St. Mary Church.

It and its successor(s) served as a beacon for worshippers arriving by boat on False River, and in 1847 the Pointe Coupée Parish Police Jury authorized the establishment of a toll ferry service across the lake, with the New Roads landing being at the cross in front of the church.

In 1858 a reference in the town's bilingual *Démocrate de la Pointe Coupée / Pointe Coupée Democrat* newspaper identified this area of the river bank as *La Place de la Croix*, French for "Square of the Cross." A succession of crosses stood on the site throughout the 19th century, and the tradition was revived during the pastorate of Rev. Frank Uter in 1983.

Though religious faith and patriotism have been closely linked in Pointe Coupée Parish since the early years of Americanization, it is interesting to note that the request of a group of "young people of False River" to have a "speech" in old St. Mary Church on Independence Day, 4 July 1841, was respectfully denied by the marguilliers.

FR. MITTELBRONN AND THE CIVIL WAR

The last pastor of St. Francis to administer to St. Mary as a mission chapel was Rev. Francois Christophe Mittelbronn. During his tenure, many of the Pointe Coupée Parish population initially supported the Confederate cause during the Civil War. Mittelbronn, the owner of two enslaved persons, supported the Southern cause and was recorded as offering Holy Mass and blessing the flags of local Confederate troops departing for the theatre of war.

Three such ceremonies were reported by the bilingual *Démocrate de la Pointe Coupée/Pointe Coupée Democrat* of 8 June 1861. On the previous Sunday, the annual feast of *Fete-Dieu* (Corpus Christi) was celebrated with "great pomp." The procession bearing the Blessed Sacrament from St. Mary Church to a *réposoir* (station of repose) erected by Joseph Richy was escorted by the *Gardes de la Fausse Riviere* (False River Guards company), who afterward offered a military salute. Sunshine prevailing, a "great assembly" of the faithful were in attendance.

That same afternoon, the blessing of the flag of the Island Guards, of which O. (Octave) Jewell was captain, was hosted by the ladies of the community, during which Captain Jewell offered the ladies "some ardent and patriotic words."

Figure 15: Father Mittelbronn, Civil War Pastor

The 8 June 1861 *Démocrate/Democrat* also related that on the 13th of the month, which had been designated by Confederate President Jefferson Davis as a day of prayer, Rev. Mittelbronn would offer High Mass at St. Mary Church, and the various military companies of the parish were expected to "assist at the solemnities" in great number.

Later that year, the 28 September issue of the same newspaper told of the High Mass to be offered by Fr. Mittelbronn at 3 p.m. on 30 October, for the intention of the Pointe Coupée Cadets, a company of young men. A banquet was to follow at the home of Monsieur (Julien) Michel, local attorney who lived in the old Dispau de Savarie home, subsequently Samson & Co. drug store and Claiborne & Claiborne law office.

Fr. Mittelbronn's support of the Southern cause did not go unnoticed by the Federal troops who occupied Pointe Coupée Parish in 1863, in connection with the Siege of Port Hudson, across the Mississippi River from Hermitage. In March 1863, while he was supposedly performing his "priestly duties" to *Créole de couleur* parishioners, at the site of the never-completed St. Joseph Chapel on the Lower Chenal, he and some of the parishioners were arrested by members of the 2nd Louisiana Infantry (Federal) and Rhode Island Cavalry.

The pastor was imprisoned first on the Winter Plantation downriver in West Baton Rouge, Parish, and ultimately in Baton Rouge, from where he was released. He returned to St. Francis to find that both the church and presbytery had been pillaged and desecrated by crew members of the Union gunboat *Switzerland*. Mittelbronn subsequently received an apology from the crew, but like many others in the parish, and across the South, Fr. Mittelbronn filed suit for damages against the Federal government in the French and American Claims Commission.

In his case, No. 17, "Francois Christophe Mittelbronn versus the United States, he claimed $37,285 in damages, issuing from his arrest in March 1863 and the theft of books, clothing and other movables by the Federal crew in April 1863. He testified to paintings, fixtures and vestments stolen from the church and furniture, silverware, chinaware, clothing, bed linens, bank notes and gold coins and Madeira and Port wines taken from the presbytery.

In their search for money, Mittelbronn continued, the crew had overturned his bookcases, holding the extensive library he had purchased from Poydras College upon its closing. About a quarter of his books were taken and the remainder torn apart in the misbelief that more money was hidden within.

The pastor's house servants, identified as Joe, Paco and Mary, reportedly protested again the looting and destruction, but the crew urinated and defecated on the pile, and wiped themselves with pages from St. Thomas Aquinas and Voltaire.

It is possible that a volume or volumes of the sacramental records of St. Francis and its mission of St. Mary at New Roads were apprehended or destroyed at this time, as well. If so, this deprivation might explain the several lacunae that appear in the chain of baptismal, marriage and burial records for the community, particularly during the 1810s-1830s period.

Fr. Mittelbronn's testimony as to being abused while in captivity was not supported, however, by some of the witnesses upon examination. An award was made in his favor, in the much-reduced amount of $300, at five percent interest from 1 April 1863. Twenty years elapsed before he received on 13 October 1883 the sum of $615, representing $300 in principal and $315 in interest.

Fr. Mittelbronn, meanwhile, had left Pointe Coupée for New Orleans in 1866. There, he founded the church parish of St. Rose de Lima, and became famous through generations in glorified versions of what he had endued during the War.

The former pastor of St. Francis also filed suit in the Pointe Coupée court in 1867 for a monetary judgment against the defunct Corporation of the Church of Pointe Coupée. Mittelbronn stated that as the Corporation had ceased to exist (it had expired 8 March 1865), he asked the court to appoint "a manager or receiver" to attend to its debts "and to wind up all its affairs." The court appointed Charles Poydras to the office of Receiver of the defunct Corporation, and Mittelbronn filed suit against him, a month after his initial suit.

Fr. Mittelbronn claimed that the Corporation owed him a total of $5,325 for 64 drafts made out during the year 1863 for his salary and stipends. Judgement was rendered in the prelate's favor in 1869, two years after he filed suit, in the amount sued for, plus eight percent interest, from 1 August 1863.

Another creditor of the Corporation was former New Roads resident Adélaide Mars, the Catholic wife of noted New Orleans Jewish jeweler and silversmith Eugéne Katzenstein. Back in 1863, Jean Pierre Courrége had received from the Corporation a note for $400 for his services as sexton of St. Francis.

Likely needing cash, or being indebted in some manner to Mrs. Katzenstein, Courrége conveyed the note to her. With neither receiving payment from the Corporation, Courrége filed suit on behalf of Mme. Katzenstein against Charles Poydras, as Receiver of the Corporation. In 1869, she received judgment in the prayed-for amount, plus eight percent interest from 12 January 1863.

A third creditor of the Corporation, Stephen Van Wickle of Pointe Coupée, sued Charles Poydras in 1868, claiming he (Van Wickle) was owed a considerable sum by the Corporation and that Poydras in his office as Receiver had acted contrary to the interests of Van Wickle and the two other creditors. Van Wickle stated that Poydras had erred by not filing suit against the Corporation's debtors and had left out some of the assets in advertising the church properties for public sale. The court ruled in late 1868 against Poydras, and sustaining the injunction filed against him by Van Wickle.

Van Wickle sued Poydras a second time, stating that the Corporation owed him "several thousand dollars," repeating the charges he made against Poydras in the earlier suit, and lamenting that one of the chief assets of the Corporation, "the church [St. Mary] on False River is in a dilapidated condition." Two months later, the court ruled in Poydras' favor and against Van Wickle.

Meanwhile, St. Mary of False River had been elevated to independent church status on 19 March 1865, and Rev. Joseph Philibert Gutton dispatched as first pastor. His first four years at the post were his most difficult, being marked by back-to-back floods of the Mississippi River, epidemic, the abandoned and deteriorated state of his church, and the judgments rendered against it and St. Francis of Pointe Coupée as the assets of the defunct Corporation of the Church of Pointe Coupée.

Diminutive in size, *Père* Gutton proved more than equal to the task, and persevered, seeing the church and community through their darkest days and expanding the ministry of the Church.

ERA OF THE MARGUILLIERS

The Catholic Church experienced its most difficult time during the early 19th century, with the *fabrique* (vestry board) system often causing dissention and opposition to clerical authority. Three pastorates of St. Francis of Pointe Coupée and its mission of St. Mary of False River, in particular, those of Revs. Jean Martin, Jean Rogalle and Francois Mittelbronn, were affected by actions by the *fabrique* which sorely tried and polarized clergy and parishioners.

Though incorporation into the American nation provided liberties, privileges and participation in government to the general population unknown in the previous colonial period, the United States government did not recognize the authority of the Church as had the French and Spanish authorities of the 18th century. Church parishes had to be incorporated and administered by a *fabrique* (board) of *marguilliers* (vestrymen or wardens) who were elected civilly.

Acting for the Corporation, the marguilliers received and disbursed monies in its name. They set a *tarif* or schedule of fees for funerals, burials and entombment and collected same, and received annual rentals for the church pews, which were auctioned to highest bidders annually.

The Corporation also paid the salaries of clergy, cantors, sacristans and anyone hired to work on church properties, and paid for repairs and improvements to churches, presbyteries and cemeteries. Though paid by the Corporation, the clergy was assigned by the bishops, and subsequently archbishops, of New Orleans.

The Corporation could, and often did, file suit in the local courts for nonpayment of fees as outlined above, though it did make concessions such as the free burial of the indigent and cancellation of fees owed by insolvent successions.

On 3 March 1814, the Louisiana Legislature passed an "Act to incorporate a congregation of the Roman Catholic Church in Pointe Coupée," in which it was specified that all free (white) males aged 25 and above were eligible to hold office.

Parish free (white) voters aged 20 and above cast ballots for six to serve as marguilliers, two each for the districts of Pointe Coupée, i.e., the old settlement along the Mississippi River, False River, and the Island of False River. The term of the corporation was 10 years, periodically renewed and its authority restated through similar legislative acts as late as 1852.

A fascinating volume titled "Corporation of the [Religious] Parish of Pointe Coupée" is rich in detail of the temporal state of the local churches during the period from 1814 through 1843. It was translated from the original French to English during the 1970s by Mmes. Martha Becnel Miller and Edna Morrison Scatterty and Miss Celeste Didier, parishioners especially fluent in languages. In essence the minutes of the Corporation, as compiled by the marguilliers, the volume it is a matter-of-fact rendering of building and repair, hiring of personal, monetary receipts and disbursements.

FR. MARTIN'S TRIBULATIONS

An interesting item in the minutes of the Corporation is found under the date of 17 October 1831, when the marguilliers agreed to have the presbytery, then vacant due to no pastor having been assigned, repaired and let out to the Pointe Coupée Parish Police Jury for use as the local and parish courts, until the arrival and location therein of a new pastor.

Meanwhile, period correspondence between local clergy and laity to and from ecclesiastical authorities of the era, preserved in the Archives of Notre Dame University, witness in candid form prejudices, hostility, and, at times, sacramental abuses which occurred in Pointe Coupée's churches.

The minutes of the Corporation begin with the election of the first-known wardens: Antoine Beauvais,[1] Simon Croizet, Martin Bourgeat, Vincent Porche, and Dr. Auguste Provosty. Croizet was elected president by his colleagues. They adopted the basic statutes by which the religious parish would be administered.

From the above list and subsequently-elected marguilliers, it is apparent that the marguilliers were all men of economic means and political influence. Pastors frequently in correspondence to the bishops and archbishops cited individual wardens as being apathetic about religion at best and openly irreligious at worst. The marguilliers often reduced salaries of the clergy, in essence rending the priests to the role of hired employees.

Rev. Jean Martin, who was pastor from 1834 to 1842, was in regular correspondence with Bishop Antoine Blanc in New Orleans, and Fr. Martin's letters are fascinating in that they depict the labors of a devoted priest in what was still, in many respects, a frontier community. Writing the bishop on 2 August 1839, Martin reported that he had said Mass at the home of Antoine Decuir (present-day Austerlitz Plantation on False River) where he baptized "18 to 20 Negro children and one white," returned to St. Francis to baptize several children in the evening, then doubled back to spend the night in New Roads.

Fr. Martin continued that he had three or four more days devoted to minister in outlying areas, but that he "dreaded the sun."

In relating the news of the larger community, the pastor of Pointe Coupée related that a billiard parlor had been built across the street from Jean Laurans' house, a block from St. Mary Church, and the construction of a dance hall was underway. Chilling was his report that on the previous Friday, "they" (authorities, or a mob intended?) had "hung an *Américain* [French term for non-French white] who had killed two children with an axe in the parish, at Raccourci."

Most of Fr. Martin's correspondence with Bishop Blanc involved the actions of the *fabrique* of the Corporation of the Church of Pointe Coupée and the increasingly hostile relationship pastor and marguilliers. As early as 1835, within his first year of pastorate, Fr. Martin informed the bishop about the marguilliers' three successive choices of sacristans, one of whom was an enslaved person who had yet to receive his First Communion, and all of whom Martin thought were inappropriate for employment.

In the following year, 1836, Fr. Martin wrote the bishop that the fabrique refused to reimburse him $3,000 for "furniture" he had acquired for St. Francis and St. Mary. Three years later, in 1839, the pastor informed the bishop that two of the marguilliers refused to have needed repairs made at St. Francis, but that he had the work done, through the monetary contributions of ladies of the parish, and with the assistance of the sacristan, Francois Bineaud. The two marguilliers then threatened Martin with a lawsuit, he continued.

---

[1] Not to be confused with his relative, Arnaud Beauvais, who also served as a *marguillier*, as well as Acting Governor of Louisiana

The Corporation of the Church of Pointe Coupée appeared quite frequently in the civil suit records of the local courts, usually as plaintiff petitioning for payment of past-due accounts of its debtors. The Corporation three times filed suit against False River planter Vincent Ternant II, builder of what was later known as Parlange plantation home, for non-payment for requiem services for his late mother, Constance Lacour Ternant.

Mme. Ternant had died in 1837 and, as was customary at the time among people of means, her son continued to honor her memory and have prayers offered for the repose of her soul, through elaborate requiem Masses. One of these requiems was held, on 22 June 1839, for which the Corporation billed Ternant $83.50, itemized as for the services of a cantor, a sacristan, an acolyte (altar server), a mourning drape, a censer, 10 candles for the altar, 16 candles for the Communion rail, two candles for the marguilliers' bench, 16 candles for the "assistants" or attendees, and 24 tolls of the church bell.

Through his attorney, Sidney A. Lacoste, Ternant replied that he owed nothing to the Corporation, owing to the "irregularity in the manner of electing the church wardens of said Congregation," adding that the Corporation itself was "dissolved and extinct." Ternant continued that he had arranged with Fr. Jean Martin in which Ternant paid the priest the sum of $50. Vincent Ternant II died in 1842, without having paid the amount of the marguilliers' bill.

In 1840, Fr. Martin informed Bishop Blanc that the *marguilliers* had sold a tract of land with a "beautiful" house thereon belonging to the church (the 1816 Chéssé donation at L'Anse, upriver of Morganza) to adjoining landowner Charles Morgan for $6,000, yet allowed Martin only two boxes of candles to serve the parish's two churches for five years, and they had contracted with Claude Favre to make repairs at St. Mary for $1,200, then a considerable sum.

In the following year, 1841, as the tension between the *fabrique* and pastor continued, a petition was circulated and signed by 116 parishioners asking that another priest be hired for St. Francis. Martin responded by transferring residence to New Roads and offering Sunday and weekday Mass exclusively at St. Mary. Having accepted the hospitality of Michel Olinde and family, Martin told the bishop he intended to have a small residence built next to St. Mary.

Mindful of his flock nearer St. Francis Church, however, Fr. Martin accepted invitations to baptize, but did so in the homes, and for burials, but he read the funeral service before, in St. Mary. The pastor offered Mass at least once at the old settlement, in the home of Clément Enéte.

Martin's chain of letters to Bishop Blanc stated that a certain *marguillier* boasted several times that the *fabrique* did not accept the authority of the bishop and they could send away any priest as they desired.

TAKEN TO THE COURT

Fr. Martin filed suit against the Corporation, presenting the above testimony, alas his claim that the marguilliers were spreading false claims about him in the community was declared invalid by the court. The Corporation countersued him in the amount of $3,000 for "damages" but, the court dismissed their case, and ruled that the books of the Corporation be handed over to the *bedeaux* (church beadles) for safekeeping.

One of Fr. Martin's most loyal parishioners, Francois Bineaud, wrote Bishop Blanc in Lent of 1842, stating that the marguilliers asked him to inform the bishop of the election of new marguilliers to fill the vacancies of those who had resigned amidst the difficulties. Bineaud mentioned among the new members a man who on the previous 26 June (1841) had "looted" St. Mary Church. The marguilliers, in an attempt to minimize the discord, offered the key to the presbytery of St. Francis to Fr. Martin, but he refused it, according to Bineaud.

A month later, Bineaud wrote the bishop of a "scandalous scene" that had taken place at Easter, claiming Coustait (sic), a beadle, and two others, robed in cassocks and surplices, held a "service" similar to those of the "French Catholic Church" in France. "Coustait" was Louis Antoine Coustaix, who had been hired as sacristan, cantor and *bedeau* (beadle) by the marguilliers in 1839 and appeared several times as party in contemporary lawsuits.

In 1841, Fr. Martin had written Bishop Blanc, claiming Coustaix was "the cause of all the trouble" by delivering a petition signed by "5 or 6" ladies of Pointe Coupée to a Mrs. Stall in St. Francisville, urging the latter to add her signature and write to the bishop about Martin's suspension of Mass at St. Francis.

Fr. Martin, Bineaud continued in his Easter 1842 letter to Bishop Blanc, had celebrated Palm Sunday, Holy Thursday and Easter at the home of Michel Olinde in New Roads, but attending worshippers appeared fearful and others expected did not come, afraid of disturbances.

Bineaud declared in the letter that the situation of the churches of Pointe Coupéean reminded him of the French Revolution of "of [17]89," and begged Blanc to visit the parish and intervene. Bineaud suggested that the bishop's first Mass in the parish should be "a High Mass of reparation."

On their part, the marguilliers wrote Bishop Blanc twice, stating that they desired peace and harmony to be restored in the parish, and requested that he dispense them from paying an "enormous amount" Martin demanded of them via law suit, including salary to date and expenses he had supposedly paid on behalf of the churches. The fabrique claimed that he had not been in their employ since the beginning of the controversies back in 1835.

The two lawsuits filed by Fr. Martin against the Corporation and the latter's countersuit against him were consolidated by the local district court, which ruled in favor of Fr. Martin, and the Congregation was condemned to pay him the sum of $6,734.76 for withheld salary and expenses he paid on behalf of the churches, plus costs of court.

The Corporation appealed to the Louisiana Supreme Court, which in 1845, found no evidence for the expenses Fr. Martin claimed, beyond the washing of the church linen. The higher court annulled the judgment of the local court, and the Congregation was declared to be indebted to him in the reduced amount of $550.76.

FR. ROGALLE'S WOES

Rev. Jean Rogalle, pastor of St. Francis and St. Mary during 1848-1853, had difficulties with the marguilliers as did his predecessor, Rev. Jean Martin. Fr. Rogalle intended the proposed chapel on the Lower Chenal, on land donated by Leufroy Decuir, to be independent of their control. He thought they assumed him to "have too much money" at his disposal, as soon after Archbishop Blanc visited and departed from Pointe Coupée in 1850, the wardens reduced Fr. Rogalle's salary from $1,000 to $800.

In reporting the above motion to the archbishop, Rogalle stated he intended to proceed with construction of the chapel at the Lower Chenal. He added that he opposed the marguilliers' appointment of a Protestant and jailor to the post of beadle for St. Mary. Rogalle, stating it was his authority to hire beadles, said he did not want one and the one hired would only cause disturbance in church.

Early in the following year, 1851, the marguilliers moved to cut the pastor's salary by $160, but he proposed to make the matter known to the congregation, who seemed dissatisfied with the wardens, and proceed with work on the Lower Chenal chapel. Rogalle then wrote the marguilliers, protesting the salary cut, asking them to pay the ¾ balance due him, demanding that inventories be made of church properties, and informing them of his intended departure if his requests were not granted.

Acquiescing, when three vacancies became vacant among the marguilliers, the *fabrique* appointed three of Fr. Rogalle's choosing as replacements. In 1853, however, Fr. Rogalle, physically ill and weakened by two years of difficulties with the marguilliers, was allowed to resign the pastorate of Pointe Coupée. He was assigned to Abbeville, Louisiana, and the two priests there, Revs. Hubert Thirion and Francois Mittelbronn, sent to replace him at St. Francis and St. Mary.

FRS. THIRION AND MITTELBRONN

Not long after the arrival of Revs. Hubert Thirion and Francis Mittelbronn in Pointe Coupée Parish, the latter wrote Archbishop Blanc, calling former pastor, Fr. Jean Rogalle, a "scandalmonger" in the latter's reporting of playing cards found in the Abbeville presbytery, and countered that Rogalle had taken a vestment and a horse from Pointe Coupée as well as six *piastres* (dollars) from the marguilliers there.

Mittelbronn continued that he found in Pointe Coupée a burse with corporal "thrown into a corner" of a provision room, and that he had to burn seven or eight "rotted" purificators, apparently neglected by Rogalle. On that same day in 1853, Fr. Thirion wrote Archbishop Blanc as well, offering his own defense that he never played cards.

In 1858, Rev. Mittelbronn succeeded Rev. Thirion as pastor in Pointe Coupée, owing to the latter's physical and mental decline. In September of that year, Fr Mittelbronn wrote Archbishop Blanc asking that His Grace inform him of Thirion's whereabouts, as Thirion had left Pointe Coupée without settling their temporal affairs.

Mittelbronn told the archbishop that a three-page letter was being sent to His Grace, listing grievances against Mittelbronn, including claims that he was spreading news that Thirion was demented and that he had thrown coffee in Thirion's face. Mittelbronn further informed the archbishop that Thirion had on three occasions drank coffee before saying Mass, had baptized without the holy oils, and ate meat on a Friday at the home of Dr. (P.G.A.) Kaufmann.

Fr. Mittelbronn wrote Archbishop Blanc in the following year, 1859, "chagrined" to have received a letter from Blanc that His Grace intended to send Fr. Thirion back to Pointe Coupée as his replacement. Mittelbronn said if Thirion returned, he would likely discontinue the mission at Chenal, and Mittelbronn would receive nothing the marguilliers owed him.

Mittelbronn pointed out "Old Knaps," i.e. Guillaume Knaps, proprietor of the *Café des Habitants* (a.k.a. Planters' Coffee House, a saloon and billiard hall) diagonally across the street from St. Mary Church, as the "prime mover" among the petitioners asking for Thirion's return, and "his [Knaps'] reasons are ignoble."

The prelate continued that blacksmith Michel had visited Thirion, telling the priest that the parishioners wanted his return, to which Thirion said a petition to that effect should be circulated; Michel conveyed the information to Knaps, who undertook the petition.

Fr. Mittelbronn remained at Chenal until 1863, and his capture and imprisonment by Union occupation forces for blessing the flags and men of Pointe Coupée leaving for service in the Confederate Army. He returned upon release, but in 1866 relocated to New Orleans.

Mittelbronn, largescale planter Stephen Van Wickle and St. Francis sexton Jean Pierre Courrége were among the principal creditors of the Corporation of the Church Pointe Coupée, and each filed suit against it. As the Corporation was virtually bankrupt, and had legally expired on 8 March 1865, the civil cases against it dragged on for years. Details of these cases and their outcome are located in this work at the end of the chapter entitled "St. Francis: Mother Church of Pointe Coupée" and the beginning of the chapter "Beloved *Pére* Gutton."

BELOVED *PÉRE* GUTTON

During the Union occupation of Pointe Coupée Parish, St. Mary of False River chapel at New Roads was fortunate not to have suffered pillage and desecration as had mother church St. Francis on the Mississippi River. In January 1865, troops of the 2nd New York Cavalry, U.S.A., camped opposite St. Mary on the Place de la Croix.

They succeeded in capturing several Confederate soldiers who were hidden in the town, some as close as beneath the Gebhart residence, across St. Mary Street from the church, and forced citizens to open the safe in the Graugnard store. The several thousand dollars therein which they took was the property of Charles Parlange of New Orleans and the False River plantation of that name.

Contradicting the manner in which Rev. Francois Mittelbronn claimed he was treated by the Federal occupation troops, he, after imprisonment and release, reportedly went to the Union commander and had most of Parlange's money returned.

With Fr. Mittelbronn's departure, New Orleans Arch-bishop Jean Marie Odin sent Lyon native Rev. Joseph Philibert Gutton to Pointe Coupée Parish. On St. Joseph's Day, 19 March 1865, St. Mary of False River was elevated to independent parish status, and Fr. Gutton named first pastor.

Eleven days prior, on 8 March, the charter of the Congregation of the Church of Pointe Coupée had expired, but its bankrupt affairs were to be the source of ongoing litigation involving several parties.

St. Mary was the second mission of St. Francis to be raised to independent church parish, Immaculate Conception at Chenal being the first, in 1861. St. Mary's territory included both sides of the upper part of False River and the Upper Chenal. On the west bank of False River, it extended as far as Austerlitz Plantation, near the head of Bayou Lanquedoc and the neighborhood which would be called Wolff's Bend.

FIGURE 16: REV. JOSEPH PHILIBERT GUTTON

On the opposite, or Island, side of the False River, St. Mary's lower limit was the downriver boundary of Ventress' Caledonia Plantation. The Mississippi River bound St. Mary parish on the east, and the *cypriere* (cypress swamp) on the north, beyond which was the remainder of St. Francis church parish.

Southwest of False River, the outer limit of St. Mary parish was vague, but most of the Catholic population of upper Bayou Grosse Tete and lower Bayou Fordoche attended, when possible, services at St. Mary and buried their dead in the church's cemetery established on New Roads Street in 1865.

The seal adopted by St. Mary church parish features an image of the church of 1823, fronted by a picket fence, and with a large cross on the bank of False River (alas, the lake bends in the wrong direction). Written around is the legend: "*Sancta Maria Interrupto Flumine,*" Latin for "St. Mary (of) False River." This image is perpetuated each week in the St. Mary *Parish Bulletin.*

POSTWAR POINTE COUPÉE

A couple weeks after his arrival in New Roads in the spring of 1865, Rev. Joseph Philibert Gutton, who was to be endearingly known for generations as *Pére* Gutton, wrote Archbishop J.M. Odin in New Orleans, attesting to the "deplorable" condition of St. Mary Church. The prelate stated that the roof was "entirely rotted," and the marguilliers had taken the church revenues but made no repairs.

Of St. Francis of Pointe Coupée, Gutton stated that he visited whenever Dr. J.H. Wiendahl could loan him a horse. Gutton pronounced that church to be in "passable" state, though the abandoned presbytery "suffered daily" from the constant passage of troops, and it had been robbed "of everything but chairs."

He continued that the late affair of the marguilliers and Fr. Mittelbronn was purely a "political" one, as the marguilliers were "less than religious" and enjoyed opposing him. Gutton continued that Mittelbronn left fond memories in the parish, but at times had been too "sharp" with the marguilliers.

Fr. Gutton declared the presbytery at New Roads as small, but the town was the center of population, and the nearest house to St. Francis was a mile and a half distant from the latter church. He stated that he left his provisions at the home of an elderly widow in New Roads, and that she prepared his daily meals.

Of the sacramental records, Gutton related that Frs. Thirion and Mittelbronn had kept separate records, on loose sheets

FIGURE 17: REV. JOSEPH PHILIBERT GUTTON

of paper, and that neither had deaths been recorded since early 1862 nor baptisms of "Negroes" for five years.

Gutton stated that he needed to travel to New Orleans to buy nails for a new church roof, as both armies had "left not a one" in the parish. An armistice had been in effect between the opposing sides, but the Federal government had stopped all communication and boat traffic on the Mississippi. In the same letter, Fr. Gutton informed Archbishop Odin that a new board of church trustees had been appointed the day prior, on 3 April 1865, and feared that "the old system will prevail" of the trustees keeping the revenues and making no material repairs.

A week later, Gutton informed the archbishop that the trustees guaranteed him a salary of $1,200 and an additional $300 should an assistant be assigned, alas the treasury was empty. He closed by repeating that the greatest need at the time was six barrels of nails, for a new church roof, but the Federal occupation forces considered nails "contraband" and would authorize only Odin for their acquisition.

The new president of the trustees, False River planter Louis Amazan Hubert of present-day Pleasant View Plantation, wrote the archbishop as well, praising Fr. Gutton's "high moral qualities" and confirmed the pastor's report on the state of finances.

Fr. Gutton's May 1865 communication to Archbishop told of the flooding of the parish due to the Mississippi River breaking its levees. A breach had occurred near St. Francis Church (the Scott Levee), as well as the Morganza Levee upriver, and a dyke (Patin Dyke) east of New Roads had given way under pressure of the floodwater, severing communication between New Roads and the Mississippi River port of Waterloo.

Due to the flood, burials were being made at homes, Gutton continued, and the trustees, having come into some revenue, decided to purchase land for a church cemetery. They rejected the property of the Pointe Coupée Parish Police Jury, behind the Courthouse, as they feared future difficulties, but were interested in a tract along the "highway" (i.e. the New Road, now New Roads Street).

In the summer of 1865, an anxious Fr. Gutton visited the Archbishop in New Orleans, telling of engineers' plans to "raze" St. Francis Church and Cemetery in order to build a new levee through church property. Fortunately, this work did not take place, and the church and cemetery existed until the site caved into the river a quarter-century later.

Upon an announcement of Fr. Mittelbronn's return to Pointe Coupée, the new board of church trustees disbanded and the money was kept by the treasurer, as supposedly they feared the closing of the churches. Gutton informed the archbishop of the above, and surmised that it may have been his (Gutton's) own strict accounting which caused them to resign.

ST. MARY CEMETERY ESTABLISHED

On 1 September 1865, Rev. Gutton purchased from Jean Baptiste Lejeune II and wife, née Pérrine Chenevert, a tract along the east side of the New Road for $1,500, to be paid in gold coin owing to the scarcity of acceptable currency. To pass the sale legally, permission had to be granted by Union Gen. Edward Canby, who was the government authority for the region.

The sale had to made relatively quickly, Gutton informed the archbishop, owing to "the transfer of the graves," likely meaning the disinterment of temporary burials made at homes during the flood and their reinternment in consecrated ground. More than 23 cemetery plots had already been sold, Gutton continued.

Fr. Gutton almost immediately conveyed the entire tract to Archbishop Odin, who accepted it on behalf of the Archdiocese of New Orleans. The property was two arpents wide and 36 arpents in depth, commencing four arpents north of East Main Street and extending as far as the common 40-aprent line of it and adjacent properties in the *cypriere* to the north. The eastern boundary was the land of the Parish of Pointe Coupée, along which line Courthouse (now Court) Street would be opened in 1900.

The cemetery proper was located several blocks north of the south line of the property Gutton had purchased, and the interval between the lower boundary (about where the New Roads Post Office stood in 2023) as well as the land north of the cemetery was sold or donated in lots well into the 20th century, thereby providing the church with a means of income.

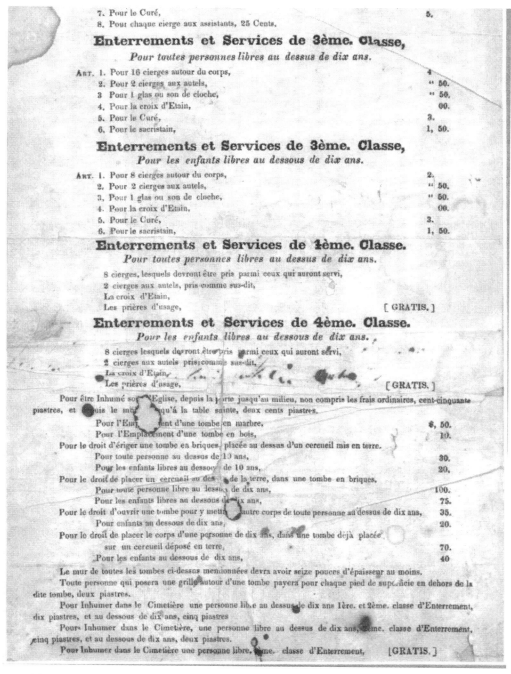

FIGURE 18: ST. FRANCIS AND ST. MARY CATHOLIC FUNERAL FEES, 1842

Auguste Provosty II, like his father, Dr. Auguste Provosty, before him, had been president of the old *fabrique*, before the war. Auguste II was a member of the Louisiana Secession Convention of 1861. He and his family suffered the loss of their fine home near St. Francis Church, when troops dismantled it for the lumber it contained to build quarters, according to Fr. Gutton.

The prelate might have been referring to the building of the Federal fort at Morganza, which took place in 1864, with materials obtained from plantations along the Mississippi River. Among the residences also dismantled for the purpose was the former two-story residence of the late Benjamin Poydras which had been contemplated as location of a convent and school for the Sisters of St. Joseph of Bourg and had become the property of free woman of color Fannie Riché in the 1850s.

Of Provosty, Fr. Gutton informed Archbishop Odin toward the end of 1865 that he (Provosty) was supposedly holding $6,000 of the church treasury, claiming it was owed him by the trustees.

Around Christmas 1865, a severe storm completely removed St. Mary's roof, and Fr. Gutton was obliged to "dismantle" (i.e. deconsecrate and remove) the altar. The new cemetery remained unfenced, and burials were being made at St. Francis. In the new year of 1866, Gutton informed the archbishop that parishioners did not want to worship at St. Mary, where there was no shelter from rain.

In order to avoid conflict with the trustees, he advised His Grace that the St. Francis and St. Mary properties be sold and a new church built on the land Gutton had bought on the New Road, i.e. near the new cemetery.

Fr. Mittelbronn, visiting Pointe Coupée, and others suggested that a judicial inventory and evaluation of the properties of St. Francis and St. Mary be made, as he and other creditors of the old Corporation of the Church of Pointe Coupée demanded their due.

During Lent, Fr. Gutton informed Archbishop Odin that a fence has been built around St. Mary Cemetery, and he suggested the digging of trenches (sic) to facilitate burials. The first burial had occurred there on 7 February 1866, of Amélina Olinde, child of A.T. and Estelle Bergeron Olinde of New Roads.

On 8 March, Jean Pierre, an African American man of free status before the Civil War, was buried on 8 March., both of the acts being recorded in the new sacramental record of burials.

Among the first, and largest tombs erected in St. Mary were four built by the extended Samson family, and which continued to stand near the East Fifth Street fence in the 2023. They are of the Samson- Gosserand family; of the families of brothers Jean Clair and Jean Baptiste Cazayoux; of the Chenevert family; and the *Famille des deux frères Lieux* (Family of the Two Lieux Brothers, i.e. Jean Francois and Jean Pierre).

Such large mausolea inevitably held the remains of more persons than those with epitaphs, as old stones disintegrated or were painted over through the years, or no markers installed in times of limited finances. Typical of tombs built in other places, such as New Orleans, and other Latin communities of South Louisiana, each tomb had below it a *caveau* or pit, into which older remains and coffin remains are reverently placed as the upper vaults received newer occupants.

SETTLING DEBTS

In the year of flood and epidemic that was 1867, Fr. Gutton informed Archbishop Odin in New Orleans that Charles Poydras had been appointed liquidator to settle all claims against the old Corporation of the Church in Pointe Coupée, upon the urging of Auguste Provosty II. Poydras was in favor of keeping St. Mary Church and having it repaired, alas Gutton feared that "Negro preachers," who had become active in the parish since the end of the war, would buy it on the day of public sale.

Later in the year, Archbishop Odin visited Lyon, France, and paid two calls on Fr. Gutton's widowed mother, née Parat, who lived at Fourviere, the height above the city and near the home of the late Blessed Paulin-Marie Jaricot who had founded the Propagation of the Faith and the Universal Living Rosary of St. Philomena apostolates.

After his return to New Orleans, Mme. Gutton wrote the archbishop, thanking him for his visits and for the gift of a Rosary blessed by the Pope (Blessed Pius IX, born Giovanni Maria Mastai Ferretti). Mme. Gutton sent, by way of Odin, to her son a photograph of herself and two little altar vases donated by an acquaintance for the church in New Roads.

In February 1868, the St. Francis and St. Mary properties were set for public sale by court order, but the auction was postponed owing the objection of one of the creditors. Fr. Gutton informed Archbishop Odin that Charles Poydras expressed his wish to be rid of his duties as liquidator, as the process was "full of too many intrigues."

On the day after Palm Sunday 1868, a storm lifted one-third of the new roof on St. Mary Church, and Fr. Gutton had to rent three tarpaulins as cover for the services of Holy Week. He informed the archbishop of such, and wrote him again a month later, stating that every rain caused the wall plaster to fall. The pastor estimated $750 for materials and labor would be required for pressing repairs and $400 for the more simple ones.

On 28 May 1868, determined to emphasize the necessity of work at St. Mary, Gutton authorized three local building experts, brothers Joseph and Auguste Richy and Henri Demouy, to inspect and make a detailed report of the conditions, and had their findings entered in the conveyance records of the Pointe Coupée Parish Clerk of Court.

A year later, on 12 May 1869, the movable and immovable effects of the churches of St. Francis and St. Mary were finally sold at public auction. The creditors were identified as Fr. Mittelbronn for salary and other past due amounts, Fr. Gutton for his salary, Stephen Van Wickle for work and materials, Jean Pierre Courrége for salary as sexton, and Mary Calvin, for money loaned.

The last-named was a woman of color, who according to testimony subsequently filed against the Succession of Charles Poydras, had been married to Poydras in a "religious ceremony" (as before the 1868 Louisiana Constitution lifted the ban on interracial marriages, they would have not been able to procure a license from the parish). Court costs amounted to $1,116.14.

The church of St. Mary (meaning lot and building) were sold for $750 and its "ornaments" for $40, the church of St. Francis for $825 and its ornaments for $100, for a total of $1,715. As highest bidder, Archbishop Jean Marie Odin was adjudicated all of the above, in the name of the Archdiocese of New Orleans.

Donations were received from the creditors, the legal officials involved and others, in the following amounts: $860.54, from Fr. Mittelbronn, through his power of attorney granted to New Roads lawyer Pierre Antoine Roy; $100 from Archbishop Odin, per contribution of 15 January 1868; $400 from Pierre Antoine Roy; $61.30 from Fr. Gutton; $7.90 from Mary Calvin; $11.00 from Clément E. Roy; $10 from Parish Judge Alcide Bouanchaud; $833 from notary Charles Hebert; and the amount of accounts receivable of the old Corporation which had been bought at the sale by Miguel Basso, as his contribution.

CHURCH RESTORED

The 21 August 1869 *Pointe Coupée Echo* newspaper recounted the joyous news of the substantial completion of repairs and renovations to St. Mary Church, and the celebration of Holy Mass therein on the previous Sunday, 15 August, its patronal feast of the Assumption of the Blessed Virgin Mary. The journal recounted the poor state of the hallowed structure, "a ruined shell," and its closure for the previous four years while in the hands of its creditors.

The *Echo* told that soon after the purchase of the property by Archbishop Odin, the ladies of the congregation began circulating subscription lists for financing the required work as well as enlargement of the sacred edifice, which had become too small for its congregation. What was left of the old roof was removed, the church lengthened by 30 feet, the walls repaired, and the altars decorated. When the required 40,000 shingles arrived, so many men arrived with their hatchets and nails that the roof was completed in two days, according to the *Echo*.

Despite the increased space, the church was filled to overflowing for its first celebration of the Mass in years, the account continued, and aisles and doorways were filled with standing worshippers. Among the new furnishings, the reporter noted in the sanctuary a handsome carpet at the foot of the altar, which was a gift to the ladies of the congregation from Sam Stafford & Co., cotton factors[2] of New Orleans.

In the following year, 1870, in February, a mission was held in St. Mary Church by the Redemptorist Fathers, followed by a number of weddings and validations of existing civil marriages. Among these was the wedding of Michel Olinde, widower of Julie Bergeron, and Marie Rosa Michel, a woman of color, who parented a well-known family. Theirs was one of more than a dozen marriages between white men and African American or *Créole de couleur* women between the time the 1868 Louisiana Constitution lifted the ban on

FIGURE 19: REV. J. P. GUTTON

---

[2] In antebellum and Reconstruction-era South, most cotton planters relied on cotton factors (also known as cotton brokers) to sell their crops for them.

"interracial" marriage and the repressive laws of the Jim Crow era.

Signing as witnesses to the Olindes' wed-ding were Fr. Jean Arthur Poyet, then pastor of St. Francis Church, and Rev. Egidius Smulders, C.SS.R., native of the Netherlands and the noted former chaplain of the 8th Louisiana Infantry regiment of the Confederate Army.

It is significant that toward the end of the Reconstruction period, during the violent campaign and contested elections of 1876 that the False River area was seen as a safe haven for African American and other potential voters for the Republican party who were harassed, beaten and, in several instances, killed by the all-white "Vigilance Committee" operating in Ward 4, upriver of Morganza and behind the community on Bayou Fordoche.

Perpetuators of the intimidation and violence were named in the subsequent Congressional Hearing in New Orleans, and such actions were predominantly undertaken by Protestant, Anglo-Saxon men. Alas, even in the New Roads area, members of the Vigilance Committee, a.k.a. "Bulldozers," pursued fleeing African Americans. At least one white woman, who refused to give the location of hidden African Americans, was tortured, unsuccessfully, by Committee members on the Claiborne plantation just west of New Roads.

The more tolerant "Créole" atmosphere of the False River area, where Catholics of various ethnicities, including the *Créoles de couleur*, was undoubtedly the reason persons in flight rested there in their ultimate exodus to New Orleans and other communities.

Fr. Gutton recorded mention of the 1870 mission by the Redemptorist Fathers in the sacramental record of baptisms, as he did the benediction of "the large mission cross" which was presented to the church, likely by the Redemptorists, at the close of the mission.

It is logical that this cross is the large wooden one with metal corpus appearing on the second eastern column from the sanctuary indicated in a photograph of the church's interior, likely in the 1880s. This same cross was transferred to the new St. Mary Church completed in 1907, and restored and hung in 1989 on the first full column from the sanctuary on the eastern side of the nave.

A third item listed by Fr. Gutton in the baptismal records of 1870 was the solemn installation of the Stations of the Cross in the church, in October. No description has been found to indicate if these Stations were paintings, engravings or of sculptural composition.

The Archives of the Diocese of Baton Rouge includes within its collection for St. Mary of False River a colored, Gothic-bordered *tarif* or schedule of fees for five classes of burials for adults and four for children, cemetery entombment and interment, cemetery plots, burial and entombment, requiem Masses and wakes, and four classes of wedding ceremonies.

At the bottom of the artifact is New Orleans Archbishop Napoléon Perché's signature of approval, dated 13 March 1872, as well as those of parishioners Ami Landry Mahoudeau, Hubert Patin, Alcide Bouanchaud and Jean Baptiste Lejeune, likely the church council members of that time.

The sacramental records of St. Mary Church during the Reconstruction period include many marriages of formerly enslaved parishioners and the legitimization of their children born prior. Among Fr. Gutton's most touching entries is that of the marriage on 19 February 1870 of Zephyr Jean-Baptiste and Clarisse (no surname), elderly natives of Africa. Prominent white congregants signed as witnesses: Aug. (Auguste) LeCoq, C. (Constant) Guillaume, A. (Auguste) Richy, and Eug. (Eugene) Poydras.

In the 1880 United States Federal Census, the venerable M. and Mme. Jean-Baptiste were enumerated as living near Patin Dyke, Zephyr Jean-Baptiste, age given as 100, and whose occupation was "sells *gombo*," and Clarisse, age 80. M. Jean Baptiste's commodity remains unclear, as *gombo* is the Créole term for "okra" as well as the soup with which is it often made.

Ages given in censuses and other enumerations often have little or no primary source documentation, if the person has no record of being baptized in childhood. In a striking example, the *Pointe Coupée Banner* of 2 April 1931 solemnly reported the death of beloved False River Road resident Augustine Alexis, "at the ripe old age of 116 years." The journal contended she "remembered when Julien Poydras died in June 1824, being at the time a girl of about ten years of age." The 1880 United States Federal Census attributed an age of 38 to her, thereby suggesting she was born circa 1842.

Evidence is clear that Mme. Alexis had resided in the immediate vicinity (present-day intersection of False River Drive and Hospital Road) for most of her life, on or near the Poydras Plantation, which was owned in succession by Julien Poydras, his nephew Benjamin Poydras de la Lande, and their cousin Charles Poydras. As Benjamin Poydras died in 1851, his death would have been the one she would have logically remembered, and her approximate age of nine years at the time – based on the 1880 Census would confirm her age at death as about 89, rather than 116.

Fr. Gutton's ledgers and the archival files of the *Pointe Coupée Banner* attest to many ceremonial and devotional observances which marked his long and inspiring pastorate. These included special liturgies and communal celebration on major feasts of the Church and the patron saints of the parish and its religious organizations, Blessing of the Crops during Rogation Days, Corpus Christi processions on West Main Street of great beauty and accompanied by brass band music, Blessing of the Graves on All Saints' Day, parish missions by visiting priests of various religious orders, and solemn First Communion and Confirmation ceremonies, the last-named in conjunction with archiepiscopal visits to New Roads.

Reaching out to the faithful beyond New Roads proper and the decaying center of the old Pointe Coupée settlement, Rev. Gutton established a number of mission chapels, and sponsored the organization of several lay associations, both national and local in structure.

His pastorate was likewise marked by the installation of a new church bell, christened *Maria Seraphina Clara*, and the opening of the first Catholic school in New Roads, for African American children. All four of these topics are treated in individual chapters later in this work.

ENHANCED REAL ESTATE

The real estate of St. Mary Church proper was augmented from the original 1823 donation by Marie Pourciau northward and westward in the wake of the Civil War. In two records which represented an act of exchange in 1871, Archbishop Perché conveyed to Pérrine Lacour, et al, *Créoles de couleur*, a tract fronting one arpent on the New Road/New Roads Street by depth of two arpents to the land of the Pointe Coupée Parish Police Jury (ultimately Court Street). Bounding neighbors to the south, fronting East Main Street, were Joseph Richy and Jean Clair Cazayoux, while to the north was the balance of the archdiocese's land.

In return, the Lacours conveyed to the archbishop a lot measuring one superficial arpent directly in the rear of St. Mary Church, fronting on the west side of St. Mary Street, bounded on the west by Rosina Michel Kern Weil and north by Auguste LeCoq. This lot is historic as during 1866-1867 it was the site of New Roads' second-known Freedmen's Bureau school, which was open to white and well as African American pupils.

In 1884, Fr. Gutton purchased in his own name from Joseph Richy the lot immediately west of the St. Mary property, measuring one arpent front on West Main Street by a depth of two arpents, bounded west by John Yoist, and north by the remainder of Richy's property. The lot transferred had been acquired by Richy in 1884 from Rosina Michel, widow in first marriage to Nathan Kern the elder and divorced in second marriage to Benjamin Weil, all Jewish.

This lady of influence had acquired the land in 1865 and operated a general store thereon, being succeeded by her nephew-by-marriage Nathan Kern the younger and he by Pierre Courtis. The sale from Rosina to Richy had included all buildings thereon, except for the store.

This lot would eventually become the "rectory lot" of St. Mary Church, occupied by buildings which would be replaced by the present rectory in 1924.

In 1895, the Congregation of St. Mary Roman Catholic Church was officially incorporated. In the following year, 1896, Archbishop Janssens donated to it: the St. Mary Church lots, the remaining land on the east side of New Roads Street, being 72 arpents in area, the property of old St. Francis Church and Cemetery on the Mississippi, and the lots of St. Philibert Chapel on False River and St. Claude Chapel at Waterloo.

Fr. Gutton died in 1896, and by terms of his last will and testament, bequeathed to St. Mary Church the two-arpent lot he owned directly to the west of the church on West Main Street, now known as the "rectory lot." St. Mary would acquire additional, contiguous property to the west and north at the turn of the 20th-21st centuries.

Most inspiring is the fact much of Fr. Gutton's work, and the congregation's support of his projects and ministrations, were made despite great adversity. The yellow fever epidemic of 1867 was especially deadly, with more than 100 victims being buried in St. Mary Cemetery. Likely, hundreds more were buried in other cemeteries as well as at homes across the parish.

SUFFERING THROUGH FLOODS

Frequent and disastrous were the *crevasses* or breaks in the Mississippi and Atchafalaya River levees in time of spring high water. The great rivers, whose alluvium it deposited in ancient times, were responsible for the great fertility of the soil and, therefore, the parish's agricultural prominence which, alas, was checked by 18 major floods between 1780 and 1927.

The most critical point in the levee system was at Morganza and Grand Levee, immediately southeast. There, more than 40 percent of the waters carried by the great river from the central part of the United States is funneled between the levees of the west (Pointe Coupée) bank and highlands beyond the east bank. The strain on the Morganza and Grand Levees is terrific in times of extreme high water, and these levees' repeated failures affected not only Pointe Coupée but numerous parishes to the south, as far as the Gulf of Mexico.

During the pastorate of Fr. J. P. Gutton, levee breaks and floods of increasing severity occurred in 1865, 1866, 1867, 1869, 1882, 1884, and 1890. These disasters washed away crops, buildings and other improvements, took the lives of thousands of livestock and several humans, and were often followed by illness and epidemics.

The precise number of human lives lost to drowning in Pointe Coupée Parish might never be known, as government officials tended to downplay the citizens' reports of deaths, especially of African American residents. Major newspapers in New Orleans, Baton Rouge and other cities of the nation reporting on the events were the most consistent sources of the death toll, and Pointe Coupée's known losses related by them included: three in 1850; three in 1882; three in 1884; eight in 1890; more than 65 in 1912, the parish's greatest disaster ever; and two in 1927.

The United States government, including the military occupation and the Freedmen's Bureau in the years immediately after the Civil War, provided some flood relief to the nonplussed population.

This relief took the form of provisions, medicines, clothing, hats, shoes and blankets, as well as fodder for their livestock.

Deprivation existed on a wide scale, however, and months after each flood event monetary and material assistance from business firms and individuals in New Orleans, Baton Rouge, and the cities of the American North was critical.

The levee breaks of March 1867 brought unprecedented flooding of Pointe Coupée and numerous civil parishes to the south. Fr. Gutton wrote Archbishop Blanc that Pointe Coupée was "an incalculable ruin," with floodwater having spread south as far as St. Mary Cemetery. Soon after, Gutton wrote His Grace that Pointe Coupée had been transformed into "an immense lake" from the flooding, and the waters of the Mississippi and False River had "met," signifying the overbanking of False River due to the southward sweep of the flood, and houses on Bayous Grosse Tete and Maringouin had been washed away. The federal government provided some aid to the suffering population, but Gutton and Fr. Gavard, pastor of Immaculate Conception at Chenal, petitioned the archbishop for further assistance.

During the flood of 1874, water issuing from a major breach in the Morganza Levee and a smaller one at the Morrison plantation downriver sent thousands of citizens in flight from their inundated homes again. In the former Poydras College building on False River, Fr. Gutton found a large number of women and children, nearly naked, starving, and ill.

The distressed prelate journeyed to New Orleans for assistance, and in a tearful plea in St. Ann Church immediately received from Archbishop Napoléon Joseph Perché the personal sum of $50. St. Ann's pastor, Rev. Hyacinthe Tumoine, allowed the use of the church for a fundraising concert in the following week, which netted $351 for the suffering of the New Roads area, according to the subsequent issue of the city's *Morning Star and Catholic Messenger*.

Due to lack of government funding, the Morganza breach remained open until 1882, and each year's spring rise of the Mississippi River sent floodwater into Pointe Coupée Parish, cutting off New Roads and False River from the old Pointe Coupée settlement, Morganza and northern or Upper Pointe Coupée in one direction and from Bayous Grosse Tete, Fordoche and Maringouin in the other direction. In the "best" of these years, only the first six arpents, or a swath of land about 1,200 feet wide extending back from False River, was available for habitation, agriculture and commerce, and cypriere had to be crossed by boat.

In recounting the services of Easter Sunday 1876, the 22 April issue of the *Pointe Coupée Republican* told how Fr. Gutton offered Holy Mass at St. Mary and St. Francis Churches. St. Mary's service was at 9 a.m. and St. Francis' at 11 a.m., and in journeying from one church to the other, Fr. Gutton, maintaining his Communion fast throughout, had to cross by skiff a two-mile-wide swath of "backwater."

During the epic flood of 1882, water rushed through the gap at Morganza as well as the collapse of the Scott Levee directly north of New Roads and the Patin Dyke east of town. Water rose four feet above New Roads' Main Street, and five feet in St. Mary Cemetery. Meanwhile, *Pére* Gutton was ill in New Orleans, and for the first time in memory, services were held neither during Holy Week nor on Easter at St. Mary. Archbishop Perché ordered the church opened for the accommodation of the citizens whose homes were flooded or had washed away.

A remarkable funeral was held at St. Mary during the height of the 1882 flood, the 25 April 1882 report of the Baton Rouge *Daily Capitolian-Advocate* being copied here in its entirety for its rich detail:

"A Sad and Impressive Scene"

On Friday afternoon the 14th, we attended the funeral of Mrs. Philogéne Langlois [née Laure Pourciau, sister-in-law of *Pointe Coupée Banner* editor L. B. Claiborne], who had died the evening previous. The corpse was brought to the church in a small flat, and after the ceremonies in the church had terminated, it was again placed in the same boat, when the funeral cortege, composed of about twenty-five boats of all descriptions, such as boats, skiffs, pirogues and dugouts, started for the cemetery. The white robed priest - Father [Pierre] Berthet - being in a skiff in front accompanied by a young boy holding aloft the cross, then followed the boat containing the remains of the deceased lady and after this the other boats composing the cortege.

The route taken was about half a mile in length and lay through yards, gardens and across fields to the rear of the cemetery, where the flood had washed up the plank fence, then across the cemetery amongst floating crosses and headboards, winding amongst tombs and over the tops of shrubbery till the tomb was reached where the remains were to be deposited. Here the water was over five feet deep and the side of the boat was on a level with the opening in the upper vault, which was to be the last resting place on earth of Mrs. Langlois. A cold drizzling rain was falling at the time and a stiff north wind blowing, which lashed the water into waves. A few brief prayers were said and as the priest's final *requiescat in pace* was said, the wind and the waves seemed to catch up the words and waft them on to the gulf and thence to God in a thousand sighs of *requiescat in pace*.

As a member of the extended Samson family, Mme. Langlois was likely entered in one of their tombs located near the East Fifth Street side of St. Mary Cemetery, all of them being tall and having upper vaults which would have been above a five-foot flood level.

Returning to New Roads as soon as possible after his recuperation, Fr. Gutton requested authorization from Auxiliary Bishop Francois Xavier Leray for the payment of at least $150 to $200 required for repairing the church's flood damages. Fr. Gutton also petitioned Archbishop Perché for the extension of time for the faithful to make Easter Duties, to 3 June, the date Gutton proposed to offer First Communion with the assistance of Rev. Antoine Pompallier, S.M.

In 1884, levee failures and flooding were slightly less severe, with the breaking of the newly-completed Morganza Levee as well as the collapse of the front, community-maintained levee and the rear, State levee at Waterloo. The overbanking of False River caused a rise of floodwater two feet above Main Street, but property owners, including St. Mary Church, had small protective levees built around their yards in time.

Mass continued to be offered at St. Mary, and the *Pointe Coupée Banner* reported that worshippers arrived by boat, landing their craft at the entrance to the sacred edifice. Fr. Gutton's ledgers indicate that he spent $5 to have a levee built in front of the church, and $12 for "crossing to serve at the chapel," i.e. likely transport by boat to St. Claude Chapel in Waterloo.

The 1890 flood was marked by an unprecedented number of breaches in the Mississippi River levees and several on the Atchafalaya. As Jean Baptiste Lejeune's sugar mill in the eastern part of New Roads was mentioned by the *Louisiana Sugar Planter* journal as being flooded, it is likely that St. Mary Cemetery was inundated as well. This journal continued that the floodwater ceased to rise before reaching floor levels in the town.

The Mississippi River port communities of Waterloo and Cook's Landing, a few miles east of New Roads, met their demise chiefly due to the Mississippi River. The front levee broke at Waterloo in 1891 and again in 1892, and in 1893 the front levee at Cook's Landing gave way. In the systemic abandonment of the two communities, many families relocated, as were a few temporarily dismantled residences and commercial structures, into the town of New Roads, and thereby these citizens continued to be parishioners of St. Mary Church.

SPIRITUAL AND FOSTER FATHER

Rev. Joseph Philibert Gutton was the longest-serving pastor of St. Mary of False River, ministering to the church parish and wider community for 31 years. Over and above his myriad pastoral duties, he served as foster father to two boys, who grew to be prominent businessmen and civic leaders and among the St. Mary's most stalwart supporters ever.

Francois Gosserand, a planter on the Upper Chenal on the Island of False River, and a special agent of the Confederate Army, met an early death, at age 32, on 10 May 1865, only a month after the Civil War ended. He left a young widow, née Clémentine Samson, three small children and another yet unborn.

Pointe Coupée Parish's most noted oral historian, Murray G. LeBeau, of False River Road, related in 1987 the oral tradition that Gosserand was fatally "shot in a duel" on West Main Street in front of the Michel Olinde residence. Primary documentation regarding the affray is elusive, but it is possible that Gosserand was killed, for his past Confederate specialization, by one of the Federal occupation soldiers in New Roads.

Gosserand's posthumous child was born on 19 October 1865, and baptized Joseph Philibert the following 25 November. His godparents were Rev. Joseph Philibert Gutton, for whom he was named, and Mlle. Julie Lieux, a cousin. Fr. Gutton was given custody of young Gosserand, commonly called "J.P." or "Philibert," and he received his education at Spring Hill College near Mobile, Alabama.

Fr. Gutton was also given custody of a child of Emma Pourciau, widow of Adélard Langlois, the latter being one of six brothers, sons of Zénon Langlois II and Aspasie Pourciau, who served in the Pointe Coupée Artillery during the Civil War. All six of the brothers were captured in the Battle of Champion Hill, Mississippi, and three of them perished in Northern captivity, including Adélard, who died 4 July 1863 in Camp Norton, Indiana.

His widow's son was born 16 June 1867, a year marked by flood and yellow fever Pointe Coupée, and was baptized Joseph Charles George Pourciau on the following 28 September, with Arthur Langlois, his 10-year-old half-brother, and Amanda Langlois, sister of the late Adélard Langlois, as godparents. He was known throughout life as George Pourciau, and the identity of his father has never been authenticated.

George Pourciau was enumerated in Fr. Gutton's household in the 1880 United States Census. Pourciau's mother, the Widow Emma Pourciau Langlois, died in 1911, and the *Pointe Coupée Banner* eulogized her as a "staunch and practical Catholic."

J.P. Gosserand was engaged in mercantile and saloon businesses and, ultimately, Chief Deputy Sheriff of Pointe Coupée Parish, under Sheriff E.G. Beuker. George Pourciau, whom the *Banner* identified as the recording secretary of Catholic Knights of America No. 367 at the age of 18 years, also established his own mercantile and saloon businesses, and founded the familiar City Pharmacy in 1903.

FIGURE 20: J. P. GOSSERAND (LEFT) WITH HIS GODFATHER AND NAMESAKE REV. J. P. GUTTON (RIGHT)

Both J.P. Gosserand and George Pourciau were early members of New Roads Knights of Columbus Council 1998, the latter serving as Grand Knight. Earlier Grand Knight Charles K. Jordan, in his circa 1951 unpublished manuscript entitled "Historical Sketch of New Roads Council 1998," stated:

> Big, jovial George Pourciau succeeded Brother [Elmo C.] LaCour as Grand Knight. What was disagreeable to him he laughed off; and while he was never without a smile, he could be as hard as nails on occasion.

ON TO ETERNAL REWARD

Fr. Gutton was ill in New Orleans during the time of the 1882 Flood. In 1887, the *Banner* recorded him as suffering a painful kick to the face by his horse, but resuming duties as soon as possible. In declining health in his later years, he was summoned to his eternal home at 8 a.m., on 18 February 1896, at the of 67 years, nine months, and 21 days. As he lay dying, he was surrounded by and offered constant solicitude by his special protégées, the local Catholic Knights of America.

On the next morning, the 19 February issue of the New Orleans *Daily Democrat* in reporting Fr. Gutton's death, related that he had undergone treatment in the city's Hotel Dieu hospital and had returned to New Roads, alas in 10 days' time "he succumbed yesterday, a martyr to his sense of duty."

On 20 February 1896, *Père* Gutton's funeral Mass was celebrated at 10 a.m. at St. Mary. His was the largest funeral ever known in Pointe Coupée Parish, with the *Pointe Coupée Banner* estimating 3,000 men, women and children in and around old St. Mary Church and on the streets of New Roads.

Chief celebrant was longtime friend and former pastor of Immaculate Conception Fr. Pierre Berthet, who journeyed up from New Orleans for the occasion. Assisting were six priests, of whom Fr. Auguste Rochard, St. Mary assistant pastor, served as master of ceremonies, and Rev. Alfred Bacciochi, pastor of Immaculate Conception and future pastor of St. Mary, delivered a touching oration.

Following the Mass, the funeral procession conveyed the venerated remains to the cemetery, with the line of march consisting of a large number of children, including the entire student body of Poydras Academy bearing a harp-shaped floral tribute, the community's various religious societies, and the Catholic Knights of America conveying *Père* Gutton's remains "on a litter."

The subsequent, February 22 issue of the *Banner*, which featured a long biographical account of the life and final obsequies of Fr. Gutton, likewise carried touching tributes in his memory, including those of Catholic Knights of America Branch No. 367 and the Poydras Academy Board of Trustees.

The Catholic Knights resolved to wear badges of mourning for their late spiritual director for 60 days and to have Masses said for the repose of his soul, to be attended in a body.

PÉRE GUTTON REMEMBERED

hree years after Rev. J.P. Gutton's death, in 1899, Mme. Hélene Richy Voirin developed streets, blocks and lots from her property, north of East Second Street, as an addition to the town of New Roads. One of the new thoroughfares was christened Gutton Street, in memory of New Roads' venerated late pastor. In the subsequent renaming of streets, this designation was changed to West Fifth Street, but for years thereafter the name "Gutton Street" continued to appear in conveyance records whose acquisition clauses adhered to early nomenclature.

FIGURE 21: NEW ORLEANS ARCHBISHOP NAPOLÉON JOSEPH PERCHÉ, NAMESAKE OF NAPOLEON STREET, OFTEN MISTAKEN AS BEING NAMED FOR NAPOLEON BONAPARTE

Interestingly, two New Roads thoroughfares were named Janssens Street for New Orleans Archbishop Francis A.A.J. Janssens: the first opened in 1899 a block north of Gutton Street, and subsequently renamed Sixth Street; and another between two lots on New Roads Streets sold by the Congregation of St. Mary to Adolphus Busch in 1905. The latter "street," apparently neither dedicated for public use nor surfaced, was sold in 1959 to parishioner Louis Vilas Pourciau, whose New Roads Lumber yard occupied the former lots of Anheuser Busch beer and ice plant to north and south.

Moreover, Napoleon Avenue (subsequently Street), opened by Joseph Richy in 1900, is believed to have been named in pious remembrance of late New Orleans Archbishop Napoléon Joseph Perché, rather than the Bonaparte dictator of Europe who had imprisoned Pope Pius VI (born Giovanni Angelo Braschi). In its 5 January 1884 obituary of the late Archbishop Perché, the *Pointe Coupée Banner* attested to the esteem of the faithful for the prelate who had often visited during the bleak years of floods and other calamities, lauding him as "a great and a good man… a scholar, an orator, a high luminary of the Church… a patriot and loyal adopted son of Louisiana… a friend to whom they were wont to look up to with filial devotion."

The 3 June 1899 *Pointe Coupée Banner* ran an interesting letter in French, entitled "A Duty to Complete" and signed "X.X.X." The author contended therein the final wishes of Fr. Gutton, stating that the cherished prelate, near the end of life, had informed his godson and foster son Joseph Philibert Gosserand and friend Joseph Richy of his desire that his remains be placed in a *caveau* (vault) under the altar of St. Joseph in St. Mary of False River Church.

The correspondent continued that, to the contrary, the prelate had been buried in St. Mary Cemetery, in a "lonely place, where the passerby sees nothing to indicate the presence of the great philanthropist." The writer stated his/her hope that the coffin would be exhumed from its "place of exile" and transferred under the St. Joseph altar, an undertaking which would be easy and inexpensive, as the distance from cemetery to church was not great.

MONUMENT AND REINTERREMENT

Two more years and nearly four and a half years following the death of Rev. Gutton, elapsed until a monument was erected in his honor in the center of St. Mary Cemetery. Joseph Philibert Gutton was donor of the monument, of Georgia granite and several feet in height. To the immediate rear was erected a masonry tomb with a vaulted top which, rather than a *caveau* under the church floor, would receive *Pére* Gutton's remains which had thereto lain in a grave. Monument and vault were surrounded by a handsome iron fence.

Pére Gutton's disinterred remains were brought to St. Mary Church for a requiem High Mass, celebrated at 10 a.m. on 9 June 1901 by Chenal native Rev. Pierre Oscar LeBeau, S.S.J., pastor of Palmetto, Louisiana, assisted by Revs. Francois Laroche, current pastor of St. Mary; H.L. Pinard, associate at St. Mary; Revs. Francis Cools of New Orleans, a former pastor of St. Mary; Louis Savouré, pastor of Chenal; Peter L.M. Massardier, Chancellor of the Archdiocese of New Orleans; John Laval, Vicar General of the Archdiocese; and Mathurin Harnais, pastor of Plaquemine.

Following the Mass, Rev. Massardier delivered an eloquent and touching tribute to the memory of the deceased, and New Orleans Auxiliary Bishop Gustave Augustin Rouxel blessed the remains.

The procession from church to cemetery, the most striking and solemn in parish history, lined up as follows: hearse, acolytes, carriages of Mons. Rouxel and of visiting clergy from five civil parishes, False River Brass Band, Catholic Knights of America, St. Lawrence Benevolent Association, St. Vincent Benevolent Society, St. Joseph Society, Young Men of America society, and carriages of visitors from several parishes.

The New Orleans *Daily Picayune* of the following day pronounced the attendance at the religious ceremonies and the procession as the largest to have assembled in New Roads to date. If so, it would have surpassed the estimated 3,000 who gathered for the funeral following the much-loved prelate's death five years prior.

Many people from the countryside had reportedly arrived as early as the evening preceding the reinternment ceremonies of 1901. The city journal also pointed out how all of the societies marching in the procession had been founded under the guidance of Fr. Gutton.

The *Daily Picayune* related that when the hearse reached the intersection of Main and Cemetery (now New Roads) Streets, a horse attached to a carriage owned by prominent Jewish merchant and planter of False River, Isaac Bigman, became frightened by the music of the band, dashed into the crowd and knocked several spectators to the street. The most seriously injured was Justin "Rickett" Patin, local building contractor, who was bruised and cut around the head. His injuries, though painful, were pronounced not serious by attending physician Dr. R.M. Carruth.

In the cemetery, Bishop Rouxel blessed *Pére* Gutton's monument and final resting place, and read the ritual of the dead, thus concluding the reverent and memorable ceremonies.

An early photo of Fr. Gutton's monument and tomb and its surrounding fence also indicates to the rear or east a large wooden cross. This was, apparently, the required central cross of the cemetery until the construction of a Calvary "group" monument by Rev. John Hoes, native of Soest, in the Netherlands.

In 1932, Fr. Hoes oversaw the "reconstruction" of Fr. Gutton's tomb, apparently transforming it from its original low, vaulted roof form into a taller, flat-roofed double chamber which allowed for subsequent entombment above Fr. Gutton's remains. Stalwart parishioner Hilary "Rook" Vignes paid the $97.49 required for the work.

FIGURE 22: GUTTON MONUMENT

Only months prior to his own death, Fr. Hoes had a large, masonry Calvary "group" monument built, adjoining and fronting Fr. Gutton's tomb. The stepped altar-like structure features a Christ Crucified and flanked by the Virgin Mary and St. John, and was built by contractors John Morel and Arthur Fabre. The $775.35 cost was paid by public donations.

For years after its replacement by the Calvary monument, the Gutton Monument stood nearby, just across the aisle to the north and adjacent to the tomb of Joseph and Josephine "Madam Joe" Tuminello. In the early 1980s, with the completion of St. Mary Parish Hall in the rear of the church and the landscaping of the grounds, the Gutton Monument was transferred thereto and placed just to the southeast of the hall's front entrance and likewise facing the parking lot.

With the subsequent development of the ground between the hall on the north and the church on the south as the St. Joseph Garden, the Gutton Monument forms the northeastern corner of the garden. There, visitors may read the inscription bearing the birth, ordination and death dates of Rev. Joseph Philibert Gutton, as well as the line which translates from the French: "The Good Pastor gave his life for his sheep."

FATE OF OLD ST. FRANCIS CHURCH AND CEMETERY

In 1866, with the departure of Rev. Francois Mittelbronn for New Orleans, the pastorate of old St. Francis, mother church of Pointe Coupée, was assigned to Rev. Jean Arthur Poyet. His tenure was marked by breaches in the nearby Scott Levee in 1865 and again in 1867, the move of many parishioners, and general decline of the old Pointe Coupée Coast.

Writing Archbishop J.M. Odin in 1867, St. Mary pastor Rev. J.P. Gutton related that recent rains had rendered the roads in a terrible state, making travel even by horse impossible for Fr. Poyet. The St. Francis pastor asked Gutton to make "sick calls" (i.e., ministry to the ill and, if necessary, Last Sacraments) in his stead at Morganza.

A day later, Fr. Poyet wrote the Archbishop that he was unable to attend a planned retreat for priests in New Orleans, as he (Poyet) did not have "a cent" in his pockets, and he was daily ministering to more than 1,200 men laboring to safeguard the levee.

Poyet continued that he and Fr. Gutton had conferred with Auguste Provosty II about the tangled state of affairs of the recently defunct Corporation of the Congregation of the Church of Pointe Coupée. Poyet continued that Charles Poydras told him Provosty could not be counted upon to solve the troubles, "for the honor of his [Provosty's] family," as Provosty had authorized his own nephew to hold the pew rents of 1865 and $934 from fees for six months of that same year.

Fr. Poyet was succeeded as pastor of St. Francis in 1872 by Rev. Constantin Van de Moere, native of Belgium, who has assisted Fr. Gutton in ministering during a temporarily vacant pastorate at Immaculate Conception in the prior year.

While on a journey down the Mississippi River, Fr. Van de Moere was among several victims of the accidental burning of the steamer *Southern Belle*, which had just departed Marionneaux Landing a mile or so above Plaquemine, Louisiana, on the night of 10 October 1876.

Fr. Van de Moere's remains were retrieved only weeks later, and his funeral and burial took place at St. Francis on 10 November. Frs. Gutton and Broquere of Pointe Coupée Parish were among five pre-lates who signed the register of burial, as did prominent parishioners, Mssrs. Vamalle Basile, F.L. Claiborne, Jules Labatut, and Valery Ledoux.

Fr. Gutton served as administrator of Fr. Van de Moere's succession, the inventory of which included the deceased prelate's personal affects, a quantity of wine and hams, as well as cassocks, Roman Missals, books, and scores of sacramentals. The latter included: crucifixes, statuettes, rosaries in black, blue and white, medals and medallions, framed pictures, chromolithographs by the bundle, and holy water receptacles. It is likely that he had purchased these in bulk for distribution at First Communion and Confirmation ceremonies as well as sale to individuals, as religious objects were rare in contemporary inventories of Pointe Coupée Parish merchants.

Rev. Gutton, Rev. Patrick R. Glendon, pastor of Our Lady of Seven Dolors church at New Texas Landing, and several lay men and women were purchasers of the sacramentals as well as personal effects of the deceased. The sale of the sacramentals suggests that they had not been blessed.

The proceeds of the public sale of Fr. Van de Moere's goods netted $509.45, but the privileged and ordinary debts of the succession, and Fr. Gutton's two and a half percent (2.5%) commission as administrator, reduced the net value of the estate to the extent that its creditors received, *pro rata*, considerably less than they were owed.

MOTHER CHURCH BECOMES MISSION CHAPEL

Rev. Pierre Berthet, who succeeded Fr. Van de Moere, was destined to be the last pastor of venerable St. Francis of Pointe Coupée as an independent parish. In the 1880 United States Census, Rev. Amable Doutré (misspelled therein as "Emile Donutte") was indicated as living with Fr. Berthet, this being prior to Doutré's assuming the pastorate of Our Lady of Seven Dolors church upriver at New Texas Landing. Five years later, owing to the temporary incapacity of Fr. Poyet in 1885, Rev. J.P. Gutton, pastor of St. Mary in New Roads, ministered at St. Francis.

August and September of 1885 were marked by several strong rainstorms and lightning strikes in the New Roads area, documented by the *Pointe Coupée Banner*. In the first incident, lightning struck and demolished to its base the chimney of the Dutrey home near the Lower Waterloo Dyke, smashing the mantel mirror, and the survival of the six persons in the house was considered miraculous.

Similarly, the escape from injury of several ladies of the Dupéron family occupying a large house on pillars in the area of present-day Gisele Street was also considered providential. A severe rainstorm weakened the structure, then belonging to the Estate of Michel (and likely the former residence of the late Artémise Chustz), precipitating it to the ground, but the occupants were reportedly unharmed.

In between the two above incidents, on the evening of 11 August 1885, the funeral of a young African American boy was being held at old St. Francis when a thunderstorm struck. The steeple was "badly broken" and the corpse, resting on trestles on the gallery of the church, "was knocked several feet into the yard," the *Banner* related, adding that several people suffered considerable shock, including one who "bit his tongue nearly in two." The report solemnly, and accurately, concluded: "This is the oldest church in the State."

LOST TO THE RIVER

The systematic caving of the river bank and set back of levees spelled the unavoidable end of old St. Francis of Pointe Coupée. As early as 1870, the *Pointe Coupée Echo* newspaper told of a movement to disinter for reinternment the remains of the community's most noted citizen, Julien Poydras, as his burial place was located at the front of the cemetery, and the bank of the river was crumbling.

Poydras' remains were not transferred until 1891, however, with the coffin being moved first into the "chancel" of the church, and subsequently to an unmarked tomb in the rear of the cemetery. Though a plot had been procured for the purpose in St. Mary Cemetery, Poydras' remains were ultimately reinterred that October beneath a handsome monument on the front campus of Poydras Academy, following services in St. Mary Church.

Another noted transfer from old St. Francis to St. Mary Cemetery was the elaborate Ternant – Parlange mausoleum which, like Poydras' tomb, had been at the front of the old cemetery. In 1888, the Parlange family contracted with Van Matthews to dismantle the tomb and transfer its elements for re-erection in St. Mary.

Once arrived in New Roads, however, Matthews left the wagon with the tomb's elements in front of the cemetery, and proceeded downtown where he encountered a cousin, J.B. Woodruff. The two exchanged pistol shots in East Main Street, in front of J.P. Gosserand's Rich Forest Saloon, allegedly in a confrontation regarding family property, and Matthews was killed.

The incident was witnessed by future District Attorney Ferd L. Claiborne, then a boy on his way to class in the Poydras School of New Roads at New Roads and First Streets.

According to oral historian Murray LeBeau, the elements of the Ternant – Parlange tomb remained in New Roads Street for several weeks until the Parlange family successfully contracted with another man to re-erect it in St. Mary Cemetery.

Despite the abandonment of St. Francis Church and Cemetery and the transfer of remains therefrom, a few burials continued to be made on the site as late as 1892. Fr. Gutton's ledgers mention the interment on 9 July that year of a son of Robert Maurice at the "Pointe Coupée Church." The deceased is recorded in the sacramental records of burial as Joseph Maurice, age 17 years.

The 26 April 1891 New Orleans *Daily Picayune*, in a lengthy feature on the doomed church and cemetery, listed names seen by the reporter on tombs as including:

Gosserand, Porche, Gremillion, Carmouche, LeBeau, Major, Robillard, Tounoir, Bourgeat, Poydras, Dayries, Pourciau, Langlois, Joffrion, Ledoux, Cooley, Bergeron, Van Wickle, Morgan, Falconer, Swain, Lejeune, Decuir, Jarreau, Allain, Trénonay, Boisdoré, Boudreau, D'Hauterive, Bara, Labatut, Lagrange, Chenevert, Samson, Olinde, Olivier, Gauthier, Provosty, Lacour, Armstrong, Désormes, L'Hermite, Lecoq, Jewell, Lacoste, Plantevignes, Laurans, Labry, Beauvais, Bouis, Plauché, Gondran, Du Bertrand, Croizet, Berza, Labbe, Dormenon, Riche, De La Roulliere, Chustz, St. Cyr, Fabre, Monceret, Favre, Labauve, Le Bedel, Saizan, Aguillard, Guerin, Robin, Vignes, Decoux, Janis, St. Germain, Delage, Enete, Delamare, Fuselier, Sicard, Mourain, St. Eloi, Bush, Lamathe, Démourelle, Trinidad and Nugent (Note: The reporter's misspellings corrected by the author of this work).

Perusal of the sacramental records of St. Francis of Pointe Coupée reveals several thousands of persons, of various ethnicities, as having been buried in the cemetery of 1764, and it is likely that many more interred there escaped record. Despite the vast number of persons committed to tomb or grave at St. Francis, relatively few can be identified as having been relocated, based on news accounts and the present location of the markers in local cemeteries.

An exacting count by this author in 2023 totaled 97 individuals who had been moved to St. Mary, the present St. Francis, and Seven Dolors (and subsequently to St. Ann) cemeteries, and the Catholic cemetery in St. Francisville, across the Mississippi from Pointe Coupée. Of the latter, the remains of several members of the Lebret, Martin and Grisham families, some of the last to be retrieved, were transported to St. Francisville in 1892.

Complicating the transfer of more remains was that a new levee was built behind the church and cemetery in 1888, and the fear of many in disturbing the tombs of victims of the cholera pandemic of the antebellum period. Likewise, it is obvious that several families had no means to transfer the remains of ancestors, other families had moved far from Pointe Coupée Parish, and still others had no knowledge of family buried there, owing to lack of markers or social amnesia.

A small levee was built at the front of the site, alas, was taken by the river in 1890. Extensive feature articles appeared in local as well as New Orleans newspapers, complete with historical references, and in the case of the New Orleans *Daily Picayune*, woodcuts of the doomed church and burial ground. In addition to these sketches in the city paper, the 30 May 1892 *Pointe Coupée Banner* told of photographer T.T. White's image of the church in water as being for sale, alas no known copy of such a priceless view is known to exist.

New Roads attorney and *Pointe Coupée Banner* owner and editor Albin Provosty (son of former *margullier* Auguste Provosty II) spearheaded a movement to dismantle and rebuild the church at a more stable site, and headed the local fundraiser effort through a subscription list. Meanwhile, in New Orleans, wholesale grocer Lucien A. Ledoux, uncle of Mrs. Albin Provosty, née Adele Ledoux, and Albin's own cousin, headed a collection in the city, to which individuals and businesses, including Jewish firms, contributed.

It was hoped the old church could be dismantled and its materials used to build a new church, at a safer site, alas when demolition work was begun by Mssrs. Désormes & Garon (Ephraim Désormes and Louis Garon) in the summer of 1892, little of the material was found to be sound for reuse. Some of the remaining timbers on the site were carried by the high water of the great river, and retrieved by enterprising parties several miles downriver in front of Nina Plantation, immediately below Cook's Landing.

FIGURE 23: ORIGINAL CAPTION: "PICTURED ABOVE ARE MR. JOSEPH OLIVIER ST. DIZIER, AN UNIDENTIFIED GENTLEMAN, REV. JOSEPH PHILIBERT GUTTON, REV. ALFRED BACCIOCHI, FIRST AND FOURTH PASTORS OF ST. MARY AND REV. AUGUSTE ROCHARD. THIS PHOTOGRAPH WAS TAKEN IN THE LATE 1800'S IN FRONT OF THE OLD RECTORY."

ST. FRANCIS CHAPEL

New Orleans Archbishop Francis Janssens assigned the building of the third, and present, St. Francis of Pointe Coupée to hands of Rev. J.J. Ferguson, pastor of Our Lady of Seven Dolors church at New Texas Landing, in which parish all of the Mississippi riverfront was included. Meanwhile, the collections solicited by Albin Provosty in New Roads and Lucien A. Provosty in New Orleans, and contributions of individuals living in Iberville Parish totaled approximately $848.

The area around St. Maurice Landing, about four miles upriver of the old St. Francis was selected, and offers of land were made by parishioners Jean Baptiste Cambre and Pierre Félicien Bourgeois, the latter being on Stonewall, formerly Hopkins, Plantation, and where Hopkins Chapel had been in service a decade prior.

The 12 May 1894 *Pointe Coupée Banner* announced a three-day fundraiser would be held for the new St. Maurice (sic, Francis intended) church: an Arthur Theatricals drama, "A Midnight Mistake," was set for 17 May at the St. Maurice Warehouse, and again on the 18th at the American Legion of Honor "theatre" in New Roads, with refreshment tables to be presided over at the latter by the P. S. Circle ladies' organization, and a ball to follow; and on the third day of the fundraiser, 19 May, the African American committee would stage a ball in the Charity and Honor Hall.

A couple weeks later, on 5 June 1894, cotton planter Jules Labatut donated to the Archdiocese of New Orleans a lot near the northwestern corner of his plantation, measuring one arpent front on the public road along the Pointe Coupée or "Levee" Road, by a depth of four arpents, bounded west by land of Joachim Frederick and east and south by the remainder of Labatut's property.

Thereon was built, at a cost of only $648, a frame church of Gothic revival inspiration, the third church of St. Francis of Pointe Coupée and familiarly known as

FIGURE 24; FATHER FERGUSON

"St. Francis Chapel" into the 21st century. Labatut and family were given two lots in the new cemetery and perpetual use of one pew – the closest to the sanctuary on the eastern side – free of rent for perpetuity.

The church was dedicated on 29 May 1895, in the presence of an immense attendance. The subsequent, 1 June edition of the *Pointe Coupée Banner* related that "fully one half of the population of the lower portion of the parish and also many from New Texas, Raccourci and elsewhere."

While that *Banner* archival issue is somewhat damaged, it is evident that New Orleans Archbishop Francis Janssens officiated; Rev. Alfred Bacciochi, then pastor of Immaculate Conception of Chenal, offered a High Mass; and Rev. (John M.) Pendergrast of Natchez, Mississippi offered a homily. Obviously, Rev. J. J. Ferguson, pastor of Our Lady of Seven Dolors of New Texas Landing, parish in which the new chapel was built, was in attendance, and likely Rev. J.P. Gutton, pastor of St. Mary in New Roads, as well.

Archbishop Janssens delivered an address on the life of St. Francis of Assisi, and in a moving rite, blessed the donors of the property, Jules and Clélie Ranson Labatut, on the simultaneous 50th anniversary of their wedding, the aged couple kneeling at the communion rail.

Following the ceremonies at St. Francis, the public enjoyed a variety of refreshments on the church grounds until 3 p.m. M. and Mme. Labatut, legendary for their hospitality, their family, friends and clergy repaired to the stately Labatut House nearby, where congratulatory toasts were offered the esteemed and pious couple "from flowing bumpers of champagne."

TREASURES OF THE FAITH

Many of the sacred objects from the St. Francis Church of 1760 were transferred to the present St. Francis upon its completion in 1895. Intriguingly, documentation has yet to be found as to where they had been stored since the time of the abandonment of the old church several years prior.

These treasures of the Faith included a 1750s-vintage wooden confessional, which ranked in the year 2023 as one of the oldest surviving items of furniture in Louisiana; the cypress statue supposedly carved by Tunica parishioners in the 18th century; a small ship's bell, bearing three *fleur de lys* and the date 1719, several of the pews (which date from the time of Rev. Antoine Blanc); and the gilded crucifix and six candlesticks of the main altar.

Regarding the last-named, the provenance of the main altar crucifix and candlesticks is not definitely known, but a 6 June 1845 letter from marguilliers Gustave Delamare and Valery Ledoux to Bishop Blanc in New Orleans requested His Excellency to purchase "from the firm where he [Blanc] usually trades" six candlesticks and a cross for the altar of St. Francis, as well as a chalice and ciborium for St. Mary.

A month later, on 16 July, Bishop Blanc received a letter from Rev. Pierre Francois Beauprez, pastor of St. Francis, complaining that the Bishop had obviously "sided" with the marguilliers who had cut the pastor's salary to $800, were planning unnecessary "repairs" at St. Francis, and had foolishly bought candlesticks "for an altar in no state to receive them," i.e., deteriorated.

Four years after the 1962 transfer of St. Francis Chapel from the administration of St. Ann Church of Morganza to St. Mary of False River, an article

FIGURE 25: MARIA IMMACOLATA DI BORBONE

entitled "What's New at New Roads?" in the 27 March 1966 issue of *Dixie* magazine, featured the "new" and "old" attractions of Pointe Coupée Parish.

Included in the description of St. Francis Chapel was an old gold ciborium, of royal bequest, which was remembered by parishioners, alas has vanished from current record. The inscription on the ciborium indicates that it was the gift of Maria Immacolata di Borbone (Bourbon), Princess of Two Sicilies by birth, and Princess of Parma and Countess of Bardi by marriage.

This young lady of especially pious character, prior to her death at a youthful 19 years of age, offered considerable support to the cause of the Faith, including religious institutions, education of the poor, and gifts for the missionary work of the Church. The ciborium at St. Francis was apparently one of the latter.

While on her wedding trip with her husband, Enrico di Borbone, Prince of Parma and Count of Bardi, the princess became ill in Egypt, and they decided to return home. Landing at Marseilles, France early in 1874, they proceed to the sanctuary of Lourdes, where she was twice immersed in the blessed waters, but died soon after in the nearby town of Pau.

Search for the Bardi ciborium in recent years by this author and the clergy and staff of St. Mary and St. Ann churches as well as the staff of the Archives of the Diocese of Baton Rouge were fruitless as of the year 2023.

The altar of the 1760 St. Francis Church, familiar as tapering down from mensa to base and surmounted by a large tabernacle, survived until about the time of the transfer of the successor chapel from St. Ann to St. Mary parish jurisdiction. Having become decayed, it was removed and replaced by the old Gothic altar formerly in Holy Family Church in Port Allen, and where it stood in the year 2023.

The new St. Francis Cemetery was established to the rear of the chapel, with the first burial being recorded as that of Eli Bernard, on 27 December 1897. Transferred to this cemetery from Old St. Francis were the remains and slabs of Jean Pierre and Euphémie Bara Labatut, parents of site donor Jules Labatut, as well as remains of the Morrison family.

FIGURE 26: INTERIOR VIEW, FIRST ST. MARY OF FALSE RIVER 1823-1907

One subsequent burial, that of Mary Bouquet Ramagos, came to be covered by the chapel, when the structure was moved southward to its present location to make way for a new levee and highway setback circa 1930, longtime St. Francis sacristan Numa Loupe, Jr. stated in 2019.

Several tombs which were located on the sides of the cemetery were dismantled, Loupe stated, and the remains transferred to St. Ann Church Cemetery in Morganza in the 1960s, as were remains from the area of the present Chapel kitchen and restroom building, as the fate of the chapel and cemetery were uncertain at the time.

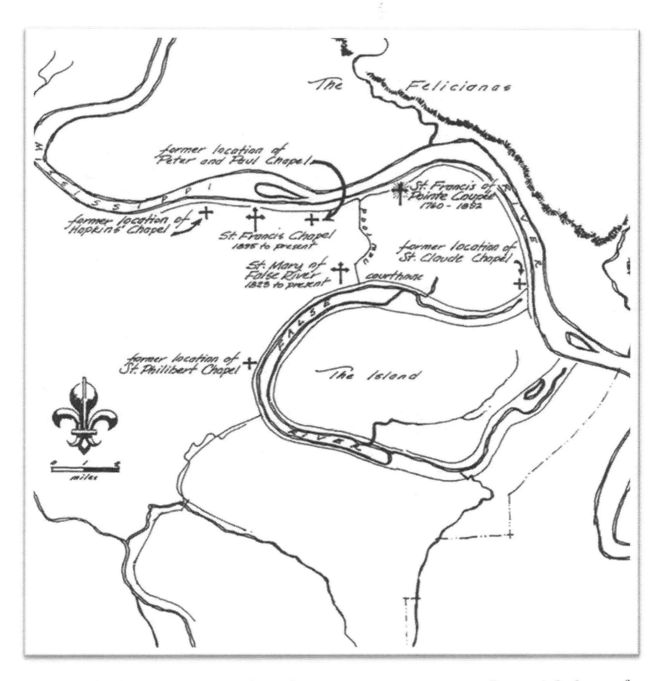

FIGURE 27: ST. MARY OF FALSE RIVER PARISH SHOWING MISSIONS OF FATHER J. P. GUTTON[3]

---

[3] Note the "Former location of Peter and Paul Chapel" item on the map is erroneous. The actual location was Lobdell, West Baton Rouge Parish.

FIGURE 28: PICAYUNE *ARTICLE TOLD OF THE PLIGHT OF THE 1760 ST. FRANCIS*

NEW CENTURY:
NEW ST. MARY CHURCH

Within 30 years after the construction of the original St. Mary of False River church in 1823, the growth of town of New Roads and congregation of the church began to outgrow the size of the hallowed house of worship. Like St. Francis Church, its wooden construction called for repairs every few years, from re-shingling of the roof, to replacement of the supporting pillars at ground level, to fresh clapboarding of the exterior walls and louvred belfry.

In 1854, the *marguilliers* resolved to make significant repairs to both churches, but Rev. Hubert Thirion, then pastor, questioned their plan for an enlarged St. Mary. Fr. Thirion wrote Archbishop Antoine Blanc in New Orleans that in lieu of having the church lengthened, the marguilliers proposed closing in the exterior galleries to either side and opening them up into the existing nave.

Thirion opposed the design, citing that it would make the church too wide and the sanctuary would not be seen by worshippers sitting at either side. Thirion asked the Archbishop to convince the marguilliers of the unsuitability of their plan.

The subsequent illness and departure of Fr. Thirion from Pointe Coupée, his successor, Rev. Francois Mittelbronn's, continued difficulty with the marguilliers, and wartime occupation and abandonment precluded any work done to the churches for another decade.

During the pastorate of Rev. J.P. Gutton, in 1869, the roofless, decaying St. Mary was extended 30 feet in depth, its walls strengthened and a new roof built. Ornamentation of the three altars was also undertaken, and a handsome sanctuary carpet presented by Sam Stauffer & Co., cotton factors of New Orleans.

Though monetary contributions of the faithful normally paid for the adornment of St. Mary, Fr. Gutton personally underwrote the acquisition of two stained glass windows in 1886. The *Pointe Coupée Banner* of 1 May that year, recounting the previous Sunday's Easter celebrations in the church, recorded his generosity for posterity, and told of the "radient" (sic) appearance of the church interior, owing to the windows.

An undated but obviously 1880s-1890s era photograph of the interior of the old St. Mary indicates floods of light issuing from a pair of windows, located to either side of the sanctuary, between it and the side altars. These were likely the windows installed by Fr. Gutton in 1886. Behind the main altar, the wall appears to be painted, or at least stenciled, to represent tiers of columns draped in garlands.

The altars to either side, that on the left featuring a statue of the Blessed Virgin Mary and that on the right St. Joseph, had reredos in the classic style of columns supporting a pediment, framing each of the statues. In the pediment of the Virgin altar was a triangle, perhaps representing the Holy Trinity and bearing the name of God in Hebrew letters, while the pediment above St. Joseph's altar displayed the twin tablets of the Ten Commandments.

On the second full column from the sanctuary on the eastern side can be seen a large crucifix, believed to be the same as hanging on the first full column from the sanctuary on the right side in the present church. Bracket oil lamps appear on the columns in the photo of the old church.

It is a blessing that neither the original nor the present St. Mary Churches were damaged, let alone destroyed, by fire, as has happened to so many churches, whether of frame or brick construction. Old St. Mary narrowly escaped conflagration around 4 a.m., 15 January 1888, when fire erupted across West Main Street from the rectory in a building owned by civic leader and stalwart church supporter Joseph Richy.

FIGURE 29: REV. FRANCOIS LAROCHE, 1899-1905

Though not stated in the subsequent, 21 January, report in the Pointe Coupée *Banner*, the structure was quite possibly the Nogués Building, which served immediately following the Civil War as Pierre Nogués' store, hotel, restaurant and bar, as well as the first location of the Freedmen's Bureau New Roads field office.

Inhabited by a "colored" family, the building had been the site of a "fair" (home entertainment) earlier in the night of the fire, but whether or not the blaze began as a result was unknown. The building, and all contents therein, were destroyed in the inferno, and of the many structures owned in the town by Joseph Richy, this was reportedly the only one which he had not covered by insurance.

St. Mary's Church bell, *Maria Seraphina Clara*, was rung as an alarm, attracting several citizens who attempted in vain to save Richy's building. The *Banner* opined that if the wind that morning had been from the south or west, it certainly would have spread the fire across the street and St. Mary would have been destroyed.

GROWING, MULTI-ETHNIC CONGREGATION

As the 19th century neared its end, the congregation of St. Mary of False River, having experienced natural increase, received the addition of several Sicilian and Syrian immigrant families. Italians from the mainland states had been in the New Roads area since antebellum times, including Bartolomeo Betlami, onetime sacristan of St. Francis Church, and families including Colombo (for whom Colombo Lane east of New Roads was named), Belozi, Sghirla, Robiote, Bestoso, Cazali, and Musso.

Garibaldi's invasion and conquest of the Papal and other Italian states and their unification under the house of Savoia as the Kingdom of Italy sent into flight many families loyal to the Papacy and the exiled Borbone (Bourbon) and Habsburg families. Subsequently others, particularly in the former Kingdom of the Two Sicilies, immigrated to Louisiana due to crop failures and infrastructural neglect by the new Italian kingdom.

Among the latter were families who settled in the New Roads area, engaging principally in the grocery, restaurant and saloon business, including: Pepitone, Tuminello, Sansone, D'Amico, Cacciatore Castellano (subsequently Costello), LoCicero (subsequently Cicero), Piazza, Rosso, Colletta, Locricchio, Rinaudo, Serio, and Affronti. Most were from the Sicilian seaport of Cefalú, while others were from towns such as Santo Stefano Quisquina, Altavilla Milicia, Vicari, and Trabia.

Cefalú native Concettina Flacommio, wife of East Main Street restauranteur Giovanni "John" Rosso, died in 1929 and was recalled in oral history of friends and neighbors to have remained flexible in death and, therefore, did not undergo rigor mortis, prior to entombment on the front aisle of St. Mary Cemetery. Such cases are rare, and the common local explanation is that the deceased was a person of great sanctity. The *Pointe Coupée Banner* did not mention the above phenomenon in its front-page obituary of the kindly Mrs. Rosso on 18 July 1929, but described her as:

> …one of those gentle creatures who meet one and all with a pleasant smile, and while not well versed in the English language, that smile conveyed volumes of kind, unspoken words … [continuing] that her "constant thoughts" were for the comfort of her husband and the welfare of their three teenaged children.

The Rosso Restaurant mentioned above was in the east half of the "divided building," at 155 East main Street, which had been two, neighboring shops of circa 1901 vintage and combined in 1921 by John Rosso. Before their ownership and occupancy, the east building had been home to the New Roads branch of the Grossman–Weinfeld millinery company, one of the parish's several Jewish-owned businesses. In January 2023, the site was occupied by St. John the Theologian Orthodox Church, the first Orthodox congregation founded in Pointe Coupée Parish.

A later generation of the Rosso family built the interesting brick, vaulted tomb, commonly referred to as "the little house" immediately south of the Calvary Monument and tomb of Revs. J.P. Gutton and John Hoes in St. Mary Cemetery. For many years, this mausoleum was opened and out-of-town family members sat therein on each All Saints Day, in time-honored Latin custom.

Most familiar and best-loved of the Italian families, and likewise natives of Cefalu, were mobile fruit, vegetable and ice vendor Giuseppe (Joseph) Tuminello and wife, Giuseppa (Josephine) "Madam Joe," née Curreri, who operated a popular "confectionery" (candy and fruit store) on East Main Street for more than a half century, and was a St. Mary parishioner of great piety. Many of the interior treasures of the church were her gifts,

FIGURE 30: "MADAM JOE" TUMINELLO, STALWART PARISHIONER

and she was frequently mentioned with appreciation by Fr. Hoes in his journal.

A daily Mass attendee, in the decades of pew rentals, Madam Joe maintained as her sitting place the first pew in front of the altar, to the east of the center aisle, while opposite her, in the first pew on the west side, sat the Sisters of St. Joseph. Widowed, Madam Joe spent her last years as a resident of the Sisters' St. Joseph Clinic, just across and down East Main Street from her former confectionery store.

The Syrians or Lebanese were smaller in number, but prominent in the dry goods, clothing and jewelry trades, having stores or peddling operations in the New Roads area. Their names included Sliman, Getany, Assfoura, Rossey, Bahry, Mansur, and Mahfouz. Most moved on to other Louisiana communities after brief local residency.

Interestingly, Syrians contributing to the fund for the building of a new St. Mary Church during 1903-1904, included in addition to the above, others who were likely living in other communities but, through their signature piety, wished to donate to a new house of worship for their colleagues in New Roads.

Smallest of the ethnic minorities, and also of short residency, were the Chinese. Of the five Chinese in New Roads, all independent laundrymen operating within two blocks of St. Mary Church, Jim Kee donated $1 to the St. Mary building fund and aided a fundraising event for same in 1904.

Following the death of the cherished *Pére* Gutton in 1896, Rev. Francis Cools, native of Belgium, was assigned to the pastorate of St. Mary of False River. In March 1898, Fr. Cools oversaw the repair and much-need expansion of the old St. Mary, in time for the arrival of two missionaries who were to lecture therein in the coming summer.

A photograph depicting the old church as well as the present St. Mary Church about 1906 indicates that the lateral galleries of the old church had been enclosed, and apparently opened into the nave for the accommodation of additional worshippers. This was obviously the enlargement of 1898.

FIGURE 31: REV. FRANCIS COOLS, PASTOR OF ST. MARY, 1896-1899

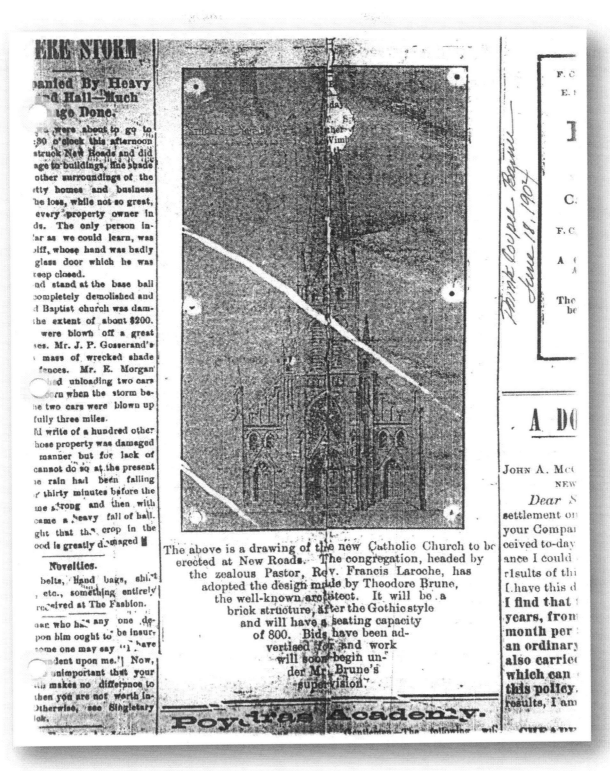

The above is a drawing of the new Catholic Church to be erected at New Roads. The congregation, headed by the zealous Pastor, Rev. Francis Laroche, has adopted the design made by Theodore Brune, the well-known architect. It will be a brick structure, after the Gothic style and will have a seating capacity of 800. Bids have been advertised for and work will soon begin under Mr. Brune's supervision.

FIGURE 32: ADVERTISEMENT FOR NEW ST. MARY OF FALSE RIVER CHURCH

FUNDRAISING FOR NEW CHURCH

The last years of the 19th century and first ones of the 20th century, a number of fundraising events were staged by the congregation of St. Mary of False River, as they and their pastors formulated plans for a new church. These events, including presentation of tableaux, plays, banquets, fairs, and raffles were relatively successful, while subscription lists circulated during 1903-1904 brought in substantial sums.

The subscription lists, which the *Pointe Coupée Banner* faithfully printed during that time, showed donations ranging from one to several hundred dollars committed by business firms and individuals, Catholic and non-Catholic, of various ethnicities, from the church parish to New Orleans and beyond.

It is significant that while Jewish citizens counted for only one percent of the population of the community, they comprised 12 percent of the businesses and individuals donating for the new church, and their contributions totaled six percent of all money raised.

In return for the contributions from Protestant citizens, parishioners of St. Mary are noted in contemporary *Banner* accounts as helping financially and materially in the establishment of Holy Trinity Episcopal Mission of New Roads and its successor church of St. Paul – Holy Trinity, a merger of St. Paul Episcopal Church of Lakeland and Holy Trinity of New Roads.

The Congregation of St. Mary also realized income from the sale of its property on the east side of New Roads Street, both south and north of St. Mary Cemetery.

J.P. Gosserand was the purchaser of several lots, the largest being a four arpent square piece, bounded south by his residence lot (present-day 208 New Roads Street), and north by the Cemetery, along which northern line Gosserand Street, later renamed East Fifth Street, was opened shortly after the turn of the century.

Gosserand purchased the property from the Congregation in 1897 and immediately established thereupon Gosserand Park, having a baseball diamond and bleachers. The park remained in operation, despite destruction of the bleachers during the 1909 hurricane, until its services were supplanted by the larger Community Park which was opened in 1927 in the eastern part of town.

FIGURE 33: THEODORE BRUNE

Rev. Francis Cools was succeeded as pastor of St. Mary of False River in 1899 by Fr. Francois Laroche, during whose tenure definite plans were made for a new church. In early spring of 1904, Fr. Laroche visited France, and on his return celebrated the Blessing of the Children of St. Mary church parish.

The *Pointe Coupée Banner* of 22 April reported that on the previous Sunday, 16 April, at 4 p.m., Fr. Laroche offered a service in which be blessed between 800 and 1,000 children, and presented each with a medal (likely the *Médaille Miraculeuse* or Miraculous Medal) he had brought from France.

The pastor then turned his attention to the proposed new church, and the 30 April *Banner* related that a building committee had been formed, consisting of Fr. Laroche, Joseph Richy, J.P. Gosserand, and subsequent Mayor of New Roads and Sheriff of Pointe Coupée Lamartine Bouanchaud. They engaged Baden native Theodore Brune to design the new church.

Talented in several architectural idioms, Brune also designed St. Joseph Church in Greenville, Mississippi, which closely resembles St. Mary in New Roads; the Cathedral of the Nativity of the Blessed Virgin Mary in Biloxi, Mississippi, whose lateral walls and apse echo St. Mary's; the classical revival Mater Dolorosa Church on Carrollton Avenue in New Orleans; and the Romanesque St. Benedict Abbey Church in Covington, Louisiana.

Apparently, some overly-zealous citizens felt that work was proceeding too slowly, as on the night of 24 May 1904, the windows of the rectory were broken and a note attached to a brick was tossed into the house. The message stated that if work did not begin on the church in 30 days, Fr. Laroche would be attacked.

The congregation voiced revulsion at the deed, an inter-community resolution posted in the *Pointe Coupée Banner*, and a reward for the capture of the culprits who, apparently, were never identified, let alone apprehended.

A few weeks later, the 18 June 1904 *Banner* featured an illustration of Brune's proposed elevation of the new St. Mary's, and in August the Koerner & Murphy Construction Company of Abbeville, Louisiana received the contract for the erection of the new church at the price of $12,182.50. The site of the new church was 20 feet to west of the old St. Mary, the latter serving until completion of its successor.

CONSTRUCTION OF THE PRESENT CHURCH

The cornerstone of the present St. Mary Church was laid 4 December 1904 by Archbishop Placide Louis Chapelle, who had arrived the previous night by train at the Texas & Pacific Railroad depot. Per the 10 December *Pointe Coupée Banner* report, "A large concourse of citizens from New Roads and all parts of the parish" were on hand to greet him, and J.P. Gosserand offered a welcoming address.

The *Banner* related that the Archbishop was assisted in the ceremonies of the next day by Revs. DuBernard (sic, J.H. DuBernard was deceased; should read J.P. Solignac), his secretary; Eugéne Royer, acting pastor of St. Mary; Henry Van Grinsven, pastor of Our Lady of Mount Carmel Church in St. Francisville; J.J. Ferguson, pastor of Our Lady of Dolors, New Texas Landing; and Louis Savouré, pastor of Immaculate Conception, Chenal.

The cornerstone is a marble block, located in the extreme southwestern point of the church, and is inscribed "Decembre 4, 1904," interesting in that the month was rendered in the French term, but with the date following, in the American manner. Inserted in the stone was a parchment attesting to the event, signed by His Grace, all of the assisting clergy, and the building committee.

The ceremonies, having begun at 3:30 p.m., were not concluded until after dark, according to the *Banner*, which added that a misty rain fell throughout that time, but more than 1,000 attendees "of both sexes" remained bare-headed in reverential observance.

On the following day, Archbishop Chapelle offered Sunday High Mass, with a homily in French, and afterward confirmed a class of 427 young people. In the afternoon, he offered another homily, in English, and was entertained at dinner by Rev. Royer. Also in attendance were visiting clergy and St. Mary's advisory and building committees. The meal ended by an expression of appreciation from Mayor Lamartine Bouanchaud, and the Archbishop and his secretary departed New Roads by the next day's 6:30a.m. train.

St. Mary, Gothic revival in style and having a classic nave and aisle plan, with apses at the head of each, has the following dimensions, as related in the 30 January 1905 *Pointe Coupée Banner*: 56 feet wide by 134 feet in length, center nave height of 46 feet, and exterior gable height of 61 feet. Topping the structure, as depicted in an architectural rendering in the *Banner*, was a spire steeple, terminating at 135 feet above foundation level.

FIGURE 34: NEW ST. MARY'S WAS BUILT 20 FEET TO WEST OF OLD CHURCH

The bricks came from New Roads Brickyard, which was capable at peak operation of producing 40,000 "cherry red" bricks per day. Other New Roads structures built of New Roads Bricks include the present, 1902 vintage Pointe Coupée Parish Courthouse; the 1906 municipal waterworks and power plant, in the year 2023 occupied by Circa reception center; and the 1909 First National Bank, home of Edward Jones agency in 2023.

New Roads contractor Wade Bouanchaud directed the interior work of the present St. Mary, with omissions of the some of its planned interior ornamentation such as columns and capitals in Gothic style, as costs soared considerably higher than expected. As such, funds were not available for the completion of the spire steeple as designed, and the bell tower remained uncrowned for more than 20 years after substantial completion of the church in 1907.

The ultimate cost of the present St. Mary Church was approximately $50,000 at substantial completion, with crowning corner spires and balustrade as well as tympanum plaques added in 1929 costing an additional $8,442.32. Adding the cost of the interior ornamentation, financed largely by the faithful, the total cost of the church was approximately $78,640 by the time Rev. John Hoes' death in 1942.

As work on the church proceeded, Fr. Laroche was succeeded as pastor by the distinguished and erudite Rev. Alfred Bacciochi, another native Frenchman and descendant of a noble Italian family. He was the first-known former associate of St. Mary to become pastor. Having also served Immaculate Conception Church art Chenal and founding St. Anthony Church in Eunice, Louisiana. Fr. Bacciochi died in Saskatchewan, Canada, where he served the last of his 61 years in the priestly ministry.

In 27 October 1949 and 8 March 1951 features, the *Pointe Coupée Banner* related that Fr. Bacciochi was fluent in French, English, Spanish, Latin and Greek, and had an extensive library, including 13th century manuscripts. Also a poet, his works included one titled "False River."

"His wealth of human kindness and understanding of his fellow men made him beloved to many," the article stated, and continued in the words of Bishop M.J. Lemieux of Gravelbourg: "This man [Bacciochi] has always found enough good in his fellow human being that he has never been known to speak poorly of any man."

FIGURE 35: REV. ALFRED BACCIOCHI

During Fr. Bacciochi's pastorate of St. Mary of False River, the present church was substantially completed, and dedicated in 1907. Old St. Mary, 20 feet to its east, continued to serve until the dedication of the new church.

Perhaps an indication that many of the nostalgic faithful whose spiritual lives and those of their ancestors had centered on the 1823 church for so long, the *Pointe Coupée Banner* reported the observance of All Saints' Day 1906 as the largest ever celebrated in the parish. The 3 November issue of the journal estimated 2,500 persons to have jammed into and surrounded the hallowed edifice for Holy Mass, and a gathering of 1,500 in the cemetery for the blessing of the graves.

An inventory of the sacred vessels, furnishings, vestments and altar linens in old St. Mary Church was made during the pastorate of Rev. Alfred Bacciochi, likely as an historic record just prior to its demolition. Included in the enumeration were: a main altar, Virgin Mary and St. Joseph altars, the latter two with statues of the saints thus honored; statues of Jesus with Sacred Heart, Our Lady of Prompt Succor, Patroness of Louisiana, Our Lady of Port. (sic, likely Bon Port or Port Louis intended), St. Anthony, a pair of adoring angels on each side of the main altar, and a (Nativity) Crib set.

The candlesticks were itemized as: a Pascal candlestick, four sets of candelabras, three sets of candlesticks, two sets of smaller candlesticks, a set of glass candlesticks, and a set of funeral candlesticks. The crosses were identified as four altar crosses and three processional crosses, while other items inventoried included 20 vases, a set of Way of the Cross images, a sanctuary lamp, a wooden catafalque and "ornaments," a pulpit, an organ, and 80 pews.

A plan to convert the old St. Mary Church into school purposes after completion of the new church did not materialize, likely owing to the aged condition of the 1823 structure, but a substantial amount of sound material was preserved during the dismantling and used in the construction of at least three West Main Street residences. These were: the Evariste Sanchez, later Dr. Edward Loupe, D.D.S., residence at No. 511, whose sills were from the old church, this house being demolished when structurally unsound in the early 21st century; the John Morrison home at No. 1007; and the largest of the trio, the two-story, English styled Ferd C. Claiborne residence at 1201 West Main. The latter, not built until 1922, included the windows as well as one panel of the great entrance doors of old St. Mary. An attraction for generations, the house was, alas, found architecturally unsound and dismantled in the year 2022.

CHURCH DEDICATION

The present St. Mary Church was dedicated on 7 March 1907 by New Orleans Archbishop James Hubert Blenk. That afternoon's New Orleans *Daily Picayune* account of the ceremonies stated that His Grace and secretary were met by "an immense delegation" upon their arrival at the Texas & Pacific Railroad depot, and escorted to the church where a welcome address was offered by New Roads Mayor and St. Mary Building Committee member Lamartine Bouanchaud.

Archbishop Blenk was assisted in the dedication rite by Revs. Jules B. Jeanmard, of St. Louis Cathedral in New Orleans, and subsequently Bishop of Lafayette, Louisiana); J.F. Solignac, dean, and pastor of St. Joseph Church in Baton Rouge; Henry Van Grinsven, pastor of Our Lady of Mount Carmel, St. Francisville; Louis Savouré, pastor of Immaculate Conception, Chenal; J.J. Ferguson, pastor of Our Lady of Seven Dolors, New Texas Landing; and St. Mary's pastor and associate, Alfred Bacciochi and Eugene Cabanel.

Following the dedication, His Grace administered the sacrament of Confirmation to the largest class in recorded Pointe Coupée Parish history, numbering nearly 500.

In its account of 16 March 1907, the *Pointe Coupée Banner* related that Archbishop Blenk had failed to make connection with his intended train out of New Orleans, and taking a later one did not arrive in New Roads until 3:30 p.m. He was, therefore, unable to offer High Mass as planned, but the local and visiting clergy did so. The *Banner* went on the state that though His Grace was fluent in several languages, he spoke entirely in English.

A fair was held on dedication day, orchestrated by the ladies of the parish, and the *Banner* reported that they netted nearly $500, for benefit of the church's building fund.

The spire steeple designed by Theodore Brune for the present St. Mary was not built as planned, owing to the lack of funding. This proved providential, as such a structure would likely have been toppled by any of the tropical storms which assaulted New Roads with hurricane force, including those of: 1909 (Grand Isle Hurricane), 1947 (George), 1965 (Betsy), 1992 (Andrew), and 2008 (Gustav). All struck with winds of about 90 miles per hour force, but Andrew had gusts as high as 110 miles per hour.

CROP FAILURES AND
WORST FLOOD IN HISTORY

As the construction of St. Mary proceeded in 1906, the boll weevil, sweeping across the American South from Mexico, arrived in Pointe Coupée Parish, decimating the parish's largest crop, and affecting future harvests for more than a decade. Severe freezes killed the sugar cane crops around False River in 1910 and again in 1911.

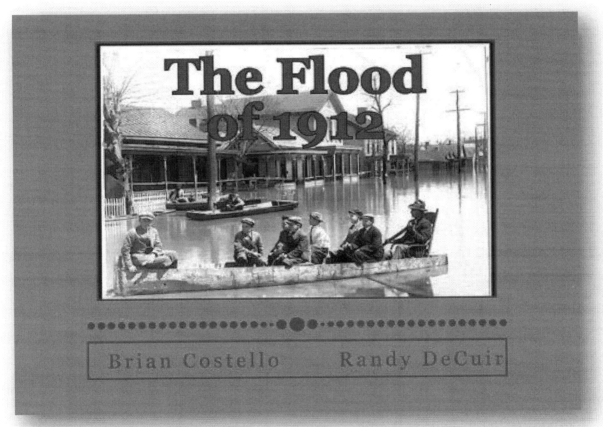

FIGURE 36: THE FLOOD OF 1912, *PREVIOUS TREATMENT OF THE SUBJECT BY THE AUTHOR*

As the *coup de gras*, in 1912 the parish suffered its worst natural disaster, with the levee breach at Torras in the northeastern corner of the parish producing unprecedented flooding and damage to Pointe Coupée and many parishes to the south. The flood covered 90 percent of the surface of Pointe Coupée from one to 20 feet deep, and of its pre-flood peak population of nearly 26,000, 17,000 were rendered homeless, of whom 12,000 were evacuated by trains and steamships to Baton Rouge and towns west of the Atchafalaya River Basin. Many, finding better educational and employment opportunities elsewhere, never returned to the parish, and the population has yet in the 21st century to regain its peak numbers of 1912.

Of the 5,000 homeless who remained in Pointe Coupée during the flood of 1912, camped atop levees or in the dry part of New Roads, south of the railroad, the Sisters of St. Joseph were among the many who journeyed by boat throughout the month to provide material and spiritual assistance.

FIGURE 37: DOWNTOWN MELVILLE, LOUISIANA DURING THE FLOOD OF 1912,
FROM THE STATE LIBRARY DIGITAL ARCHIVE (WWW.STATE.LIB.LA.US)

The Sisters had planned to evacuate, as did some 100 of the laity of New Roads, but government officials implored the nuns to stay and help bolster the hope of the townspeople. Within less than a week, the northern part of the town was inundated, from a foot deep at the Texas & Pacific Railroad embankment to 10 feet deep near the Iron Bridge crossing Portage Canal. The floodwater topped and washed out the railway west of town and began to cover the Poydras Avenue crossing, headed toward downtown when, suddenly, the inland rise reached its crest.

It is to the Sisters of St. Joseph leading the faithful in prayers to Our Lady of Prompt Succor, Patroness of Louisiana, that generations have believed the greater, southern portion of New Roads was spared the flood of 1912 and its two successors. On its part, the 13 May 1912 *New York Times* reported: "Water from Torras is surrounding New Roads, but today it was at a stand."

Untold thousands of animals drowned in Pointe Coupée in 1912, as did at least 65 men, women and children, principally in the northern and southernmost sections of the parish, and others died in the typhoid epidemic which succeeded the recession of floodwater. The parish never fully recovered from the succession of setbacks, which continued with typhoid epidemics in 1913 and 1925 and the influenza pandemic of 1918, which claimed hundreds of local victims.

A return of a sense of normalcy and material prosperity occurred in the 1920s. By 1929, sufficient funds had been collected through annual July 4 fundraising celebrations coordinated by Council 1998 Knights of Columbus and other means for the completion of a modified crowning touch to St. Mary Church, described elsewhere in this volume.

FLOOD OF 1912 PHOTOGRAPHIC FEATURE

*FIGURE 38: POINTE COUPEE PARISH DURING THE FLOOD OF 1912,
FROM THE STATE LIBRARY DIGITAL ARCHIVE (WWW.STATE.LIB.LA.US)*

*FIGURE 39: PHOTOGRAPH OF THE LEVEE BREACH AT TORRAS, 1 MAY 1912,
WHICH BREACH CAUSED THE FLOOD OF 1912*

FIGURE 41: REFUGEES ESCAPING THE FLOOD AT TORRAS

FIGURE 40: REFUGEES AT THE TEXAS & PACIFIC RAILROAD EMBANKMENT

NOTRE-DAME DE PROMPT-SECOURS,   OUR LADY OF PROMPT-SUCCOR,

hâtez-vous de nous secourir!   hasten to our help!

MIRACULOUS STATUE OF OUR LADY OF PROMPT-SUCCOR VENERATED AT NEW ORLEANS

IN THE CHAPEL OF THE URSULINE NUNS

FIGURE 42: POPULAR ICON OF OUR LADY OF PROMPT SUCCOR, INTERCEDING FOR THE FAITHFUL AGAINST NATURAL DISASTERS AS PATRONESS OF LOUISIANA

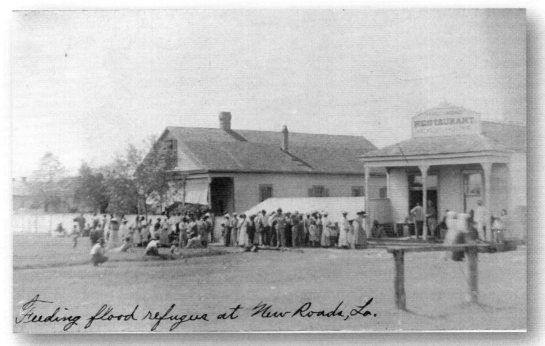

Feeding flood refuges at New Roads, La.

FIGURE 44: FLOOD REFUGEES BEING FED IN NEW ROADS

Building boats for flood relief work.

FIGURE 43: "BUILDING BOATS FOR FLOOD RELIEF WORK"

FATHER HOES:
ADORNING THE TEMPLE

J ust prior to the dedication of the present St. Mary of False River church in 1907, the *Pointe Coupée Banner* commented on the beauty of its three altars, of pure white ornamented in gold. The main altar was financed anonymously, yet oral tradition states its donor to have been merchant and planter Thomas Mix, of the False River community named for him.

Mix and wife, née Léocadie Michel, and family were among the most generous contributors to St. Mary Church, financially, and through the donation of the Eleventh Station of the Cross, "Jesus is Nailed to the Cross," and "The Assumption" stained glass window in the sanctuary.

Mr. and Mrs. Thomas Mix were especially supportive of the Sicilian families who settled in the Mix and Oscar neighborhoods, standing as godparents and as confirmation sponsors for many of the youth, and offering use of the large Mix tomb on the front aisle of St. Mary Cemetery for entombment of their deceased.

FIGURE 45: ST. MARY'S BEFORE COMPLETION OF THE BELL TOWER

Moreover, it was Thomas Mix who telephoned Baton Rouge governmental and relief authorities when the advancing floodwaters of the 1912 crevasse at Torras reached the cultivated fields of False River and "the suburbs" of New Roads on 8 May, thereby endangering some 20,000 lives.

The Mixes were strong in devotion to Our Lady of Prompt Succor, to whose intercession the sparing of the larger part of New Roads was attributed, and three of their grandchildren accepted the call to religious vocations.

Though the 8 March 1907 New Orleans *Daily Picayune* account of the dedication of the present St. Mary Church stated it to have a seating capacity of 900 persons, the maximum number of persons who can be accommodated by seating in the church is obviously much less. There are approximately 140 stationary pews, of gold oak in Gothic design, which can comfortably seat three persons per pew, for a total of approximately 420 persons, and if four squeeze into each pew, a total of 560.

In 1941, 100 folding wooden chairs were acquired, these being located in the rearmost part of the church and in the cross aisles, thereby provided additional seating. Those at the rear were usually occupied by persons with mobility limitations.

The function of these chairs was succeeded by additional wooden pews, crafted in the 1980s, which have been temporarily placed in the church in the cross aisles and adjacent to the side altars to provide for additional seating of approximately 64 worshippers for the great feasts of Christmas and Easter. More than 100 persons can be accommodated in the Parish Hall, in movable chairs, for these liturgies, which are live-streamed from the church proper.

GALLERIES AND PULPIT

In its earliest years, galleries surrounded the present St. Mary church interior on three sides, that at the rear supporting the organ and choir and referred to as the Choir Loft, and those extending along the lateral walls from choir loft to approximately the side doors to the church were remembered by late parishioner Alton Gaudin to have provided accommodation for African American worshippers, in those days of legalized segregation. As documentation has yet to be found attesting to the number of worshippers who could have occupied the galleries, the exact seating capacity of St. Mary Church at its highest remains elusive.

Speaking to the era of segregation, it is noteworthy that during the politically volatile 1920s, no Ku Klux Klan activity was reported in the New Roads area. *Pointe Coupée Banner* reports in 1922 tell of Klansmen visiting the Lottie community, in southwestern Pointe Coupée Parish. Their arrival sent local African Americans fleeing for the duration, while the Klansmen went into a white Baptist church. The nervous congregation was supposedly informed by the uninvited Klansmen that the latter was on a mission to stamp out cohabitation and bootlegging.

The lateral galleries inside St. Mary Church in New Roads were removed in 1925, after the establishment of St. Augustine Church by the Josephite Fathers, approximately a half-mile distant from St. Mary, in 1922. The majority of local Catholics of African American and mixed ethnicities became members of St. Augustine.

Also existing until 1925 was an elevated pulpit, recalled by Gaudin as being located on the first full column from the sanctuary, on the western side of the nave.

Continued sales of church property on the east side of New Roads Street helped pay for St. Mary's construction costs. In 1905, Adolphus Busch of St. Louis, Missouri purchased two lots, each fronting 200 feet, and separated by Janssens Street. The southern lot had a depth of 300 feet, and was bounded on the south the street paralleling the north side of the Texas & Pacific Railroad right-of-way, known for some time as Busch Street, but for most of its history as Railroad Avenue.

The northern lot sold to Adolphus Bush had a depth of 200 feet, and was bounded on the south by Janssens Street and north by the remainder of the church property. Busch built upon the site a huge, two-story frame building as an Anheuser Busch beer and ice plant.

In 1916, Rev. John Hoes, then pastor of St. Mary, bought the company's wheeled iron Victor Patent safe for $90, toward which devoted parishioner George Pourciau donated $45. It was placed in the old rectory, and upon completion of the present one in 1924, moved therein into a specially built brick chamber or "walk-in vault" with reinforced foundation which remains in use in the 21st century.

In 1906, Rev. Alfred Bacciochi purchased from the Congregation, for subsequent re-sale, three properties: the first, measuring 231 feet front on New Roads Street by depth of 406 to Courthouse (later Court) Street on the rear or east, bounded south by St. Mary Cemetery and north by the right-of-way of Texas & Pacific Railroad; the second, measuring 200 feet front on Busch Street (later Railroad Avenue) by depth of 300 feet, bounded east by Mrs. Auguste F. St. Didier, et al, west by Adolphus Busch, and north by an unnamed (Janssens) street; and third, a 200 by 200 foot lot directly north of the second lot described above.

AGREEMENT WITH TOWN: FREE UTILITIES

In 1906, the Town of New Roads erected its municipal waterworks plant and tower – and subsequently electric plant – on a 60-foot stretch of riverbank, encompassing the 14-foot-wide lower extension of St. Mary Street and 46 feet frontage of the St. Mary property to the west. Neither sale nor act of donation was recorded, but in a succession of officially recorded 99-year lease agreements, the Town agreed to provide the church with free utilities.

At the front of Rev. John Hoes' journal is an undated note stating that the concession of free "water and light" for the church was made in exchange for the construction of a municipal (water) pipe along the east side of the church property. In modern times, the City of New Roads abrogated the concession, and St. Mary has since paid for all of the church plant's utility usage.

STATIONS OF THE CROSS

Rev. John Hoes, succeeding Rev. Alfred Bacciochi as pastor of St. Mary of False River in 1913 due to the latter's illness, diligently saw to completion the finishing of St. Mary's interior ornamentation. Most of the fittings, statuary and adornment was financed through a number of parishioners and organizations, notably Josephine Currieri "Madam Joe" Tuminello, a much-loved Sicilian confectionery owner on East Main Street.

A sanctuary lamp and small organ were installed in 1914 and a baptismal font in the following year.

Also in 1915, fine Way of the Cross framed oils on canvas, painted by students studying the originals in Europe, were hung on the plastered lateral walls of the church. They were solemnly blessed by Fr. Hoes in the following year.

The canvases were restored and the frames shortened and crowning crosses lowered onto the face of the pediments during the 1977-1979 church renovation. The canvases were restored again in 2005, with coordination by St. Mary's staff member, Cathie H. Crochet.

Listed in counterclockwise progression, from northwest to northeast, the Stations are:

- ❖ **On western wall, from north to south:** 1. "Jesus is Condemned to Death," donated by Pupils of St. Joseph Academy; 2. "Jesus is Made to Bear His Cross," by Mrs. Marcy Lebeau; 3. "Jesus Falls the First Time," by Mrs. Ben Jewell, Sr.; 4. "Jesus is met by His Blessed Mother," by George Pourciau Family; 5. "The Cross is Laid on Simon of Cyrene," by Mr. and Mrs. J.B.H. Hebert; 6. "Veronica Wipes the Face of Jesus," by C. Cazayoux Family;
- ❖ **On southern wall, from west to east:** 7. "Jesus Falls the Second Time," by Bondy Family; 8. "Jesus Speaks to the Women of Jerusalem," by St. Mary's Branch 367 C.K.A. [Catholic Knights of America];
- ❖ **On eastern wall, from south to north:** 9. "Jesus Falls the Third Time," by Pupils of Poydras Academy; 10. "Jesus is Stripped of His Garments," by T.R. Lorio Family; 11. "Jesus is Nailed to the Cross," by Thomas Mix Family; 12. "Jesus Dies on the Cross," by Beauregard Olinde Family; 13. "Jesus is taken Down from the Cross," by Mr. and Mrs. Albin Major; 14. "Jesus is Laid in the Sepulchre," by W.O.W. and W.C. [Woodmen of the World and Woodmen Circle].

Fr. Hoes related in his journal that each station cost $25, given by the respective sponsors, and that the following also contributed to the expense of their acquisition and installation: Mssrs. Lamartine Bouanchaud, Willie Morel, Jr., Wade Bouanchaud, Jake Morrison (father of future New Orleans mayor deLesseps "Chep" Morrison) and Charles Parent, and Mmes. Alcide Bouanchaud (née Eugenia Hébert), Marcy Lebeau (née Hazilda Samson) and L.B. Claiborne (née Rosa Pourciau).

A WEALTH OF STATUES

Between 1917 and 1926, a wealth of realistically painted plaster statues was installed in St. Mary of False River, on the altars and on individual pedestals. These included the following:

- ❖ Calvary group sculptures of Jesus Crucified, Virgin Mary, St. John the Apostle, and Mary Magdalene on a wide pedestal, flanked by a pair of medium height candlesticks, originally located against a pilaster between the Sanctuary and the St. Joseph Altar, installed 1917 and financed by the Rosary Society, Anne Lejeune and Auguste Bondy; repaired and repainted 1928 with money from Mrs. Joseph Tuminello and parishioners;
- ❖ St. Anne with Child Mary, paid by public collection through Sewing (sic, Needlework likely intended) Circle, installed 1918, on west wall in front of the Virgin Mary altar, fronted by a metal votive candle stand;
- ❖ Jesus with Sacred Heart and its Gothic pedestal, against pilaster between Sanctuary and Virgin Mary altar, installed 1917 and financed by the Rosary Society, Anne Lejeune, and Auguste Bondy;
- ❖ Our Lady of Prompt Succor with Infant Jesus, both uncrowned, in the northwest corner, to the left of the Virgin Mary altar, donated by J.P. Gosserand, retouched in 1918, and he donated its fluted column pedestal in 1919;
- ❖ St. Peter and St. Paul, in the Main Altar reredos niches, installed 1918, donated by Mrs. Joseph Tuminello;

❖ St. Therese the Little Flower and its fluted column pedestal, in the northeast corner, to the right of the St. Joseph altar, installed 1928, both donated by George Pourciau in memory of his wife (née Anna Vignes);

❖ Our Lady of Lourdes, placement unknown at present; and St. Anthony, in the rear of the nave, near the main entrance, with a locked, iron Poor Box for alms on its pedestal, said pedestal financed in 1931 by Mary Rinaudo, daughter of Mrs. Frank Rinaudo; and St. Lucy, on the east wall in front of the St. Joseph altar, fronted by the metal votive candles stand (all described within the 1948 Parochial Report).

Most of these statues were removed or placed elsewhere in the church following Vatican II. The Calvary group was moved to the former location of St. Lucy against the northernmost windows on the eastern side, and ultimately relegated to the southeast entry of the church. It was set on the brick parvis of the church for a couple of Good Fridays during the pastorate of Fr. Frank Uter in the late 1970s, but the strong wind of the latter Good Friday knocked the statues to the pavement and damaged them beyond repair.

The statue of St. Lucy, memorable as she was depicted holding a dish on which were symbolically placed her eyes, was moved from the northeast part of the church to the pilaster between the main and eastern entrances into the nave in the 1970s, and ultimately lost.

St. Anthony holding the Child Jesus and a bun, on the opposite pilaster between main and western entrance, suffered the breaking and robbery of the Poor Box simultaneous with the theft of the metal corpus of the main altar crucifix in 1987; the Poor Box was thereafter replaced by a small wooden holder for alms envelopes, the latter to be placed in the ushers' baskets at Mass or hand-delivered to the Parish Office. Said statue of St. Anthony was ultimately consigned to the southwest entry of the church.

Noting throughout his long and interesting journal spanning the years 1913-1942, Fr. Hoes regularly remarked on the generosity of time, talent and treasure of the St. Mary parishioners. In 1920, he recorded the expenditure of $30 for crucifixes to be given in appreciation to "a few pious souls who zealously work for the church."

STAINED GLASS WINDOWS & SELF-GUIDED TOUR

In 1921, five stained glass windows portraying the Glorious Mysteries of the Rosary were installed in the sanctuary of St. Mary Church. These windows, purchased from the F.X. Zettler Company of Chicago, were imported from Munich, Germany. The windows cost $300 each, and were entirely financed by five parish families as related below. Fr. Hoes obviously intended to portray all of the Mysteries of the Rosary, as funds were available, and commenced in the sanctuary with the most striking decades of the devotion.

Between 1937 and 1940, stained glass representing the Joyful and Sorrowful Mysteries of the Rosary, the Transfiguration, the Miracle at Cana, and symbols of the Virgin Mary and the Church were installed in the lateral windows. These later windows, also fabricated in Munich, were purchased from the Emil Frei Company of St. Louis, Missouri. Shortly after their delivery in New Roads, the stained glass works in Munich was closed on orders of the Nazi government.

Each of the lateral windows of St. Mary are divided into two panels, and the cost of stained glass windows for each set was $640 for each "figure" (i.e. illustrative) pair and $400 for each "ornamental" (i.e. allegorical) pair. Each of the lateral door transoms cost $140, and the windows above the transoms $65 each. The four nave gallery windows, set in the façade of the church were of patterned stained glass and cost $142.50 each. The latter were replaced by art glass in 1992 as subsequently noted.

The following is a guide to the windows of St. Mary, suitable for self-guided tours of the inside of the church. This resource may also be useful in the praying of the Rosary, as the predominant theme of the stained glass in the church is the Mysteries of the Rosary.

FIGURE 46: RESURRECTION WINDOW, SANCTUARY

STAINED GLASS WINDOW TOUR OF ST. MARY & ROSARY DEVOTIONAL

ST. MARY OF FALSE RIVER

200 YEARS
1823 – 2023
OF CATHOLIC FAITH IN NEW ROADS

The following is a guide to the windows of St. Mary, suitable for self-guided tours of the inside of the church. This resource may also be useful in the praying of the Rosary, as the predominant theme of the stained glass in the church is the Mysteries of the Rosary.

GLORIOUS MYSTERIES

First, the windows of the Sanctuary depict the Glorious Mysteries of the Rosary. Of Munich glass, they were produced by F.X. Zettler and installed 1921, from west to east:

- "The Resurrection," in memory of Richard Lorio and daughter, Sister St. Vincent de Paul (Ursuline Sister);

- "The Ascension," in memory of Sister Mary Bernard (Sister of St. Joseph), née Emma Pourciau, donated by her parents, George and Anna Vignes Pourciau;

- "Descent of the Holy Ghost," in memory of Beauregard Olinde, by Mrs. Beauregard Olinde and children; and

- "The Assumption," in memory of Thomas Mix, by Mrs. Thomas Mix and family; and

- "Coronation of the Blessed Virgin Mary," donated by Mr. and Mrs. Joseph Tuminello.

SORROWFUL MYSTERIES

Next, the windows of the western wall depict the Sorrowful Mysteries of the Rosary. Again of Munich glass, they were produced by Emil Frei and installed from 1937 through 1940, from north to south:

- "Agony in the Garden" and "Scourging at the Pillar," both in memory of Albin and Amintas Major and Stella Major Bertoniere, by Mrs. Albin Major and children;

- Monstrance image and Eucharist before Pelican in Piety, both donated in celebration of Eucharistic Congress 1938, sponsored by His Excellency J.F. Rummel, D.D., by parishioners of St. Mary's Church;

- "Crowning with Thorns" and "Carrying the Cross," both in memory of Otis Louis Olinde, by his wife, Mrs. B. Olinde [mother], sisters and brothers;

- Door transom: Jesus blessing children image;

- Above door transom: "J" monogram; "The Crucifixion," in memory of Albert Vignes Family, by Mr. and Mrs. Hilary Vignes;

- "The Transfiguration," in memory of Mr. and Mrs. John L. Vignes, by Mr. and Mrs. Herbert Harrell;

- "Gate of Heaven" and "Tower of Ivory," both donated by members of Holy Name Society;

- And lastly, southwest window bricked in for heating and cooling system.

JOYFUL MYSTERIES

The windows of the eastern wall depict the Joyful Mysteries of the Rosary. Of Munich glass, they were produced by Emil Frei and installed from 1937 through 1940, from north to south:

- "Annunciation" and "Visitation," both in memory of George Pourciau Family, by the children;

- "I Have Chosen You" with Pax image and "teaching, Offering and Administering" with fountains pouring from Eucharist and altar, both in commemoration of 25th anniversary of Fr. Hoes' appointment to St. Mary's Church, 1913-1938;

- "Birth of Jesus" and "Presentation of Jesus," both in memory of I.G. Morgan, by Mrs. I.G. Morgan and daughter, Trina; door transom: Guardian Angel with two children on bridge;

- Above door transom" "M" monogram;

- "Finding Jesus in the Temple" and "Marriage at Cana," both in memory of Joseph Philibert Gosserand, by Mrs. J.P. Gosserand and children;

- "Ark of the Covenant" and "House of Gold," both donated by parishioners of St. Mary's Church, sponsored by local Council K. of C. [Knights of Columbus]; and

- Last window of lighter, patterned glass without image or inscription.

FIGURE 47: ASCENSION WINDOW, SANCTUARY

The newest stained glass windows are located in the façade, facing outward, and illuminated by back lighting at night. Designed by stalwart parishioner and artist Glenn C. Morgan, they were produced by the Laukhuff Stained Glass Company of Memphis, Tennessee and Mitchell-Marionneaux of Maringouin, Louisiana. The scenes depict the history of the Church in Pointe Coupée from the arrival of the Iberville party of explorers in 1699 to the dedication of the first St. Mary Church in 1823, and are, from west to east, as follows:

- ❖ "Iberville at Pointe Coupée," donated by Nelsi and Mary Bondi;
- ❖ "Baptism of the Natives," by Jeff and Doris David;
- ❖ [Reverend] "Jean Baptiste Blanc Dedicating the New Church," by Morel and Rose Lemoine;
- ❖ "Gifts to the New Church," by Tom and Dorothy Jewell;
- ❖ "Mary, Mother of the Church," by Hewitt and Pauline Fontaine;
- ❖ [Rev.] "Antoine Blanc Offering the First Mass," by Lynn and Gertrude Schexnayder;
- ❖ "The New Road From St. Francis" [Church], by Pearl and Garner Haydel; and
- ❖ "Mission Church" [first St. Francis], donated by Ludovic and Helen Patin.

ALTAR APPOINTMENTS

The large gilt candlesticks which adorn the main and side altars in the present St. Mary Church are each of separate pattern, and have been moved from one altar to another periodically based on 20th century photographs. The set of four reeded candlesticks, on the eastern altar in the year 2023, is possibly the oldest of the trio.

The four tall candlesticks on the western altar are of a set of six, the two others, both smaller in size, having been relegated to the church rectory dining room mantel at an indeterminate modern date. This six-piece set was acquired in 1925 and adorned the main altar. They were financed by the Catechism Class of 1926 and Mrs. Stephen Garrett (née Aimée Bondy).

The six tall, bulbous column candlesticks, Baroque in design, on the main altar reredos in the 21st Century, are likely the newest of the three sets.

"TABERNACLE OF THE VIRGINS"

A significant addition to St. Mary's interior was made by substitute priest Rev. Francois J. Baissac, a native of Lyon, while Fr. Hoes was on a four-month sojourn in Europe. The *Pointe Coupée Banner*, in its issue of 13 August 1921, stated: "We note with pride another step taken by Father F. Baissac, acting Rector of St. Mary's Catholic Church," and outlined a nine-point justification, apparently submitted by a committee, as to the origin of a new, second tabernacle.

Signed by "The Secretary and Treasurer," the account stated the purpose of the undertaking was "To commemorate the passage of Father F. Baissac in this parish of New Roads," with "something of beauty, usefulness and lasting character." The object selected was "A safe-Tabernacle as per illustrated description." The donors stated their "Caution" was "Not to interfere with Father J. Hoes' work but prepare for him another pleasant surprise."

The cost of the tabernacle was given as $250, plus $25 freight and labor, for which 275 young ladies were to contribute $1 each, and others were invited to add their own donations in memory of any deceased "friend of the fair sex."

The tabernacle was to be known as "The Tabernacle of the Virgins," and as Fr. Baissac "begs the honor of leading and working" to make it reality, the *Banner* article closed: "We are hoping for the best and trust the girls of the community and vicinity will not fail him."

On his part after his return to St. Mary, Fr. Hoes noted in his journal in December 1921 that the tabernacle installed by "my wonderful substitute," i.e., Fr. Baissac, had cost the congregation $400, adding: "This action was in my opinion such a flagrant transgression or violation of pastoral rights, that I only wish to mention this act of arrogance as a matter of record."

It is likely that the Tabernacle of the Virgins was, until 2022, that one in the reredos of the western altar. This altar originally had a statue of Our Lady, Queen of Heaven, but since the 1977-1979 renovation of St. Mary Church, the altar has been referred to as the Blessed Sacrament altar and this tabernacle is the only one in the church.

In Advent 2022, Rev. Christopher Decker, responded to several parishioners' long prayed-for goal of having the Blessed Sacrament returned to the place of honor in the main altar reredos by moving the "Tabernacle of the Virgins" thereto.

Fr. Hoes' note of expenses paid by Fr. Baissac, in addition to basic necessities of the church and rectory in 1921, also indicate Baissac's "self-arranged" salary of $532.50, and the installation of a telephone, likely in the rectory. Four years later, Hoes made note of Baissac's death, in 1925, while pastor of Kenner, Louisiana, at the age of 43, adding "R.I.P."

Chalice at St. Francis Chapel dates from 1696 and was the gift of Jean-René Bauwens van der Boyen, Baron de Neeryssche , whose coat of arms is incribed with the date on the base.

FIGURE 48: NEERYSSCHE CHALICE

NEERYSSCHE CHALICE OF 1696

The oldest treasure at St. Mary of False River, normally kept in safekeeping, but used on occasional celebratory occasions, is a silver, gold-lined chalice inscribed with the date 1696 and the name and coat of arms of Jean Réné Bouwens van der Boyen, Baron de Neeryssche. Fr. Hoes referred in his journal to its being re-gilded in 1918, but its provenance is unknown.

Popular sentiment among descendants of the original settlers from Hainaut, now part of Belgium, who arrived at Pointe Coupée in 1720, is that the sacred vessel may have been gifted to the colonists by the Baron, he being a prominent nobleman of present-day Belgium.

Of even more obscure origin is a small silver repoussé ciborium. However, other items which are evidenced in Fr. Hoes' journal and still in use in the year 2023 include: a gold ciborium donated in memory of Joseph Tuminello by his wife, "Madam Joe" Tuminello; a Gothic "ostensorium" or monstrance, acquired in 1918 and bearing a strong resemblance to St. Mary's main altar reredos in its early form; a censor, donated in 1922 in memory of Bérthold Patin; a processional cross, of 1926; an ornate brass Missal stand; a brass altar gong, which might be either one of the other of sets of "chimes," the first, donated by Misses Emilia Pourciau and Kathryn O'Conner in 1922, and the second donated by Mrs. Joseph "Madam Joe" Tuminello in 1930; and four marble holy water stoups, located to either side of the main entrance into the nave and beside the western and eastern doorways and installed in 1920.

As was mandatory in all Catholic churches until the Vatican II era, a communion rail of Gothic design stretched in front of the three altars in St. Mary, with a double gate at the head of the central aisle. Attached by rings on the sanctuary side of the rail was a white communion cloth, which altar servers, one at each end, flipped over at communion time.

Communicants knelt at the rail and, with arms under the cloth, brought it to their chins so that if a consecrated host accidentally fell during the distribution of Holy Communion, it could be caught by the administering priest before touching the floor.

FIGURE 49: NEERYSSCHE COAT OF ARMS DETAIL

ANGELS AND SAINTS
OVERHEAD

In 1922 the apsidal vault above the main altar of St. Mary Church was frescoed by an artist as-yet unidentified at a cost of $400 to represent cherubs in a pale blue sky and rays surrounding the Sanctuary Lamp connection. In 1937, $600 was expended as artist A. Schnyder frescoed medallions of the Twelve Apostles framed by garlands in the arched panels of the nave vault.

This fondly-recalled ornamentation remained until unfortunately being painted over under direction of a substituting priest during the pastorate of Rev. J.W.A. Janssen in the 1950s. Also painted over at the time was the scored effect on the upper walls of the church, which simulated cut stone above the wainscoting, and the slender vine or garland effects framing the sanctuary arches.

RECTORY

While continuing to ornament the church interior, Fr. Hoes in 1924 saw to completion the building of a new, two-story rectory, in classic revival style and fronted by lower and upper galleries, on the site of its old predecessor, immediately west of the church. Built at a cost of approximately $12,000, local builder John Morel was contractor for the project, and Fr. Hoes personally paid a substantial part of the bill.

The upper gallery was screened not long after completion of the rectory, and the lawn was planted with palms, giving a Caribbean feel to setting. In the 1960s, during the pastorate of Rev. A.J. LeBlanc, both galleries were enclosed, and the St. Mary Parish Office operated for many years in the eastern portion of the enclosed lower gallery.

According to late New Roads businessman Humphrey T. Olinde, Jr., the old rectory – a classic Créole cottage - was moved to Napoleon Street at the time of construction of the present rectory. The cottage stands at 543 Napoleon at the present time, beautifully restored by the Olinde Properties corporation and occupied as a rental residence.

FIGURE 50: PRESENT RECTORY, BUILT FOR FATHER HOES (RIGHT)

A concrete walk connecting the rectory front steps with the West Main Street sidewalk was laid in 1931. In 1978, a commemorate marble base, supporting a large metal urn, and the latter crowned by a statue of St. Francis of Assisi, was erected on the walk, midway the rectory and street, in commemoration of the 250th anniversary of the "Church in Pointe Coupée."

Fr. Hoes resumed work in the church in 1925, installing boxing around the wooden chamfered columns which had never been completed with the rich Gothic detailing originally intended. That same year, the lateral galleries which had formerly accommodated African American worshippers prior to the establishment of St. Augustine Church in 1922, were removed, as was the elevated pulpit. The old pulpit base was recalled by parishioner Glenn Morgan as subsequently being in the southwest entry to the church when that area served as the baptistry until the 1970s.

ELECTRIC LIGHTING AND ADORING ANGELS

In 1927, electric lanterns in a Gothic design, suspended from the lateral arches between nave and flanking aisles, were installed in the church. Their cost of $500 was paid through the fundraising efforts and personal contributions of St. Mary's Catholic Daughters of the Americas court. Fr. Hoes' journal, however, relates that the first electrical lighting in the church occurred in 1917, with the installation of the candelabra supported by the Adoring Angels to either side of the main altar, first lit on Christmas Night that year, and additional "electric work" was undertaken in the church in 1922.

Likewise in 1927, the Rosary Society paid for six "funeral candlesticks" or torches, which were set to either side of the catafalque placed in the main aisle during requiem services. These torches were found along with a silver processional cross, the church's three altar stones, and two *ex voto* thanksgiving plaques when a makeshift vestment closet was removed from the vesting sacristy during the 2016 renovation.

At the end in 1927, Fr. Hoes installed a set of double, swinging doors, topped by a glass transom between the main church doors and the nave, at a cost of $91.25. Mrs. Marcy Lebeau (née Hazilda Samson) contributed $50 and Mrs. Albin Major (née Marie Langlois) gave $25 toward the cost, and Fr. Hoes personally contributed the balance. These doors and transom above were removed during the 1977-1979 renovation of the church

TOWER AND FAÇADE COMPLETED IN 1929

In 1929, the completion of St. Mary's bell tower was achieved according to the designs of Theodore Brune. Rather than the 60-foot steeple spire he had designed back in 1904, it consists of four corner spires, capped by cusps, and connected by an openwork balustrade, all in gothic revival style complementing Brune's overall design.

The 17 July 1929 *Pointe Coupée Banner*, reporting on the commencement of construction of the spires and balustrade, stated, "The plan borders on the Moorish [sic] style of architecture," and identified the Castone (sic) Co., supervised by a Mr. (F.) Simonson, as contractor for the work.

Included in Rev. John Hoes' invaluable journal is the copy of the contract entered by St. Mary Church with the Architectural Cast Stone Co. of New Orleans, La., represented by Victor Lachin (president), to "furnish and erect all materials necessary for completion of the tower to be erected on the above building [St. Mary], in strict conformity with the plans and specifications."

Simultaneous with the work on the tower and the placement of four small spires on the buttress caps of the façade, sculptor Angelo Lachin installed tympanum plaques above the three front doors of the church. That in the center depicts the Assumption of the Blessed Virgin Mary, patroness of the church, while those to west and east display, respectively, Alpha and Omega monograms.

Fr. Hoes' journal identified Angelo Lachin, father of Victor Lachin above, as "designing and sculptor [sic] artist for St. Mark's cathedral at Venice, Italy."

The 1929 additions totaled $8,442.32, according to Hoes' notes, toward the payment of which nearly $5,000 was contributed by New Roads Council 1998 Knights of Columbus. The latter had realized the sum through a succession of Independence Day parades and related fundraising activities during 1920-1925.

The completion of St. Mary's tower and façade embellishments coincided with that completion of a new St. Joseph Academy and Convent on Richy Street. Fr. Hoe's journal relates, "The 19th of September 1929 was a red letter day for the Parishioners of St. Mary's," with the blessing of the tower and new academy/convent by Rt. Rev. (Francis L.R.) Gassler, Dean of Baton Rouge, who had been delegated for the service by His Grace (New Orleans Archbishop John W. Shaw).

In the opening High Mass, Monsignor. Rev. Gassler preached "extolling the good will and magnificent spirit of the present generation," Fr. Hoes continued, and a procession of St. Joseph pupils, the congregation and attending clergy was thereafter made to the new academy/convent. After ceremonial dedication of the new building, a "sumptuous dinner served by the undersigned ladies, " to wit, Mmes. Ernest (née Dora Hadowal) Morgan, Trina (née Morgan), widow of Otis L. Olinde, Hilary (née Élise Guérin) Vignes, Cherie (née Neff), Mrs. Berthold Patin, and J.C. (née Bertha Seibert) Roberts.

Also signing were: Monsignor Gassler, "Delagatus ad Hoc," Rt. Rev. A. (Andrea) de Maurizi; longtime pastor of Our Lady of Prompt Succor, White Castle, Louisiana; Rev. Louis Savouré, pastor of Immaculate Conception, Lakeland; Rev. G. (Gerard) Bosch, pastor of St. John, Plaquemine; and Mssrs. George Pourciau and Lamartine Bouanchaud, parish trustees.

TRADITION OF MUSICAL EXCELLENCE

One of Father Hoes' later projects was the purchase and installation of a magnificent 433-pipe tracker organ from the Hinners Organ Co. of Pekin, Illinois in 1931. It is a 1917 model, whose installation required an expansion of the choir loft forward, into the nave, and supported by two columns.

Through the years, the liturgy at St. Mary's has been enhanced by the talented organists and pianists including Mme. Charles Hébert, née Virginie Eva Bondy, and Dr. Charles Marie Menville in the old St. Mary, and Miss Celuta Jewell, Mmes. Louise Bowles, Elsie Heck Olinde, Chloe Lefebvre White, June Gaudin Allor, JoAnn Busse, Patricia Olinde Laurent, Sarita McDonald Bouanchaud, and Daryl Chauvin in the present church. Miss Lily Martinez added to St. Mary's beautiful musical tradition her talent as a violinist in the early 21st century.

The St. Mary Choir was famed as early as the 1870s, when parishioner Jean Baptiste Alcide Bondy is recorded in period news accounts and oral history to have drawn persons of various and no beliefs to Sunday Mass, by his commanding voice and Stradivarius violin he had brought during his immigration to Pointe Coupée from the island of Martinique.

The 31 March 1883 *Pointe Coupée Banner*, recounting the previous Easter Sunday liturgy at old St. Mary, told of Senator Charles Parlange, native of False River but resident of New Orleans, as singing with the choir and offering a moving rendition of "Crois en Dieu." In the previous year, 1882, he was tireless in efforts to get provisions and other needed supplies to the flood sufferers in Pointe Coupée and neighboring parishes.

Reared on the family's False River plantation, Charles Parlange was described by Rev. J.P. Gutton in an 1866 letter to Archbishop Jean Marie Odin as "a charming and well instructed young man" of 16 (sic, actually 14) years old who had recently made his First Communion. Fr. Gutton wrote that Mme. Parlange (née Virginie Trahan) asked if His Grace could have her son confirmed in New Orleans, as the young man was about to depart for college (Centenary, a Methodist institution located in, at that time, Jackson, Louisiana).

In his later years, Charles Parlange served as a United States attorney, Lieutenant Governor of Louisiana, and as an associate justice of the state's Supreme Court.

Older New Roads residents of the 21st century recall the deep bass ("Down to the floor!" per now- deceased Olinde S. Haag) of Réné Lejeune, an impeccable gentleman and longtime clerk at the town's iconic Morgan's Department Store. He and sister Miss Anne Lejeune, a generous benefactor of the church and cemetery, and nurse to countless newborn children and their mothers, were two of the 12 siblings who, along with both of their parents, had been born in the stately Lejeune House on East Main Street.

None of the Lejeune siblings married, and most of them, as their parents before them, Francois and Alice Samson Lejeune, died in the old mansion. Francois Lejeune, affectionately known as "L'Ami" (friend) was also a St. Mary choir member and a spiritual directee and close confidante of Rev. John Hoes, while Mme. Lejeune was remembered as having an extraordinary charism in rearing her children to be Catholic ladies and gentlemen.

In one of several examples of inter-faith relationships in Pointe Coupée, at least two known Jewish citizens, Mrs. Aaron Baum, née Julia Simon, and their only child, Simon Baum, of a prominent Jewish merchant family of present-day Rougon, Louisiana, sang in area Catholic choirs. Mother and son were regular members of the old Immaculate Conception of Chenal choir, the turn of the 19th-20th centuries, and Simon Baum is recorded in 1911 *Pointe Coupée Banner* accounts as soloist for weddings at St. Mary in New Roads as well as old Immaculate Conception.

By the third quarter of the 20th century, St. Mary Choir, consisting of adults, was part of an expanding musical ministry, with a newly-organized children's choir, bell choir, and folk group, the latter of which featured guitar and typically post-Vatican II music. The newest musical ensemble is the Men's Choir, which debuted at the 7 a.m. Sunday Masses at St. Francis Chapel, and added to the majesty of Midnight Mass in St. Mary in 2022. Their repertoire includes Southern spirituals, folk hymns, and Latin liturgical music.

FIGURE 51: MISS ANNE LEJEUNE HOLDING THE YOUNGEST OF HUNDREDS OF BABIES SHE CARED FOR, FUTURE MAJOR GENERAL STEPHEN DABADIE[4]

---

[4] Major General Stephen Dabadie is the son of Brigadier General Levy Dabadie. Together, they are the only father and son pair to both hold the rank of general in regional history.

AIR COOLING AND HEATING

The earliest air-cooling in St. Mary Church consisted of two large "typhoon" electric fans set in the sanctuary for the comfort of the clergy and altar servers and a fan located on the railing of the choir loft. The 27 June 1935 *Pointe Coupée Banner* told of Mrs. Joseph Philibert Gosserand, née Amanda May Morgan, being injured the previous Thursday night when the fan on the choir railing fell into her pew.

The church's first known heating system consisted of eight gas heaters, installed in 1936. A central heating and air conditioning system was installed at St. Mary by Fr. Hoes' successor, Rev. J.W.A. Janssen, in 1958.

FIGURE 52: INTERIOR OF ST. MARY'S DURING FATHER HOES' PASTORATE

PARVIS, ST. MARY CHURCH PARK, AND THE "LITTLE DRAG"

Outside, the *parvis* or public assembly area at the front of St. Mary, was originally enclosed by a painted, wooden picket fence and ornamented with lawn and shrubs. A brick walk was laid from main entrance to the West Main Street sidewalk in 1915. The parvis was "paved," i.e. bricked, by New Roads mason Arthur Fabre in 1941.

During the pastorate of Rev. Christopher Springer, the parvis, or "plaza," as it was termed at the time, was repaved, with a main and diagonal brick paths leading from all three entrances to the street sidewalk and brick polygonal raised planter beds at the four corners.

To the east of the church proper, St. Mary Church Park was developed in 1915 on the site of the predecessor church of 1823, under Fr. Hoes and through the generosity of the newly-formed Mothers Culture Club of New Roads. New Roads Council 1998, under grand Knight Charles K. Jordan, and with Knight A.B. Curet, longtime County Agent, as chairman, provided for the planting of trees and shrubbery. Swing sets and a baseball playing area are remembered by older residents as being enjoyed by the town children on site in the 1940s. The cedar trees planted at the front, East Main Street, side of the park, grew to great height but were removed in the wake of hurricane damage near the close of the 20th century.

As early as 1906, the *Pointe Coupée Banner* reported on the nuisance and danger posed by the shooting of air rifles by young boys within the corporate limits of New Roads. The 29 February 1940 issue of the paper included an editorial entitled "The Air Rifle Menace," in which it lamented that birds, including the government-protected robins, suffering from the cold, were likewise shot by youth, continuing:

> But now comes the crying shame of it all. In St. Mary's Catholic church have been placed expensive and beautiful art memorial windows. This week it was found that some of the air rifle brigade have been making targets of some of these windows. Father Hoes and the church authorities have most generously given to the children of New Roads a splendid playground adjoining the church, where they may assemble and engage in the many games and exercises so dear to the heart of childhood. It is expected that the little ones play innocent and harmless games, and not convert it into a shooting range, with the windows of the church as targets, as well as endangering the eyesight of other children who gather to play.

Damaged portions of St. Mary's windows have been repaired periodically through history, and fortunately they have survived the many hurricanes which have assaulted the community since 1909. Exterior protective panels were installed in recent years, which prevent the windows from being open for interior ventilation, but the art glass itself has thereby been safeguarded.

The Mothers Culture Club, visionaries of the St. Mark Church Park, is the oldest surviving women's organization in Pointe Coupée Parish. The club was formed in 1914, and active in a number of cultural undertakings, including the founding of New Roads' Mardi Gras afternoon parade in 1932,[5] the acquisition and annual installation of decorative holiday illuminations on Main Street for the Christmas season, and the erection of Nativity figures that were placed in the Church Park, in front of the Grotto.

---

[5] The Mothers Culture Club was succeeded as sponsor of the New Roads' Mardi Gras parade by the New Roads Lions Club in 1941.

Opposite the church property, a traffic turn-around was created on the West Main Street perimeter of the former Place de la Croix through efforts of Knights of Columbus Council 1998 in the early 1920s. It mirrored, on a smaller scale, the turn-around four blocks east, in front of the Pointe Coupée Parish Courthouse. Stemming from the term "making the drag" to indicate a vehicular circuit through a downtown area, the turn-around in front of the Courthouse came to be called "The Drag," and that in front of St. Mary the "Little Drag" or "Half-Drag."

The neutral ground of the Little Drag has been successively planted in shrubbery and perennial flowers, and in the 21st century, in abbreviated form, it is the location of the statue of Jesus with the Sacred Heart, donated in memory of Gail Bueche Jarreau, and mentioned elsewhere in this volume.

FATHER HOES
IN RECORD AND MEMORY

Rev. John Hoes, one of Louisiana's most familiar prelates of the 20th century, was like his successor, Rev. J.W.A. Janssen, and their contemporary Rev. Louis Savouré at Immaculate Conception of Chenal – Lakeland, a man of strong character. While all three had loyal, and affectionate, supporters, their no- nonsense approach to the liturgy, sacraments and parochial life left strong impressions, especially upon the youth, who in adulthood recalled them as having been "strict" or "mean."

Fr. Hoes was remembered as frightening to some of the more timid youth, for his habit of "grinding his teeth" while engaged in catechetical instruction. A first-hand illustration of something of Fr. Hoes' character is presented in a letter of his parishioner and next-door neighbor, New Roads attorney and former *Pointe Coupée Banner* owner and editor, the Hon. Albin Provosty. A legendary *raconteur* and man of great joviality, Provosty wrote his daughter Sidonie Provosty, when the latter was visiting Toledo, Ohio, on 13 January 1914:

Old New Roads is truly a deserted village. The only source of excitement is the new priest [Fr. Hoes]. He is a bear when it comes to preaching and he has inaugurated a crusade against the tango, one step, fish walk [dances], etc. He said last Sunday he had been told that in these dances a sheet of paper could not go between the partners, [and] levied his opposition and condemnation. This speech created a mild sensation. Several of the Sisters [of St. Joseph] fainted and restoratives had to be applied to Mrs. [J.W.] Seibert and other leaders in the fight for morality in New Roads.

This author is indebted to Sidonie Provosty [Hall]'s grandson Rev. LaVerne "Pike" Thomas III for the above, which appears in his splendid tome *LeDoux: A Pioneer Franco-American Family, With Sketches of Allied Families* (Polyanthos, 1982), which chronicles many of the early families of Pointe Coupée in great detail and color.

Owing to the vast territory of the Archdiocese of New Orleans and its many parishes, episcopal visits were made to Pointe Coupée Parish but every few years, and confirmation was usually held in conjunction, usually with hundreds of young people receiving the sacrament. This author's paternal grandfather recalled well into advanced age the 1915 ceremonies, in which he, eldest sister and a future brother-in-law were all confirmed.

The *Pointe Coupée Banner* issue of 27 November 1915 told in detail of the gala 24-25 November visit of Auxiliary Bishop Jean Marius Laval and his secretary, Rev. Arthur Jerome Drossaerts, the latter a pioneer in the religious education of African American Catholics in South Louisiana.

The bishop having confirmed a class of 135 at Immaculate Conception in Chenal on the 24th, some 14 automobiles of St. Mary parishioners drove to meet the party in Chenal where, after partaking of a dinner, the bishop and secretary were taken on a tour of False River.

Entering town via West Main Street, the distinguished visitors were met by St. Mary's confirmation class, the parish's religious societies, and a large part of the congregation. Headed by the (Clay Camp No. 271) Woodmen of the World brass band, His Excellency and the entire entourage proceeded to the church, and entered beneath floral arches into an "artistically decorated" interior.

The two prelates were officially welcomed in the church by New Roads Mayor Lamartine Bouanchaud, then repaired to the sacristy to don their vestments. Reentering the body of the church, Bishop Laval thanked the congregation for their warm welcome and recalled his visits to St. Mary while a young priest as guest of the treasured Rev. J.P. Gutton.

His Excellency then presided over the Benediction of the Blessed Sacrament. Spending the night, he confirmed St. Mary's class of 165 young people on the following day, then departed for Raccourci for his third confirmation of the week [at Our Lady of Seven Dolors, New Texas Landing].

In addition of Catechism classes and annual First Communion ceremonies for children and periodic Confirmations during archiepiscopal visits, Fr. Hoes apparently made concessions for older youth re-questing the sacraments. This author's grandmother recalled going with other teenage girls in company of Miss Corinne Philippe, longtime clerk at Hebert's Jewelry Store, for First Communion and Confirmation "at the same time" from Fr. Hoes, in St. Mary Church in the 1920s. Another late parishioner, Jacqueline Major Saizan, recalled her Catechism class receiving First Communion and Confirmation on the same day: First Communion in the morning, followed by ice cream in St. Mary Church Park, culminating with Confirmation in the church in the afternoon, this apparently being near the end of Fr. Hoes' pastorate.

Fr. John Hoes was likely the first priest to drive, and his journal notes in 1918 the construction of a garage, and thereafter periodic expenses for gasoline and oil.

FATHER HOES HONORED

Two special liturgical celebrations attested to the esteem borne Rev. John Hoes by many of his parishioners and the community at large. In the 25th year of his ordination, 1928, he journeyed back to his native Netherlands to visit his 83-year-old widowed mother and pray

FIGURE 53: FR. JOHN HOES & MOTHER IN HOLLAND, 1928

at the grave of his deceased father. He observed the anniversary of his ordination with relatives on 12 June.

Fr. Hoes intended to celebrate his anniversary when back in New Roads with a solemn High Mass on Tuesday, 20 September. When he arrived at the rectory by automobile, he encountered a huge gathering of parishioners who had, meanwhile, planned a grand celebration, and had been joined by New Orleans Archbishop John Shaw, Alexandria, Louisiana Bishop Cornelius Van de Ven, also a native of the Netherlands, and other visiting clergy and laity.

The students of St. Joseph Academy greeted Fr. Hoes with a rendition of "Home Again From a Foreign Shore" and a special poem, and one of their number presented him a silver tray upon which lay the sum of $25, a gift of the church Needlework Club.

The students' own gift was a silver crown surrounded by silver dollar coins. A procession into the church then formed, led by the student body, and followed by 25 little girls who formed a living silver garland and 25 little boys who waved silvered palm branches.

The choir of St. Agnes Church of Baton Rouge offered a number of touching hymns during the High Mass, for which Rev. (later Mons.) Francis L.R. Gassler, Dean of St. Joseph Church of Baton Rouge, offered the jubilee homily. After recessional, celebrants and attendees posed on the front lawn of the rectory for a memorable panoramic photograph that was reproduced for the church and a number of faithful.

This panoramic photograph has also been reproduced in the next pages and split into three separate images due to its dimensions.

FATHER HOES' JUBILEE CELEBRATION PANORAMIC PHOTOGRAPH

FIGURE 54: FATHER HOES' JUBILEE CELEBRATION PANORAMIC PHOTOGRAPH, LEFT

FIGURE 55: FATHER HOES' JUBILEE CELEBRATION PANORAMIC PHOTOGRAPH, MIDDLE

FIGURE 56: FATHER HOES' JUBILEE CELEBRATION PANORAMIC PHOTOGRAPH, RIGHT

A banquet followed in the rectory at which ladies of the parish served and pupils of St. Joseph Aca-demy sang in choir. A total of 29 members of the clergy were in attendance, coming from as far away of Lake Charles, Mermentau, Lafayette, Alexandria, and Thibodaux, Louisiana.

In his journal entry of that day, Fr. Hoes began, "Tuesday was a gala day in New Roads," and recounted highlights of the celebration, included the receipt of an additional $500, being the gift of his parishioners, presented during the banquet. The good pastor promptly turned the money over to the "steeple fund," from which was paid the cost of the completion of the church bell tower in the following year.

A week after the jubilee, the 27 September 1928 edition of the Baton Rouge *State-Times* newspaper published a lengthy account of the celebration.

FIGURE 57: FATHER HOES WITH ARCHBISHOP RUMMEL

Ten years later, on 13 December 1938, Fr. John Hoes observed his 25th anniversary as pastor of St. Mary of False River with High Mass, with Archbishop Francis Rummel and several priests of the archdiocese assisting.

In total, some 35 prelates were in attendance, as were many St. Mary parishioners and visitors. Rev. A.M. Dormsdorf, of St. Amant, Louisiana, delivered the homily. A striking photograph was taken of the clergy and many of the laity outside the main entrance of the church afterward.

A banquet followed at the Lake View Hotel, where Rev. Louis Savouré, with whom Fr. Hoes had a strained relationship in his earliest years in New Roads, was toast master. Amidst the clerical gathering, 16 leading Catholic laymen of the area attended as special guests, according to the 15 December 1938 *Pointe Coupée Banner* account of the celebration.

CEMETERY IMPROVEMENTS AND END OF AN ERA

In addition to leading the spiritual and sacramental life of St. Mary church parish and the upkeep of the parish properties, Rev. John Hoes also paid attention to the parish's hallowed cemetery on New Roads Street. The fence, described in early accounts as being of "planks," was improved on its front, New Roads Street, side in 1931 with the construction of an iron fence, having brick piers at its southern and northern ends. Midway, four other brick piers anchored ornamental iron gates: a central double gate, flanked by single gates, the whole topped by masonry urns and an ironwork arch bearing the name "St. Mary's Cemetery" and crowning cross.

The iron was obtained from the Louis Ironworks of New Orleans, and the project cost $650.50, which was secured through the tireless fundraising efforts of Miss Anne Lejeune and Mmes. Herbert Harrell and John Morel. Local drayman Sam Rinaudo donated his $3 charge for hauling the materials to the site.

In 1932, Fr. Hoes oversaw the "reconstruction" or enlargement of the tomb of Rev. J.P. Gutton in the center of the cemetery to allow for Fr. Hoes' own, subsequent entombment. In failing health for a relatively short time, Fr. Hoes saw to completion in 1942 the central, life-size Calvary monument in St. Mary Cemetery, behind which he intended to be entombed beside the late Rev. J.P. Gutton.

During his final illness of six weeks, Fr. Hoes was ministered to by a "watchers attendance" committee of Council 1998 Knight of Columbus, of which organization he had been chaplain for 23 years. This service of laity for pastor mirrored that given by the Catholic Knights of America to Rev. J.P. Gutton a half-century earlier.

The tolling of the venerable church bell *Maria Seraphina Clara* signaled Fr. Hoes' passing at 10:05 p.m., on 4 August 1942. Reporting the news the following day, the Baton Rouge *State-Times* stated that the deceased prelate was survived by three sisters, two brothers-in-law and several nieces and nephews, all living in his native Netherlands which was then under Nazi German occupation.

Yet one day later, the 6 August 1942 issue of the *Pointe Coupée Banner* stated: "Father Hoes is dead! We shall all miss his pleasant smile and cordial greeting." The home-town journal related that Hoes had studied in Venray (Venraij), Roosendaal and eventually the American college in Louvain. While at Louvain, he corresponded with the Archdiocese of New Orleans and expressed his desire to minister in Louisiana. He was ordained in 1903 in Louvain, and within three months began his work in South Louisiana.

"Saint Joseph's Academy was very dear to him," the *Banner* reported, "and he was a daily visitor giving out reports and making a lifelong friend of every child enrolled in the classes."

Of his Silver Jubilee in 1928, the *Banner* credited the Sisters of St. Joseph as being the coordinators, adding: "All creeds united in doing him honor." The next week's *Banner*, that of 13 August 1942, told of the Pontifical Requiem Mass offered for the repose of Fr. Hoes' soul, offered in St. Mary Church by Archbishop Rummel.

Forty members of the clergy were in attendance, and some served at the organ. The homily was offered by Fr. Savouré, whom the *Banner* described as a lifelong friend, eulogizing Hoes as "A spiritual man – a Christian."

Revs. Joseph Philibert Gutton and John Hoes are the only pastors of St. Mary to have their final resting places in the parish cemetery. Rev. Maynard "Tippy" Hurst, Jr., a native St. Mary parishioner who ministered in Baton Rouge, is likewise entombed in St. Mary Cemetery, adjoining the tomb of his parents and maternal LaCour relatives.

By the terms of his Last Will and Testament, dated 1933, Rev. John Hoes left all of his movable and immovable possessions to Rt. Rev. F.L.R. Gassler, then Dean of the Baton Rouge Deanery and rector of St. Joseph Church of Baton Rouge, less the following bequests: the sum of $6,000 and the remainder of any annuity policies, to Hoes' sisters and their children, he requesting of them "an occasional prayer" for the repose of his soul; $500 for improvements to St. Augustine Church and School of New Roads; $500 for improvements to St. Joseph Academy of New Roads; $200 for Masses for the repose of his soul, with a stipend of $2 per Mass for celebrant; $20 a year to Christine Paul for every year she had been in service as rectory housekeeper, and the same for anyone who might succeed her by the time of Hoes' death; $250 to the Lafon Home for elderly "colored" operated by the Sisters of the Holy Family (in New Orleans); $250 to the Lafon Orphan Asylum for "colored" boys, also operated by the Sisters of the Holy Family in that city; and Hoes' automobile, to Rev. Francis Rombouts, then pastor of St. Anthony, McDonoughville (suburban New Orleans).

Fr. Hoes specified that if either Rt. Rev. Gassler or Rev. Rombouts, or both, pre-deceased him, Hoes' bequest(s) would go to their successors.

REMARKABLE SERVICE TO CHURCH AND COMMUNITY

Throughout history, many of the Catholic laity of Pointe Coupée parish, Louisiana lived lives of exceptional service to Church and community. When Rev. John Hoes assumed pastorate of St. Mary of False River in 1913, he continued his predecessor, Rev. Alfred Bacciochi's employment as rectory housekeeper the cherished Ms. Harriette Aguillard, who, in turn, had succeeded Emiliéne Chenevert, Widow of Léonce Guého, and daughters Misses Mathilde and Estelle Guého, in the post.

Ms. Aguillard was a *Créole de couleur* native of the Island of False River, and childhood contemporary of future Josephite prelate Pierre Oscar LeBeau. After decades of selfless service at St. Mary, Ms. Aguillard and family moved to New Orleans, where she served as housekeeper first at St. Ann Church rectory and subsequently for the clergy at Jesuit High School, until retirement in 1937.

Succeeding Ms. Aguillard in St. Mary's rectory was her daughter Miss Christine Paul, who likewise moved to New Orleans and served in a similar capacity at the Josephite Fathers' rectory at St. Peter Claver Church. Returning to New Roads, she was housekeeper for the Josephite Fathers' rectory at St. Augustine Church.

A few months prior to Ms. Aguillard's death at age 97 in 1968, the national *Josephite Harvest* magazine devoted three pages to a feature on her and her daughter, stating in part:

> The story of the lives of this mother and daughter is one which breathes the spirit of devotion and love for priests which characterizes the legion of unsung heroes and heroines of so many of our Josephite missions.

In its 10 October 1968 front-page obituary of Ms. Harriette Aguillard, the *Pointe Coupée Banner* stated she had been ill but for a short while before her death in her residence at 410 Parent Street in New Roads, and marveled that "until the end she was able to thread a needle without glasses." The article continued that the "beloved… dignified, devoutly religious old lady" lay in repose in her home during recitation of the Rosary, and her funeral was celebrated the following day in St. Augustine Church, with burial in the church cemetery.

A few years earlier, in 1963, New Roads celebrated the 50 years of service of Miss Christine Paul, who had begun in the employ of Rev. John Hoes in St. Mary's rectory at age 16. She was honored at a solemn High Mass, followed by Benediction of the Blessed Sacrament in St. Augustine Church. At the reception held thereafter, Miss Paul received congratulatory gifts, cards and letters from generations of laity, clergy, Sisters and organizations. Among those who sent letters were New Orleans Archbishop Francis Rummel, Baton Rouge Bishop Robert Tracy, and Auxiliary Bishop Abel

Caillouet, the latter of whom also presented Miss Paul with a medal blessed by His Holiness Paul VI (born Giovanni Battista Montini).

FIGURE 58: "NURSE" FAZENDE, BELOVED MIDWIFE

Another remarkable lady of the *Créole de couleur* faithful of New Roads was New Orleans native "Nurse" Fazende. Born Marie Raymond, she was the wife of New Orleans, Baton Rouge and New Roads businessman Félix Fazende, both being of distinguished colonial Louisiana ancestry.

They and Mrs. Fazende's twice-widowed mother, Eugénie Bouligny Raymond Llado, moved to Railroad Avenue North (subsequently Texas Street) New Roads, opposite the Texas & Pacific Railroad depot. Mrs. Fazende, a professional midwife and obstetrician, delivered hundreds of babies of St. Mary's congregation. Mrs. Llado, meanwhile, operated a hotel and the adjacent Rail Road Restaurant and Lunch House, both popular in the days of train travel.

Prior to the arrival of the 1912 floodwater in that section of New Roads north of the railroad, Mrs. Llado's restaurant provided meals for thousands of the homeless evacuating flooded Upper Pointe Coupée and en route to refuge in Baton Rouge.

"Nurse" Fazende died in Los Angeles, California, age 86, in 1964, and was buried in that city. Her memory is fondly recalled by many of the faithful of St. Mary and St. Augustine church parishes, and Tenger Street in New Roads was renamed Fazende Street in New Roads in her honor.

Other *Créole de couleur* midwives who delivered hundreds of the faithful of St. Mary Parish on False River Road were Mme. Anatole St. Amant, née Virginie Ladmirault, a granddaughter of octogenarian Dr. Ludovic Ladmirault, native of France, under whom she was apprenticed; Mme. Sterling Rodney, née Valéntine "Ahl Zee" Gayle, on Parlange Plantation, they being the grandparents of Rev. Conway Rodney, S.S.J.; and Mrs. Robert Davis, née Elvira "Shoo Ma" Henry, who delivered approximately 3,500 babies, including several of her own grandchildren and great-grandchildren, during her ministry of nearly 60 years.

Changes and Tradition:
Vatican II and Following

Following Rev. John Hoes' death in 1942, he was succeeded as pastor of St. Mary of False River by fellow native Dutchman and close friend Rev. John William Anthony Janssen, a native of Nijmegen. One of the first important events in Fr. Janssen's pastorate occurred in 1943, with the dedication of a replica grotto bearing a statue of Our Lady of Prompt Succor, Patroness of Louisiana, in the Church Park.

The 28 October *Pointe Coupée Banner* of that year told of the shrine being blessed by Archbishop Joseph Francis Rummel, for whom the Knights of Columbus stood as honor guard. Erected in memory of the military veterans of Pointe Coupée Parish, the grotto was financed by Mrs. James Serio (née Sarah Faraci), of a well-known family of grocers of the town.

FIGURE 59: GROTTO, ORIGINALLY DEDICATED TO OUR LADY OF PROMPT SUCCOR, SUBSEQUENTLY DEDICATED TO OUR LADY OF LOURDES

Subsequently, the statue of Our Lady of Prompt Succor was replaced by one depicting Our Lady of Lourdes, which is more in keeping with the grotto representation, and the statue of St. Bernadette, child visionary of Lourdes, placed at ground level in front. The grotto featured pinnacles in stone to left and right of the statue niche, but having been damaged in the severe hurricane of 1947 (subsequently named George), the pinnacles were removed.

In 1948, the Congregation of St. Mary donated to the Town of New Roads a 10-foot strip along 14- foot-wide St. Mary Street, the church's eastern boundary, from West Main Street on the south to First Street on the north for the purpose of widening St. Mary Street. The enhanced 24-foot-wide pavement provides parallel parking for the church during services, as well as a more accommodating roadway.

As early as 1939, New Roads pedestrians have called for the installation of a traffic signal light at the "Savignol – Church" intersection, i.e., West Main and St. Mary Streets, as well as at the "Morning Treat"[6] corner, next to the grocery and coffee store of that name at East Main and Alamo Sts, per that year's 14 June edition of the *Pointe Coupée Banner*. Neither was installed, and the only light downtown has been at Main and New Roads Streets, two blocks east of St. Mary Church.

The municipal Police Department, however, has provided manpower for church-goers' safety for funerals and Sunday Masses during the late 20th and early 21st centuries. The late Pointe Coupée Parish Sheriff A.K. Smith, a stalwart parishioner, is fondly recalled to have personally directed traffic after Masses for many years.

TOWN'S FIRST GYMNASIUM

New Roads' first gymnasium was erected in the rear of St. Mary Church, fronting on First Street, in 1949. It was formerly a military barracks, located in North Louisiana, and acquired, transported

FIGURE 60: PHOTOGRAPH OF A LATER-DAY ASSEMBLY OF KNIGHTS OF COLUMBUS, 4TH DEGREE HONOR GUARD

---

[6] Morning Treat Coffee Company, founded by parishioners, the Lieux brothers, Bertrand, James, and Ivey Lieux

and re- erected on the church property by several fathers of students at St. Joseph Academy. The 12 and 26 May issues of the *Pointe Coupée Banner* that year related how the completed structure was blessed by Archbishop Francis Rummel, who offered benediction on the occasion.

The Knights of Columbus stood as honor guard to His Grace, and attendees included Mother Superior Frances, C.S.J., Sisters of St. Joseph from Baton Rouge, New Orleans and other cities, and civic officials.

The commodious frame structure measured 88 feet wide by 124 feet in depth, had tiers of bleachers to either side indoors, and was capable of seating approximately 1,200 persons. At the south side, facing the entrance opposite, was a stage, hung with velour curtains.

Through primarily used for athletic and other events by St. Joseph Academy and its successor school, Catholic of Pointe Coupée, the fondly recalled "old gym" was also employed by Poydras High School, and the scene of school graduations, pageants, and the annual arrival of Santa Claus coordinated by the Mothers Culture Club.

The last-named event, staged during the 1940s and 1950s, featured the arrival of a prominent local resident anonymously disguised as Santa Claus, who received Christmas wishes and disbursed small net stockings filled with candy to hundreds of area children. The Old Gym stood until dismantling for the construction of St. Mary Parish Hall on its site in 1979-1980.

Immediately west of the St. Joseph Gymnasium and likewise fronting First Street, opposite the foot of Poydras Street, the Congregation re-located a typical Créole cottage from another street, and it served as the residence of church caretaker Herschel "Jack" Leonard and wife, née Joséphine Webre for several years. It later served as the C.Y.O. meeting quarters, but was gone from the site prior to the dismantling of the adjacent gymnasium.

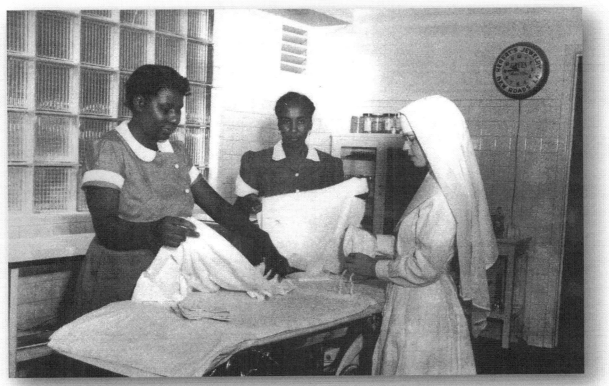

FIGURE 61: SR. MARY DAVID, CSJ, AND AIDES IN THE ST. JOSEPH CLINIC

ST. JOSEPH CLINIC

In the area of health care, in 1950 the Sisters of St. Joseph assumed the administration of the former Mosely Clinic, which had opened in 1940 on East Main Street, opposite the foot of Court Street. The facility was renamed St. Joseph Clinic, or Hospital, and the Sisters served it as well as the successor Pointe Coupée General Hospital, which opened at the western end of New Roads in 1969.

Rev. John W.A. Janssen's correspondence includes a letter referring to the completion of the Sisters' private chapel in the old hospital in 1950, it measuring 27 feet by 67 feet in area. The altar included an altar stone bearing the relic of a saint, six candlesticks adorned the altar, and a large crucifix hung behind.

A gold-plated steel tabernacle kept the Blessed Sacrament for the reception of Holy Communion, and a chalice and ciborium were kept for the celebration of Mass by ministering clergy.

The Sisters of St. Joseph staffing this hospital and its successor were a community separate and apart from the Sisters of St. Joseph at St. Joseph Academy and Convent. In 1954, new living quarters were built for the nursing Sisters at the old hospital, in the form of a two-story and basement annex located on the lower bank of False River, adjoining the rear and perpendicular to the main hospital building fronting on East Main Street.

Repairs to the St. Marry Church interior were undertaken under Fr. Janssen as pastor, at a cost of approximately $6,000, in 1953. Among new features installed at the time were foam rubber kneelers for the pews. The church was fitted with a central air conditioning and heating system in 1958.

A large portion of the Congregation of St. Mary's real estate on the east side of New Roads Street was sold in 1958. The Pointe Coupée Parish School board purchased a 12-acre portion bounded south by Ferry Road, west by New Roads Street, east by a 50-foot strip retained by the Congregation, and north by the remainder of the tract. On this tract, the School Board built Rosenwald High School.

FIGURE 62: ST. JOSEPH HOSPITAL, CA. 1956

FATHER JANSSEN'S PAROCHIAL REPORTS

Based on the Parochial Visitation Reports during Rev. J.W.A. Janssen's pastorate of St. Mary Church, the number of parishioners increased from approximately 1,700 in 1948, to 2,266 in 1954, and 2,615 in 1958. The 1958 total, representing 803 families, had been obtained through a door-to-door parish census in the preceding year.

Indicative of the mass commercialization of any-thing rural and French in South Louisiana "Acadian" or "Cajun" by mid-20th century, Fr. Janssen's description of his congregation metamorphosed from "French Descent. A few Italians" in 1948, to "Acadian-French descent. Some Italians" in 1954; and to "Acadian-French descent" in 1958. Fr. Hoes' reports of 1919, 1923 and 1935, to repeat, identified St. Mary's congregation to be "Creoles" or "Creole," to which ethnicity the majority of the population has consistently identified, owing to their ancestors' origins in mainland France and other Francophone countries.

Fr. Janssen, who suffered from limited sight and hearing, underwent the surgical removal of one eye, but resumed his pastoral duties as soon as possible. He continued at St. Mary until retirement in 1962. Shortly before the community bid farewell to him, the civil parish of Pointe Coupée and all Catholic churches therein became part of the new Diocese of Baton Rouge, formed from the northernmost part of the Archdiocese of New Orleans in 1961.

FIGURE 63: ARCHBISHOP FRANCIS W.A. JANSSENS, FROM THE RAYMOND GARRETT COLLECTION

Vatican Council II and the modification of liturgy, church environment, and a certain disdain for many customs of the past was met by mixed reaction of clergy and parishioners alike. Rev. Arthur J. LeBlanc, Jr., a native of Lockport, Louisiana and the first native-born American to serve as pastor of St. Mary of False River, succeeded Fr. Janssen in 1962.

The erection of the Diocese of Baton Rouge resulted in some changes in administration of churches and chapels, and St. Francis Chapel, third church to bear the name, and built in 1895, was transferred from its status of a mission of St. Ann of Morganza to St. Mary. Several Masses were offered daily at St. Mary, and officiating clergy offered Mass at St. Francis on Sundays and on Christmas Day.

HOLY MASS IN THE VERNACULAR

The most profound change in the Catholic Church, universally, during the pastorate of Rev. Arthur J. LeBlanc, Jr. was expressed in a new liturgical format, with Mass being offered in the vernacular, a detached altar of sacrifice relocated to the center of the sanctuary, and the priest facing the congregation from the opposite side of this altar.

The 26 November 1964 *Pointe Coupée Banner* related that on the following Sunday, 29 November, the changes would take effect, "in promoting a more full and active participating of the people in the worship services."

In addition to the construction of a modernistic altar of sacrifice in the center of the sanctuary, the elaborate main altar reredos was shortened at either end, and pushed back against the rear wall. The three ornamental spires above were removed, but the tabernacle remained in the central place of honor, in the reredos for more than a decade.

The donation of a red carpet for the center aisle of the church, leading from inner entrance doors to the steps of the sanctuary, was made at this time anonymously, but the donor is believed to have been late parishioner Verna Vignes Rittler, daughter of St. Mary stalwarts Hilary and Elise Guérin Vignes.

During Fr. LeBlanc's pastorate, the lower part of the sanctuary wall, below the wainscot, was likewise painted red, supposedly in keeping with the carpet. The carpet was removed and the sanctuary wall painted white during the pastorate of Rev. Frank Uter, to the vocal appreciation of many of the congregation.

FORMER PLACE DE LA CROIX

Though no record of conveyance or right-of-way is to be found in the Conveyance records of the Pointe Coupée Parish Clerk of Court from any vendor, St. Mary of False River was one of several adjacent property owners in downtown New Roads whose riverfront was paved and designated Morrison Parkway in 1965. This public area accommodates automobile parking and boat launching at water's edge on the "lower bank" of False River.

In connecting the Parkway with West Main Street above, a public street was built to link the two, on St. Mary property historically known as the Place de la Croix. Additionally, most of the former "little drag," or planted neutral ground and vehicle turn-around (as opposed to the "big drag" in front of the Pointe Coupée Parish Courthouse) to the west, was paved for parking as well, leaving but little grassy area of what had been in the 19th century the church's Place de la Croix.

Upon the remaining neutral ground was located a marble statue of Jesus with the Sacred Heart, donated by longtime Police Jury Secretary and New Roads Troop 66 Boys Scouts master Joseph Harry Jarreau in memory of his late wife, née Gail Bueche.

In the next decades, the local Kiwanis Club built a pavilion at the edge of the escarpment, dubbing the area "St. Mary Kiwanis Park," and a neighboring owner built a camp "down the hill" and closer to water's edge which encroaches upon St. Mary's property. No legal action has been pursued by the Congregation to date to determine boundaries of its remaining riverbank property.

Meanwhile, St. Mary Church received additional income during Fr. A.J. LeBlanc's pastorate through the sale of the northernmost part of the Congregation's tract on the east side of New Roads St. In 1968, real estate developer Alton "Billy" Ducote purchased the tract bounded on the north by the mutual 40-arpent rear line of St. Mary's and adjoining properties, south by land of the Pointe Coupée Parish School Board, on which Rosenwald High School was located, west by the extension of New Roads Street, and east by the Gaudin Subdivision.

Portage Canal bisected the tract, and between the canal on the north and St. Augustine Street was developed Pecan Acres West subdivision, which, like the adjacent Pecan Acres East were subjected to successive flooding by the overbanking of the canal in heavy rainfall, necessitating a buy-out of the most of the property owners and their moving elsewhere.

FIGURE 64: HISTORIC PLACE DE LA CROIX, SOUTHERN PORTION OF WHICH IS PRESENTLY DESIGNATED ST. MARY'S KIWANIS PARK

INTO THE 1970s

Fr. LeBlanc resigned from the pastorate of St. Mary in 1974, citing the numerous changes which the Church had undergone through the decade. After laicization, he married Catherine LaBorde, widow of Albin Major, Jr. of New Roads. The LeBlancs were consistent supporters of St. Mary Church, and Mr. LeBlanc ministered as a lector for Sunday Mass.

Following Fr. LeBlanc as St. Mary's pastor was Rev. Christopher Springer, who served from 1974 until 1976. During this time, simplification of the church interior was made through the move or removal of a number of statues and other ornamentation. The rebricking of the church parvis — described as a "plaza" at the rime - began during his tenure.

RENOVATIONS AND EXPANSION

The last quarter of the 20th century and beginning decades of the 21st were marked by renovations in St. Mary Church and expansion of parish plant, ministries, and participation by the laity. The pastors and the parish's increasingly larger staffs strove to balance priority of liturgical and sacramental observance with the technological and social changes of the time.

Charismatic and antiquarian Rev. Francis M. "Frank" Uter served as pastor of St. Mary of False River from 1976 until 1982. His pastorate was marked by increased participation in the liturgy and sacraments, and several examples exist of many who had not been to church in years becoming regular attendees and generous contributors of time, talent and treasure.

Fr. Uter supervised a major renovation of the St. Mary church interior, lasting from 1977 until 1979. He completed the liturgical changes mandated by Vatican II by working with St. Mary as it was, and employing many of its existing artistic treasures and returning others which had been removed. While work proceeded in the church, Holy Mass was offered in the St. Joseph Catholic High School Gymnasium, facing First Street behind the church.

FATHER UTER'S RENOVATIONS

St. Mary's three altars were reworked and painted in *faux marbre* (false marble), and to the truncated reredos of the main altar, two spires from the altar of St. Francis Chapel were added, to restore something of the appearance of St. Mary's altar before its post-Vatican II mutilation. A taller, central spire was not replaced as had existed before, but the space thus left open provides for an unhindered view of the striking, central, stained-glass window: "The Descent of the Holy Ghost."

The Virgin Mary altar in the western apse had a gold-plated tabernacle that was likely the so-called "Tabernacle of the Virgins" installed in 1921 during the substitute pastorate of Rev. Francois Baissac. It was transformed into a Blessed Sacrament altar and the tabernacle

FIGURE 65: FATHER UTER WITH CA. 1750 CONFESSIONALS LOCATED AT ST. FRANCIS CHAPEL

118

became the only one in the church, upon the removal of the principal one from the main altar reredos.

The terra cotta depiction of the Last Supper from the main altar was moved to this one, the work on the western altar being financed in in memory of Corinne Morrison Claiborne Keller Jacobs, mother of Hon. Corinne "Lindy" Claiborne Boggs, United States Representative and subsequent Ambassador to the Holy See.

Dame Boggs had received her sacraments of Baptism, First Communion and Confirmation in St. Mary Church, and boarded at St. Joseph Academy until her graduation therefrom in 1931. She subsequently married Hon. Hale Boggs in St. Mary, and periodically returned to visit the church and cemetery, in the latter of which lay her predeceased parents, grandparents, and the Boggs' infant son.

With the Blessed Sacrament now reserved on the left side altar, an old processional cross was resized through a reduction in the staff length and set on a base in the place of the former tabernacle in the main altar reredos. After the original metal corpus of the crucifix was stolen by unknown parties in 1987, it was replaced by an antique ivory one from the renowned *Atélier* Heckman of Paris, given and mounted in memory of Mr. and Mrs. Lloyd Vivien by daughter Aline Vivien Hebert.

The eastern, St. Joseph altar was redeveloped as a Holy Family altar, by joining the existing statue of St. Joseph holding the Christ Child and a lily to that of the Virgin Mary statue from St. Francis Chapel. St. Mary's statue of the Virgin as Queen of Heaven proved too tall in proportion to aesthetically pair it with that of St. Joseph, so the Marian statues of St. Mary and St. Francis were exchanged to complete the Holy Family unit. Below the Holy Family statue, a lighted, glass-fronted ambry was fashioned for safekeeping of the holy oils.

The mensas of the two side altars were removed and joined back-to-back to form an altar of sacrifice in the middle of the sanctuary, the work being financed in memory of late parishioner Verna Vignes Rittler. A new mensa was made for the altar of sacrifice.

Rather than installing thereto the old altar stone with relics within, Fr. Uter had the religious education students from both Catholic Elementary and the parish C.C.D. program insert their handwritten notes of blessings for which they were especially grateful. These were retrieved when a new mensa, complete with the altar stone, replaced the deteriorating one of the late 1970s in 2016.

Another treasure, St. Mary's suspended brass sanctuary lamp, which had been saved from salvage by parishioner Dr. Leon "Boobie" Monceret, Jr., D.D.S., was polished and rehung in the church, albeit not in its original position from the sanctuary arch, but, instead, before the tabernacle in the western altar.

Fr. Uter oversaw the transfer of the baptismal font from the southwestern entry of the church to immediately in front of the Holy Family altar. The domed cover of the font was turned upside down to form a rosette for the chandelier in the main entrance of the church, though the figure of Jesus being baptized by St. John the Baptist which had crowed it was retained. The latter was to stand on the edge of the font when not being used, and moved onto a specially built ledge at the foot of the Holy Family altar at the time of baptismal ceremonies. The expense of the font renovation was covered in memory of Mr. and Mrs. Albin Major.

A pair of matching Gothic statue pedestals, one of which had borne the statue of Jesus with the Sacred Heart, were reworked into an ambo for proclamation of the Gospel and lectern for the First and Second Readings and for the cantor. This work was financed in memory of the late Mr. and Mrs. Ernest Morgan and the late Mr. and Mrs. Joseph Philibert Jewell.

In the entrance, the swinging double doors to the nave and transom above installed by Fr. Hoes a half-century before were removed. The arched passages from the main entrance to those on the west and east were enclosed, and a Reconciliation room created in the room thus formed on the west and an ushers' room in that of the east. The electrification of the bell *Maria Seraphina Clara* did away with the long rope hanging from the bell tower, through the choir loft and into the entrance where it had been used by the altar servers to sound the hours of services and the Angelus.

The church interior was painted in off-white, to highlight out the pure white of the altars, and the hardwood floors and pews were refinished. Much of the renovation work was done by parishioners, including the family of Lynn and Mildred Bourg Langlois, who refinished the pews by hand. New lighting including Williamsburg style chandeliers to replace their semi-globular predecessors, and spot lighting toward the sanctuary were installed, as well a new sound system, a piano, a carillon bell system, and carpeting of the sanctuary and north-south aisles.

COMMEMORATIVE CELEBRATIONS

Rev. Frank Uter's vibrant pastorate at St. Mary was highlighted by special liturgical celebrations, including the 250th anniversary of the Church in Pointe Coupée in 1978, and a Mass in 1979 marking the 75th anniversary of the present St. Mary Church, the arrival of the Sisters of St. Joseph in New Roads and the establishment of the local Catholic school system. The 75th anniversary Mass, celebrated by His Grace William Borders, Archbishop of Baltimore, was also marked by the dedication service in which the walls of St. Mary's were marked with holy chrism in 12 places.

In commemorating the latter, small, colored metal rosettes were set in each of the 12 places marked by chrism, and a brass and glass candle wall sconce above each. Several elements of the latter were accidentally damaged and removed through the years, and had yet to be replaced as of early 2023.

PARISH HALL

Toward the close of the eventful year of 1979, on 9 December, Fr. Uter oversaw the laying of the cornerstone of St. Mary Parish Hall. The building was designed by local architects and parishioners A. Major Hébert and Glenn C. Morgan, on the site of the dismantled St. Joseph gymnasium in the rear of the church, but facing St. Mary Street and with paved parking at front and north side.

Though not intentional, according to Morgan, the hall – which was completed in 1980 – bears a striking resemblance to the St. Francis Church of 1760, being a gable fronted structure surrounded on three sides by exterior galleries.

The Parish Hall and front parking area occupy the historic site of New Roads' second-known Freedmen's Bureau School, which was open to white as well as African American students and in operation during 1866-1867.

St. Mary's Parish Hall has been used for large parish functions, such as meetings, receptions, religious education and youth events, and for the monthly Shut In Mass and Social for persons whose mobility prevented them from attending Mass in the church. The hall is also the meeting place of the Knights and Columbus, is fitted with seating for additional accommodation of worshippers at the major feasts of Christmas and Easter, and is rented out to the public for wakes and various community and private functions.

FIGURE 66: IMAGES OF THE PRAYER GARDEN, INCLUDING BLESSED MOTHER STATUE AND ONE OF THE STATIONS OF THE CROSS WALLS

PRAYER GARDEN

The grounds surrounding church, hall and rectory were landscaped, and St. Mary Prayer Garden established as an oasis of serenity for meditation in the rear of the Parish Hall. A ground-level monument made of salvaged masonry and a cross from demolished tombs in St. Mary Cemetery bears an engraved marble tablet in memory of the late Dr. James Cleveland Roberts and wife, née Berthe Seibert, whose descendants sold the south one-half and donated the rear or north half of the tract on which were built the Parish Office and Adoration Chapel.

Other memorials in the Prayer Garden include two placed by Council 1998 Knights of Columbus: one for its longtime financial officer J. Jeff David, and the other for the victims of abortion, both of them being located at the foot of a statue of Our Lady of Fatima.

A nearby statue of St. Jude was erected in 2022 by John and Stacie Arcement Allen in memory of the late Rev. Danny Roussel, who died during Hurricane Ida as it wreaked unprecedented destruction through his native community of Vacherie and much of southeastern Louisiana in 2021.

As Deacon Danny Roussel, he has previously ministered at St. Mary through the time of social restrictions owing to the Covid-19 pandemic. The Prayer Garden was one of the places where he could visit with and minister to the faithful, in a socially-distant setting, during the trying months when public liturgy and reception of the sacraments was suspended.

The Prayer Garden is flanked on south and north sides by brick panels bearing ceramic Stations of the Cross created by art students of the late much-loved Sister Anne Constance Livaudais at Catholic High School of Pointe Coupée. The panels and park benches were donated in memory of the C.E. Hebert family.

The maintenance and continued natural growth of the St. Mary Prayer Garden and the grounds of the church, rectory, adoration chapel and parish office were for years the ministry of Mrs. James M. Bouanchaud, née Sarita McDonald. Her donation of time, talent and treasure in and around St. Mary was given in addition to her roles as organist and pianist for church, school, and the C.C.D. and Summer Bible School programs.

BUILDING FUND

Mindful of the financial obligations of the parish incurred through the years of renovation and expansion, Fr. Uter oversaw the establishment of the St. Mary Building & Maintenance Fund, a monthly collection which helped to retire the Parish Hall construction debt within 10 years and continues to cover the cost of material improvements.

A special Building Fund collection is passed in St. Mary at Masses one weekend of each month, and the fund has likewise received a number of memorial donations.

FIGURE 67: PROLIFIC ARTIST AND INSTRUCTOR, SISTER ANNE CONSTANCE LIVAUDAIS, CSJ

CROSS BESIDE THE RIVER

Largely due to the various renovation projects, Fr. Uter's pastorate was also marked by a new appreciation of St. Mary's and St. Francis' rich past. Historical research, in which he was assisted by parishioner Glenn Morgan, led to the installation in 1983 of a large cross across the street from the church, on the bank of False River.

A cross, or succession of crosses, had stood on the site, officially La Place de la Croix, from 1843 to at least 1891. None appears in the heirloom photograph of West Main Street in the "St. Valentine's Day Snow" of 1895. The new cross erected in 1983 was the gift of the J.C. Langlois family, who operated Main Street Service Station adjacent to the west, and the park-like area was once again called by its original name, *La Place de la Croix*. Plans for the erection of yet another, successor cross were underway in early 2023.

The J.C. Roberts property to the west of St. Mary's rectory, totaling 5.488 acres, was acquired in 1984, the front half through purchase and rear half through donation by the Roberts descendants. Included on the site was the old home built for the Albin Provosty family in 1905 and known as "Provosty Hall," prior to being acquired by Dr. J.C. Roberts later in the 20th century. Toward the rear is the former Roberts family tennis court, one of the earliest in town, and whose concrete base remained in the year 2023.

Extending as it does from West Main to Napoleon Street, the rear of the former Roberts property allows for additional parking for the Catholic of Pointe Coupée school campus located across Napoleon.

In the late 19th century, civic and church supporter Joseph Richy's fine home stood on the site of what would later be the Provosty – Roberts residence, and in the front yard Richy built New Roads' first fire engine house. A Corpus Christ *réposoir* or station was located there by parish ladies for the 1885 procession.

PRESERVING ST. FRANCIS CHAPEL

While restoring, preserving and expanding at St. Mary, Rev. Frank Uter directed the renovation and continued viability of the parish's hallowed mission chapel, St. Francis of Pointe Coupée. The 1895 vintage building, the third to bear the St. Francis name since 1738, was placed on the National Register of Historic Places in the active year of 1979, as a monument to the Faith. Holy Mass continues to be offered there in the 21st century each Sunday morning.

By the year 2020, structural renovation work was deemed necessary in the historic chapel by Dr. Eddie Cazayoux, A.I.A., a native of St. Mary church parish, retired university professor and specialist in historic preservation. Likewise, concerns were voiced for the chapel grounds and cemetery, which, like most properties along the Mississippi riverfront, tends to drain slowly owing to the water table and collection of rainwater beneath the chapel. Some work toward remediation of the chapel's sill structure was undertaken by 2022.

FIGURE 68: ENTRANCE TO ST. MARY'S CEMETERY PRIOR TO THE LOSS OF TREES IN HURRICANE GUSTAV

ST. MARY CEMETERY RENOVATION AND EXPANSION

Turning his attention to the aged St. Mary Cemetery, Fr. Uter sought to identify families having abandoned and decaying tombs in the hallowed burial ground in hopes that descendants would have them repaired. With the assistance of male students of Catholic High of Pointe Coupée, several unclaimed tombs were dismantled, including those of the LeBeau – Demourelle family, notable as two vaults in height but six vaults in width; the large, multi-vault Joffrion family tomb, topped by a masonry cross of rustic design; and the tomb of Luiggia Fiorenza, native of Castelvetrano, Sicily.

While *Signorina* Fiorenza's remains were interred on the site and topped by the slab of her demolished tomb, most remains found in other tombs were respectfully transferred to the stately Ternant – Parlange mausoleum, which the Parlange family had donated to St. Mary, thus becoming as ossuary.

On the former site of the LeBeau – Demourelle tomb, another branch of the family, the Echelards, erected a large and handsome new tomb, while the F.A. Smith family had a new tomb built on the site of the demolished Joffrion tomb.

Tragically, in the succeeding pastorate of Rev. Victor Messina, the Ternant – Parlange tomb was despoiled of its elaborate temple-like superstructure of six classic columns supporting a starred canopy and crowning urn, with ornamental sarcophagus enshrined therein. The mutilation took place, Glenn Morgan informed this author, on the urging of a member of the church's Cemetery Committee, the latter being "afraid" of a potential collapse of the monument, though it had withstood more than 140 years of hurricanes and other calamities.

FIGURE 69: TERNANT TOMB

The original slabs bearing the names of the Ternants who had been entombed therein were returned to the Parlange family. The artistic ornamental iron fence formerly surrounding the tomb was placed for a brief time between St. Mary Church and the Parish Hall, but ultimately returned to the Parlange family, as well.

The massive "society tomb" of the long-defunct St. Vincent de Paul Society in the cemetery was spared the demolition suffered by many of its neighbors, to be repaired by St. Mary, and has since served as the last resting place of indigent deceased.

As is likely in any un-mapped burial ground where markers no longer exist, some newer burials and tomb construction have occurred in St. Mary Cemetery through the years on the site of earlier burials. Persons employed to dig new graves or lay foundations for tombs have informed this author that any human remains found are respectfully interred on one side of the plot.

More than a century after its establishment, St. Mary Cemetery was finally mapped, in the last quarter of the 1900s, for locations of existing burials and availability of new ones, largely through the

FIGURE 70: TERNANT TOMB INSCRIPTIONS

efforts of parishioner Anna Lee Swindler Jewell, and plotted by Glenn Morgan. The St. Mary Cemetery Association was formed to help guarantee the upkeep of the old burial ground though annual dues, and a Perpetual Care program initiated for periodic, long-term care of tombs, monuments, and plots.

As a matter of note, should the facts be lost to historical record, the Scott L. Smith family tomb, of early 21st century construction, stands atop the burial plot of the Santo Piazza family, natives of Trabia, Sicily. This author's paternal grandfather, a godson of Santo's son Ignazio Piazza, periodically pointed out the plot as such in the early 1970s, while it was still surrounded by a substantial iron fence, and further stated that all of the family had long since moved to California.

In recent years, the urn containing the cremated urns of late parishioner Henry Mars was interred, without ceremony, by a grandson of the deceased in the aisle, adjacent to the coping of the vault of the decedent's first wife, Ethel St. Romain Mars, after repeated requests to have a church staff member meet the family to arrange a proper interment and blessing were not honored.

Two mausoleums have been built by St. Mary Church for the entombment of multiple parishioners, some of them being "double" vaults in which couples can be entombed. For decades, a ditch running north – south dividing the cemetery into halves existed to receive runoff rainwater, but by the 1970s had become a ground for discarded floral offerings, vases and other rubbish. Fr. Uter's work included leveling of low spots and filling in the old ditch.

North of the central west – east aisle, where the ditch had been filled, the first mausoleum was built. It is located, however, on what may have been one or more burials. A descendant of the late James "Jimmy" Boudreau, founder of the city's Community Center Carnival parade, the state's oldest outside New Orleans, stated that upon his death in 1949, he was buried, with neither presence of clergy nor recordation in the St. Mary burial records, in an unmarked grave. She is of the opinion that it likely was in the area now occupied by the mausoleum.

A second mausoleum was built by St. Mary some decades later, on a lot immediately north of the old cemetery and facing New Roads Street, on a property formerly owned by the Olinde commercial enterprises.

Longtime St. Mary staff member Wilfred "Hot Coffee" Fabre is recalled as devotedly attending to the cemetery maintenance and systemically painting tombs covered by Perpetual Care in time for each year's All Saints' Day ceremonies.

Upon Fr. Frank Uter's transfer to other diocesan assignments in 1984, he was succeeded by Rev. Victor Messina. During his three-year tenure, Fr. Messina inaugurated a $34,000 painting and water-proofing project on the church, and continued the reduction of the cost of a decade of physical improvements and growth at St. Mary.

In ministering to the needy, St. Mary's Service Center, a volunteer, goodwill project, was begun during Fr. Messina's pastorate, and operated from the adjacent Provosty-Roberts home, which had become church property.

Other highlights of Fr. Messina's tenure included the reorganization of the St. Mary Altar Society, by which men were welcomed into membership, and the institution in 1985 of annual Blessing of the Boats on False River festivities, established by the by Council 1998 Knights of Columbus in conjunction with Memorial Day. Hundreds of decorated watercraft participate each year on the Sunday prior to Memorial Day, and a lakeside ceremony honors living and deceased veterans.

EUCHARISTIC AND MARIAN DEVOTION UNDER FATHER MILES WALSH

Rev. Messina resigned as pastor of St. Mary in 1987 to continue his ministry in spiritual direction. He was succeeded in the pastorate by Rev. Miles Walsh, who had served as associate pastor at St. Mary during the pastorate of Rev. Uter.

In addition to continuing the ongoing maintenance of both St. Mary and St. Francis Chapel, Fr. Walsh directed the refurbishment of the altars and restoration of paintings in both of the historic churches. Much of the maintenance at St. Francis was performed through the dedication of parishioner Francis Gauthier, and his family continued to be active in his footsteps in the 21st century.

Mr. Gauthier, in addition to his regular duties as building and grounds keeper at St. Francis, installed statues of the Blessed Virgin Mary as appearing on the Miraculous Medal and inscribed stones representing open Bibles which he placed on a number of tombs.

FIGURE 71: REV. MILES WALSH, S.T.D.

Fr. Walsh's pastorate was marked by the purported apparitions of the Blessed Virgin Mary at Medjugorje, in Bosnia and Herzegovina. He and several parishioners were among the untold thousands of pilgrims to the small town, and returned to share in the parish and beyond a renewed devotion to the Blessed Sacrament and Mother Mary.

In 1990, parishioner and artist Glenn C. Morgan designed art windows portraying the history of the Catholic Church in Pointe Coupée for installation in the church facade. These are backlit and offer a striking panorama of key episodes in the local Faith journey.

Produced by the Laukhuff Stained Glass Company of Memphis, Tennessee, and Mitchell-Marionneaux of Maringouin, Louisiana, the windows were dedicated in 1992 in the presence of Baton Rouge Bishop Stanley Ott and His Eminence Albert Cardinal Decoutray, Archbishop of that city with so many ties to the history of Catholicism in Pointe Coupée: Lyon, France.

A new religious complex, designed by Morgan and fellow architect A. Major Hébert for additional meeting and office space was built to link the rear of the church with the south side of the Parish Hall. Christened the St. Joseph Center, in honor of the ministry of the Sisters of St. Joseph in New Roads since 1904, the building was dedicated in conjunction with the blessing of the church's new art windows by Cardinal Decoutray on 19 September 1992.

Construction of the St. Joseph Center was financed by parishioners of St. Mary and in memory of the late Hewitt L. Fontaine, Gertrude Schexnayder, Lawrence and Mathilde Bizette, Felton Bizette, Reynolds Bizette, and Eddie Langlois.

In that same year, Fr. Walsh inaugurated the devotion of Perpetual Adoration of the Blessed Sacrament at St. Mary, one of the first parishes in the Baton Rouge Diocese to do so. A small building adjacent to the rectory was dedicated as an Adoration Chapel, and hundreds of parishioners have since committed to at least one hour of prayer each week before the Blessed Sacrament.

Simultaneous with the completion of the St. Joseph Center, the parish dedicated the contiguous St. Joseph Garden, in thanksgiving for the Sisters of St. Joseph's "Many Years of Loving Service to God and this Community."

The garden is fronted by the parking lot on the east, and bounded west by the St. Joseph Center, south by the church and north by the Parish Hall. In addition to the Gutton Monument at its northeastern corner, the St. Joseph Garden includes statues of the Foster Father of Jesus in the northwestern corner; an Angel, installed in memory of Blake Chustz, in the south-western corner; and, to the south, at the rear of the church apse, a statue of Our Lady of Prompt Succor and the Infant Jesus, both uncrowned, and financed in memory of Nolan Curtis Miller by his wife, sister, and children.

Rev. Mark Alise was named pastor of St. Mary of False River in 1994. During his tenure, work continued toward the maintenance of the aged church, which by that time counted 1,200 families in its congregation.

FIGURE 72: ORIGINAL ADORATION CHAPEL AT ST. MARY, ESTABLISHED BY FR. WALSH

COMMEMORATING DONOR MARIE POURCIAU

In 1995, a worker engaged in extermination of destructive insects discovered a subterranean brick vault under the floor of the western, then the Blessed Sacrament, apse. What appeared to be a human cranial fragment therein correlated to oral tradition in the Humphrey T. Olinde and Alton Gaudin families that Marie Pourciau, their ancestress and benefactress of old St. Mary, upon her death in 1833 was buried beneath the Virgin Mary altar in the original church, and her remains transferred to beneath that in the present church during its construction in 1904-1907.

Marie Pourciau was born on False River in 1747, a daughter of Jean Baptiste Pourciau and Marie Thérèse Chalin. Her paternal grandfather, likewise named Jean Baptiste Pourciau, was a native of the County of Hainaut, in present-day Belgium from whence he and fellow citizens were recruited in 1719 as engagés for the Ste. Reyne Concession, opposite the Mississippi River from Pointe Coupée. His prolific progeny pioneered in the False River, Island, Lower Chenal, and Bayou Grosse Tete areas of Pointe Coupée.

Twice widowed, Marie Pourciau was married first, at age 13, in 1762 to 32-year-old Charles Robillard, who hailed from the Illinois *poste*. Their numerous descendants comprise a large percentage of the 21st century St. Mary congregation. Charles Robillard died in 1790, leaving a substantial estate, including a plantation which comprised in the 21st century the locations of St. Mary Church and parochial buildings, the Catholic High School complex, and the Julien Poydras Centre (formerly Poydras High School).

A year later, on 8 July 1791, enslaved Ado laborers of George Olivo informed him of a plot of enslaved Minas on the plantation of Widow Marie Pourciau Robillard to revolt. On the following night, 9 July, parish magnate Claude Trénonay de Chanfret was murdered at his dinner table, on his plantation near St. Francis Church, by his Ibo enslaved laborer LaTulipe. Sixteen Mina, from various plantations, were apprehended and tried on suspicion of a planned inter-Mina rebellion.

During the proceedings, on 14 July 1791, the Widow Robillard, aged 43, was married to her next-door neighbor to the east, Barthelemi Olinde, age 20. Theirs was likely a marriage of convenience, and apparently she was an unhappy woman, as she filed civil suit for separation from him, on grounds of abuse and character defamation. Barthelemi Olinde died in 1818. The Olinde family of New Roads, who have consistently been active and contributing members of St. Mary Church and St. Francis Chapel, descend from Euphrosine Robillard (daughter of Charles Robillard and Marie Pourciau) who married Pierre "Pelisse" Olinde, older brother of Barthelemi Olinde above. The intertwined and multiple relationships in this family is common in most early families of Pointe Coupée Parish.

After the finding in 1995 of what appeared to be Marie Pourciau's disinterred cranial remain, it was relegated to a small plastic bag in the Parish Office for several years. Finally, preservation-minded parishioner Glenn Morgan was authorized to have a small casket made in which the bone fragment was placed and respectfully returned to the vault beneath the church floor. A trap door was let into the floor nearby, to allow for easier access whenever work under the church is required.

In 2010, Morgan and this author designed a marble "Merci" or Thank You tablet, in memory of Marie Pourciau and in thanksgiving for her benevolence. It was cut by the B. & D. Marble and Granite firm of Port Barré, Louisiana, and affixed to the wall immediately to the left of the Blessed Sacrament altar, beneath which her remains are located.

During the 2016 church renovation under Mons. Robert Berggren, two small marble *ex voto* plaques, one marked "Merci" and the other "Thanks," were returned to this area, and placed atop the Marie Pourciau tablet. Though their donors are unknown at present, they are similar to ex votos in other old churches of French Louisiana and Europe.

Among Morgan's last works for St. Mary was the design and installation of a matching Gospel stand and hymn board, to either side of the sanctuary arch, and in Gothic style; and a pair of similar boards at the entrance to the nave, one of which gives a brief history of the church, and the other the St. Mary Church Mission Statement, both in gilt letters.

Fr. Alise resigned from the pastorate of St. Mary in 1996, and was subsequently laicized and married. He was succeeded at St. Mary by Rev. Michael J. "Mike" Schatzle, who was pastor from 1996 until 2004.

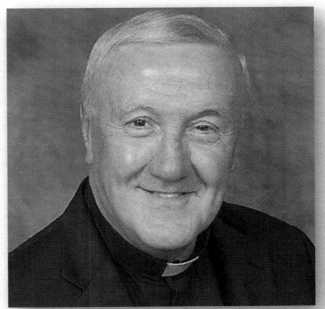

Figure 73: Father Michael J. "Mike" Schatzle

EXPANSION UNDER FATHER SCHATZLE

During Fr. Mike Schatzle's tenure, the Congregation of St. Mary Church in the year 2002 donated to the Congregation of St. Augustine Church the last of St. Mary's property on the east side of New Roads Street that had been purchased back in 1865 by Rev. J.P. Gutton.. This was a 5.45 acre tract, bounded west by New Roads Street, east by Court Street, north by Ferry Road, and south by the existing property of St. Augustine and location of its cemetery.

In 2003, St. Mary purchased the former lot and residence property of Miss Louise Laurent, located north of the existing church property, and occupying the southwest corner of Poydras and Napoleon Streets. With this acquisition, the St. Mary church holdings came to front on five streets, West Main, St. Mary, Poydras, First and Napoleon, and limited on the west side by the former Poydras High School property.

Miss Laurent's modern cottage residence became the home of the remaining Sisters of St. Joseph in New Roads, for whom the living area of their convent at the corner of Napoleon Street and Louisiana Avenue had become superfluous.

The Sisters of St. Joseph of Bourg who remained in teaching ministry in New Roads in the last quarter of the 20th century included Sr. Constance Livaudais, a native of New Orleans, art instructor, and noted regional artist in her own right, and Sr. Marilyn Saltamachia, who taught Catholic school students during the week and parish C.C.D. students on Saturday mornings.

FIGURE 74: PICTURED LEFT TO RIGHT ARE SISTERS OF ST. JOSEPH: THE LATE SISTER AGNES JEWELL, SISTER RITA LAMBERT, AND THE LATE SISTER MARILYN SALTAMACHIA

In 1977, a reorganization of the Sisters of St. Joseph in the United States and Europe was affected, in which the American contingent was renamed the Sisters of St. Joseph of Medaille. The new name was that of the Jesuit Rev. Jean Pierre Médaille, who helped organize the Sisters of St. Joseph in LePuy, France in 1650.

After the disbanding of the congregation and martyrdom of several Sisters during the French Revolution, the Sisters of St. Joseph reorganized in 1807 in Lyon, France, city with so many links to Pointe Coupée Catholicism, by Mother St. Jean Fontbonne and Joseph Cardinal Fesch, Almoner and Prince of France, Coadjutor of the Prince-Archbishopric of Dahlberg, and maternal half-uncle of Napoléon Bonaparte. A decrease in vocations by the turn of the 20th-21st centuries combined the Sisters of St. Joseph of Bourg and Medaille into the Congregation of St. Joseph in 2007.

With the withdrawal of the Sisters of St. Joseph from the faculty of the Catholic school, they became active in other areas of parish spirituality and life, including Srs. Rita Lambert and Mary Anne

Hébert, successively in parish ministry at St. Mary. In the year 2023. Sr. Janet Franklin, residing in St. Mary church parish, continued the order's charism of retreat direction.

A Sisters of Saint Joseph tomb is located near the central Calvary monument in St. Mary Cemetery, and several Sisters are entombed therein. Other, native Sisters are buried in family tombs elsewhere in the cemetery.

PARISH OFFICE AND ADORATION CHAPEL

Until the turn of the 20th-21st centuries, St. Mary's parish office was located in the space afforded by the Rectory's former first floor gallery. The staff long consisted of a secretary, who worked in that area, a housekeeper and cook for the clergy, and a maintenance man for the church grounds and cemetery.

The increase in parish ministries and staff required more spacious and modern facilities. Moreover, many church parishes in Louisiana, as well as throughout the world, were being paired and or discontinued. It was generally viewed by clergy and laity alike that St. Mary would, perhaps, become one of a few parishes in the region, and the expansion of ministries would require more space and staff members. Among those employed by St. Mary at this time was parishioner David C. Olinde, who provided sacristan and other services for several years.

During the pastorate of Rev. Mike Schatzle, the former Provosty – Roberts residence west of the Rectory was dismantled and on its site were built a Parish Office and new Adoration Chapel in 2004. Both designed by parishioner architect – artist Glenn Morgan, the Office is of utilitarian but trim design, while the Adoration Chapel embodies the Créole architecture of colonial Pointe Coupée.

The Office and Adoration Chapel were financed largely through a half-million dollar bequest of the late False River landowner Murphy "Dack" Porche, son of pre-deceased Adolphe and Roberta Aguillard Porche.

Descendants of the Provosty family attended the ceremonial dedication of the Parish Office and Adoration Chapel, described elsewhere, and expressed pleasure that their ancestral home site had become one of continuous prayer before the Blessed Sacrament.

Rev. Robert "Bob" Stine succeeded Fr. Schatzle as pastor of St. Mary later in 2004. During his tenure, he and parishioners helped to welcome and minister to approximately 5,000 citizens of New Orleans who moved to the New Roads area owing to catastrophic Hurricane Katrina in 2005.

Though most of the individuals and families who took refuge in Pointe Coupée Parish at the time eventually returned to New Orleans or established new homes elsewhere, many remained in the New Roads area, some of whom became dedicated parishioners of St. Mary and have contributed to local civic and cultural life.

Pointe Coupée, in turn, suffered Hurricane Gustav, in 2008. Though its winds, maxing at 91 miles per hour, were of less intensity than Hurricane Andrew's 110 miles per hour in 1992, Gustav's were of longer duration and its torrential rainfall flooded parts of New Roads adjacent to Portage Canal.

The last of the cedar *allée* which had once bisected St. Mary Cemetery from west to east was toppled, crushing the New Roads Street entrance gates. All remaining cedars were removed, and the gateway rebuilt and commemorative tablet of cemetery history restored thereon.

In 2017, through the generosity of parishioner Todd Perrault, a new crowning arch bearing the name "St. Mary Cemetery" was erected above the brick pillars to replace the 1940s original which had been mangled by Gustav.

MAJOR RENOVATION UNDER MONSIGNOR BERGGREEN

Just after announcing his plans to retire from active ministry, Mons. Robert H. Berggreen followed Rev. Bob Stine as pastor of St. Mary in 2011. His charisms of educator, pastor and administrator provided guidance for a capital campaign and major, eight-month-long renovation of the church interior and exterior, which was completed in 2016. The cost was approximately $1.5 million, for which one-third of St. Mary's parish families pledged the funding.

The renovation was complete in time for Christmas 2016, and a celebratory Mass was held in the following year, for which Baton Rouge Bishop Robert Muench officiated. He was assisted by Msgr. Berggreen, pastor; Rev. Nicholas "Jack" Nutter, assistant pastor; St. Mary deacons Mssrs. Tom Robinson and Mike Thompson; former St. Mary pastor Rev. Michael "Mike" Schatzle; former St. Mary

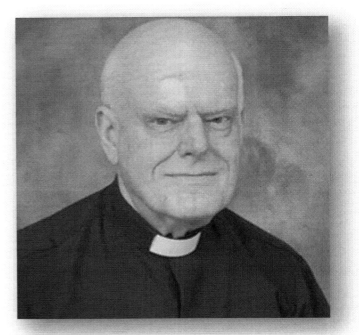

FIGURE 75: MSGR. ROBERT H. BERGGREEN

associate pastor Rev. Peter Dang; St. Augustine Church pastor Rev. Patrick Healy, S.S.J.; St. Ann Church of Morganza pastor Rev. Brent Maher; and Rev. Joseph Doyle, S.S.J., novice master of the Josephite Fathers' Mary Immaculate Novitiate in nearby St. Augustine church parish.

A special welcome was extended the former and visiting clergy as well as novices from the Mary Immaculate Novitiate, religious Sisters and other attendees, while gratitude was expressed for all who contributed to work on the church, the financing of the project, and the celebration.

In his remarks during the Mass, Bishop Muench stated the beauty of the renovated 110-year-old St. Mary Church reflected its parishioners and their commitment to the Faith which began with their ancestors nearly 300 years ago, while Monsignor Berggreen delivered another of his memorable homilies which put practical application to the words of scripture. He stated that even the commendable praise for the church building was secondary to each person's primary purpose of praising and being proud in God.

Upon Mons. Berggren's retirement owing to health issues in 2018, he was followed as pastor of St. Mary by Rev. Patrick Broussard, Jr. A former deacon who, as a widower, completed seminary formation and was ordained, his ministry was marked by renovations at St. Mary Parish Hall and Coronavirus 19 pandemic restrictions. The latter resulted in several months of neither liturgy nor sacraments at St. Mary, and for the first time since the 1882 Flood, neither were Holy Week nor Easter observed liturgically for the public.

Of the more than 2,400 COVID-19 cases reported in the Parish of Pointe Coupee by Easter 2023, a total of 96 deaths were recorded by the Centers for Disease Control and Prevention.

Rev. Broussard resigned as pastor of St. Mary in the year 2020, and was subsequently laicized and married. He was followed at St. Mary by former pastor Rev. Michael "Mike" Schatzle, who returned from retirement and assumed the assignment of administrator.

FIGURE 76: PASTORS OF ST. MARY CELEBRATING THE MAJOR RENOVATIONS, REVS. FRANCIS UTER (1976-1984), VICTOR MESSINA (1984-1987), MILES WALSH (1987-1994), MICHAEL SCHATZLE (1996-2008), ROBERT STINE (2008-2012), AND MSGR. ROBERT BERGGREEN (2012-18)

TOWARD A BICENTENNIAL JUBILEE

In 2021, Rev. Christopher Decker, whose maternal ancestry is from the Frisco community in Ward 10, Pointe Coupée Parish, was assigned pastor of St. Mary. His tenure has been marked by catechetical emphasis through the liturgy, the Catholic school, and other aspects of parish life, and a return to the dignity in liturgical practice and environment fondly recalled by many from past generations.

Gifted in technological and artistic realms,[7] Fr. Decker's earliest accomplishments included the compilation of a "Prayers and Devotions, With Chants for the Holy Mass" booklet for use of the congregation and the resumption of novenas following the weekday noon Masses at St. Mary. The novenas, one each on Tuesday through Friday, invoke Jesus Christ the High Priest (for priestly vocations), the Sacred Heart of Jesus, Our Lady of Perpetual Help, and St. Joseph. Fr. Decker likewise devised an "M" monogram for the church and enhanced the scope and presentation of the weekly St. Mary *Parish Bulletin*.

FIGURE 77: REV. CHRISTOPHER J. DECKER, PASTOR OF ST. MARY OF FALSE RIVER (2021-PRESENT)

The Catholic Daughters of the Americas and the Holy Name Society were reanimated with new membership at St. Mary after decades of inactivity, and a new society, the Guild of St. Stephen, was formed, all during the apostolate-rich year of 2022.

---

[7] A planned, accompanying volume to this work will feature an animated acolyte character, which Father Decker has created.

In preparing for St. Mary's bicentennial jubilee of 2023, Fr. Decker in 2022 identified the relics within the altar stone in the Altar of Sacrifice to be those of Sts. Felissimus and Jucundian, martyrs, and saw to fruition several parishioners' long-suffering desire to have the Blessed Sacrament restored to its previous place of honor in the main altar reredos.

Advent 2022 was marked in St. Mary Church by some rearrangement in keeping with many parishioners' desire for something of the beauty that characterized the hallowed house of worship prior to the dramatic changes of the post-Vatican II period. The 1921 vintage "Tabernacle of the Virgins" on the western altar, which had held the Blessed Sacrament since removal of the main tabernacle in the central reredos during the 1977-1979 renovation, was relocated from the western to the main altar reredos on the feast of St. John of the Cross, 14 December.

The statue of Jesus with the Sacred Heart, exiled from near the sanctuary to the southeast entrance of the church circa 1990, was enthroned upon the western altar, thus changing its focus again: from originally the Blessed Virgin Mary, Queen of Heaven in 1907, to the Blessed Sacrament in 1977-1979, to the Sacred Heart of Jesus in 2022.

In relieving the sanctuary of the inaesthetic mélange of chairs, tables and other objects in use since the 1970s renovation, gothic revival presider's and assistant's chairs, credence table and missal stand were installed and the redundant second lectern removed.

A prayed-for addition to St. Mary's hallowed environment is an official shrine to Blessed Kaiser Karl, last Emperor of Austria and Apostolic King of Hungary. He is increasingly invoked in the 21st century as the "Peace Emperor" for his and wife Kaiserin Zita's determination to end the First World War, and their lives of heroic sanctity since youth and into exile on Madeira, where he died in 1922. The international Kaiser Karl Gebetsliga, or League of Prayer, exists in support of his eventual canonization, as well as the cause of world peace. Blessed Karl has gained a following in New Roads and vicinity. In early 2023, a picture of Karl and Zita on their wedding day was placed at the foot of the recently-recovered Sacred Heart statue in St. Mary Church, attesting to the couple's fervent devotion to Our Lord and His Sacred Heart.

In mid-2023, Fr. Decker was assisted in the spiritual and temporal works of St. Mary and St. Francis by a staff including Deacon Patrick Witty; Patty Aguillard, bookkeeper; Lisa Chutz, director of facilities and executive secretary; Molly Cline, director of Christian formation; Jade Robillard, receptionist and *Bulletin* editor; and Mike Vaccaro, maintenance.

At that time, a total of 2,895 individuals, comprising 1,196 families, were registered as members of St. Mary of False River church parish, according to Executive Secretary Lisa Jarreau Chutz. The parish encompasses all of the 70760 (New Roads) and 70783 (Ventress) postal zip codes and the northernmost portion of 70762 (Oscar), which total approximately 10,210 persons, according to the United States Postal Service.[8]

To the above numbers are added the scores of persons in assisted living and nursing facilities, the incarcerated and hospitalized, and the estimated 5,000 weekend visitors and secondary home owners in the False River resort area who receive the sacraments and other ministrations of St. Mary in church and local institutions.

Of the approximately 20,800-person population of Pointe Coupée Parish, contemporary online sources estimated 60 percent of the total to be registered members of churches, and of their number, 80 percent or approximately 9,750 were registered Catholics.

---

[8] https://www.unitedstateszipcodes.org/70760/, accessed 1/18/2023

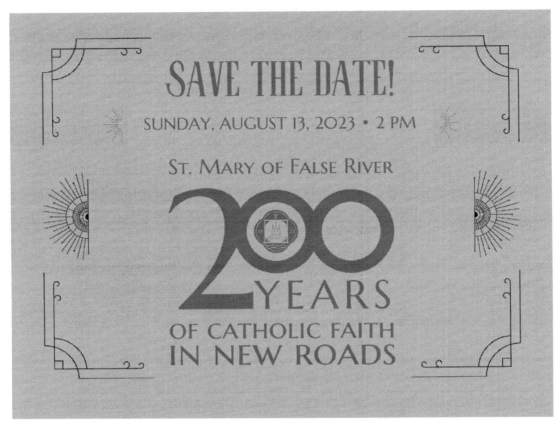

FIGURE 78: BICENTENNIAL CELEBRATION INVITATION, DESIGNED BY FR. DECKER

MISSION CHAPELS AND SISTER PARISHES

In addressing the growth in population and expansion of inhabited areas in Pointe Coupée Parish during the 19th century, the succession of clergy serving the mother church of St. Francis of Pointe Coupée and its mission chapel of St. Mary of False River frequently wrote of the need for additional mission chapels and stations for the faithful in outlying areas.

In 1857, Rev. Francois Mittelbronn, then associate pastor of St. Francis, wrote to Archbishop Antoine Blanc in New Orleans of plans for the establishment of a chapel in the Morganza area. He reported the parishioners in the Raccourci section, just above Morganza, were desirous of such, surmising, however, that when the time of payment of funds subscribed by them for the purpose would be due, "each" would have an excuse not to remit payment.

Fr. Mittelbronn continued that Mr. (Auguste II) Provosty had offered a building with dimensions of 60 feet by 30 feet by 40 feet, but was somewhat "aged" and would have to be moved from Provosty's land to that of Eugene Tircuit, the latter of whom had offered property for a church, presbytery and cemetery Three years later, in 1860, Fr. Mittelbronn wrote Archbishop Blanc, stating that he intended to begin work on a chapel near Morganza after Easter of that year. Mittelbronn likewise told of the need for a chapel at Waterloo, the parish's busiest port community on the Mississippi River, east of the parish seat of New Roads.

The pastor envisioned that with him and another priest in Pointe Coupée Parish, one could serve St. Francis Church and a mission near Morganza, and the other could administer St. Mary of False River and a Waterloo mission.

Fr. Mittelbronn's successor, Rev. Joseph Philibert Gutton, from his newly-erected parish of St. Mary of False River at New Roads, visited the Morganza area and offered Holy Mass upriver at New Texas Landing at the end of 1865. Less than two years later, in 1867, Fr. Gutton wrote to New Orleans Arch-bishop John Marie Odin, C.M., surmising that if a chapel were built at Morganza its expense could be paid off in six months.

SEVEN DOLORS AND MISSIONS

In 1872, Our Lady of Seven Dolors church parish was established, and its jurisdiction encompassed all of northern or Upper Pointe Coupée, to which was added the former St. Francis parish in 1890. A temporary church and rectory were built and a cemetery established at New Texas Landing, upriver of Morganza. During 1882-1883, when the pastorate was vacant, Seven Dolors was ministered to intermittently by St. Mary pastor Rev. J.P. Gutton and Immaculate Conception pastor Rev. Pierre Berthet. Seven Dolors was estimated to embrace 1,000 congregants, of whom 800 were white and 200 were African American and *Créole de couleur* in 1884. Construction began on a larger church in 1887, and it was completed in 1892.

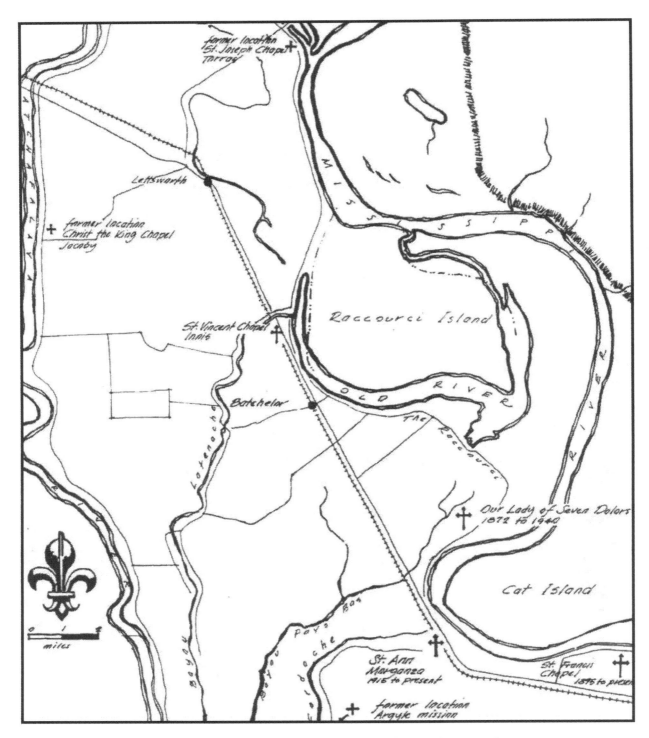

FIGURE 79: ST. ANN'S PARISH, FORMERLY SEVEN DOLORS PARISH

The pastors of Seven Dolors, alternately referred to as Seven Sorrows or The Raccourci Church, also ministered to St. Joseph Chapel and Cemetery. The latter were established by pioneer landowner and merchant Joseph Torras, native of Barcelona, Spain, and named for his patron saint, circa 1875, at Red River Landing at the northeastern extremity of Pointe Coupée Parish.

FIGURE 80: ST. CECILIA'S HALL AND ST. JOSEPH CHAPEL AT TORRAS

In 1902, Torras' grandson Torras Phillips founded the nearby town of Torras, Louisiana, which would be devastated in the infamous 1912 crevasse and flood bearing its name. The New Texas Landing and Red River Landing properties, the latter subject to reversion to the Torras family upon the discontinuance of the chapel, were held in the names of the Archdiocese of New Orleans, until their transfer to the Corporation of Seven Dolors in 1896.

Seven Dolors' pastors likewise served St. Francis Chapel on the Mississippi River northwest of New Roads since its 1895 completion, as well as mission stations at New Texas Interior and Bayou Fordoche in Pointe Coupée Parish as well as Tunica, Cat Island and the Mississippi River port town of Bayou Sara, all in West Feliciana Parish.

Meanwhile, at Jacoby, on the Atchafalaya River, Christ the King Chapel and Cemetery was established, to be served by Seven Dolors as well, and Angelo Sparacino donated the land and building to the Congregation of Seven Dolors in 1918.

FIGURE 82: SEVEN DOLORS, RACCOURCI CHURCH, DEMOLISHED 1940

FIGURE 81: RACCOURCI CHURCH INTERIOR

ST. ANN CHURCH AND ST. VINCENT CHAPEL

In 1914, Rev. Dominic Perino, assuming the pastorate of Seven Dolors, also began offering Mass in the Morganza public school. Land was acquired in the town, and a church completed in 1916, named St. Ann, at the urging of the Catholic Extension Society, who donated $500 toward the project. New Texas' increasing isolation owing to the decline of steamboat transportation and its lack of telephone and telegraph services, spurred Fr. Perino in 1916 to transfer residency to Morganza, which was served by the Texas & Pacific Railroad and benefitted from utilities and communications. The first burial in St. Ann Cemetery was that of a World War I casualty, Raoul Laiche, in 1918.

In 1921, Archbishop Francis Shaw recognized St. Ann as the church parish and Seven Dolors at New Texas Landing and St. Francis on Pointe Coupée Road as its mission chapels, though the parish continued to operate under the corporation of Seven Dolors until 1936.

St. Ann Church was damaged twice in short time: by the Hurricane of 1934, and by an unusual snowfall in 1935. It was demolished, and the present church built and dedicated in 1936. At that point, the Seven Dolors Corporation was dissolved, and St. Ann incorporated as a parish in its own right.

In 1937, a tornado damaged St. Joseph Chapel at Red River Landing – Torras, and the liturgy was suspended there, with the property reverting to the Torras heirs. The transformation of central and western Pointe Coupée Parish into the Morganza Spillway and Floodway, spelled the end of a number of communities which had to be dismantled and its population relocated in 1939. These villages

FIGURE 83: ST. ANN CHURCH IN MORGANZA

included New Texas Landing, New Texas Interior, French Settlement, Red Cross, and Ravenswood. Landowners sign an easement each year to allow the United States Army Corps of Engineers to divert high water from the Mississippi into the area, confined by levees and floodgates between Morganza and Batchelor.

Among the structures demolished and burials moved were those of Seven Dolors, in 1940. Remains of parishioners buried there were moved to the rear of St. Ann Cemetery in Morganza, and the materials of the Seven Dolors church used in the building of a hall adjacent to St. Ann Church. Furnishings retained from Seven Dolors include pews of Baroque design, which were transferred to St. Francis Chapel, and chandeliers and statutes which were relocated in St. Ann Church.

One of the oldest-known European artifacts in Pointe Coupée Parish was located in Seven Dolors Church and likely in the earlier St. Francis Church(es). A feature in the 15 January 1987 New Orleans Archdiocesan journal *Clarion Herald*, told of a mahogany crucifix, dating anywhere from about 1620 to 1700, probably Spanish in origin, and likely brought to Louisiana by Franciscan missionaries.

The article claimed that the artform had been "rescued by Father Blumel," i.e. Rev. Canisius J. Bluemel, O.S.B., "when an old chapel [sic] was being dismantled to make way for the Morganza Spillway." The crucifix was placed above the main altar of Our Lady of the Lake Church in Mandeville, Louisiana, of which parish Fr. Bluemel was pastor during 1948-1958.

St. Ann of Morganza is unique among the churches of 21st century Pointe Coupée Parish in that Holy Mass is celebrated in Spanish once a month for the large number of permanent and seasonal Hispanic members of the community.

Christ the King, familiarly known as the Jacoby Chapel for the community in which it was located (in turn, named for Jewish landowner Max Jacoby), continued to serve into the mid-20th century until its discontinuance. The chapel was dismantled, but the cemetery continues to be ministered by St. Ann of Morganza. St. Ann established a new mission in Upper Pointe Coupée at Innis, where St. Vincent de Paul Chapel and Cemetery were dedicated in 1954. A former apiary was converted to a 250-seat house of worship and a hall built adjacent. With increasing attendance, owing to a number of Catholic families from Avoyelles Parish, across the Atchafalaya River, the larger hall became the chapel, and the former apiary used as a hall.

St. Francis Chapel was transferred from the jurisdiction of St. Ann parish to that of St. Mary of False River in 1962.

Meanwhile, back in southern Pointe Coupée Parish, Fr. Gutton, who had ministered in the Morganza and New Texas Landing area, greatly increased the number of liturgical services, reception of the sacraments, and the organization of lay associations in New Roads in the postbellum period. While old Immaculate Conception of Chenal was without a pastor, from 1868 to 1871, he periodically traveled to and served that congregation, as did Rev. Constantin Van der Moere, then pastor of St. Francis.

FIGURE 84: ST. ANN'S HALL, BUILT WITH MATERIALS FROM THE RACCOURCI CHURCH

ST. FRANCES CABRINI
AND ST. CATHERINE

Turning his attention beyond False River, Rev. J.P. Gutton offered, on at least one documented occasion, Holy Mass at Livonia, on Bayou Grosse Tete, in the southern part of Pointe Coupée Parish. The *Pointe Coupée Banner* of 22 October 1881 related:

Last Sunday, Rev. J.P. Gutton celebrated mass on Bayou Grosse Tete at the saw mill of Mr. Ernest Joffrion who kindly made all the necessary arrangements beforehand. Favored by a splendid autumnal Sabbath the attendance was large and the ceremony impressive. About a hundred Catholics were assembled on both sides of the rustic altar erected for the occasion, the men on one side and the ladies and children on the other. Father Gutton exhorted them to continue their exertions to secure the erection of at least a regular mission chapel before undertaking the difficulties of a permanent organization.

Many Catholics of southernmost Pointe Coupée, living along Bayous Grosse Tete, Fordoche and Maringouin, have journeyed to St. Mary in New Roads for liturgical and sacramental participation through the decades, and most families of the region buried loved ones primarily in the cemeteries of St. Mary in New Roads, old Immaculate Conception at Chenal and the present Immaculate Conception at Lakeland.

Southern Pointe Coupée, however, was ministered to by visiting priests: from St John Church in Plaquemine, Iberville Parish, during 1889-1893; from Sts. Peter and Paul Church at Lobdell in West Baton Rouge Parish, during 1893-1906; and ultimately by St. Joseph Church in the community of

FIGURE 85: ST. JOAN OF ARC CHAPEL WAS THE FIRST CHURCH AT LIVONIA

Grosse Tete, in Iberville Parish to the south, from 1906 until the erection of St. Frances Xavier Cabrini Parish at Livonia in 1955.

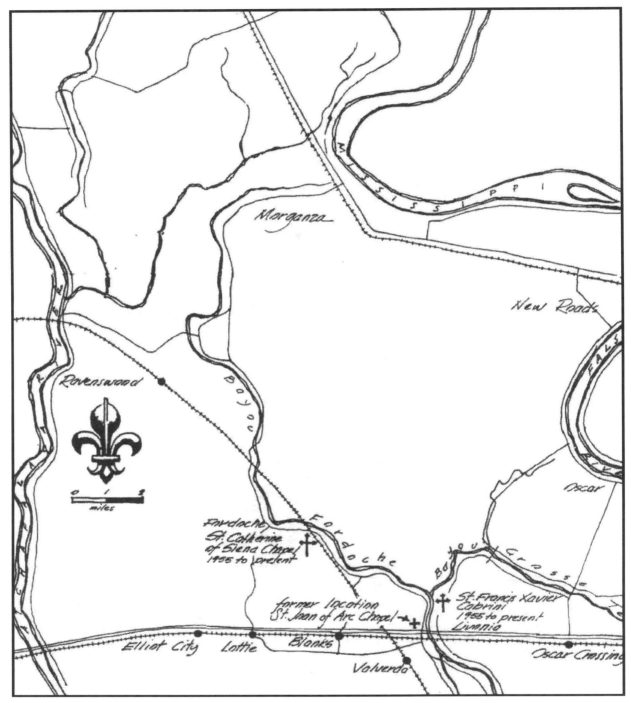

FIGURE 86: MAP OF ST. FRANCIS XAVIER CABRINI PARISH
SHOWING FORMER CHAPEL CAR MISSION STOPS

A chapel was listed as existing at Livonia since the 1893 publication of *Sadlier's Catholic Directory, Almanac and Directory* through the 1907 publication of *Hoffman's Catholic Directory, Almanac, and Clergy Directory*. The exact location, and fate, of this chapel is unknown at present. Interestingly, it was not mentioned by Rev. Francis S. Lamendola - former pastor of St. Joseph Church in Grosse

Tete, Iberville Parish, and St. Frances Cabrini in Livonia - in his 1984 publication, *The Catholic Church on the Grosse Tete Ridge*. Fr. Lamendola was, perhaps, unaware of the above sources, as he devoted considerable attention in his work to point out "errors" and "omissions" in earlier histories of the area, particularly those he ascribed to esteemed New Orleans journalist and history Roger Baudier, K.S.G., author of the monumental 1939 tome, *The Catholic Church in Louisiana*.

The clergy of St. Joseph Church in Grosse Tete, Iberville Parish, ministered to a number of mission stations in southernmost Pointe Coupée Parish in the second decade of the 20th century. These included: Fordoche, beginning in 1913; Elliot City, in 1913; Lottie, in 1913 and 1915; Ravenswood, during 1913-1915, and Lorio (Valverda Plantation), likewise during 1913-1915. Several of these communities, and others in northern Pointe Coupée, were served by the Catholic Church Extension Society's "St. Paul" railroad chapel car, as is related elsewhere in this volume.

Following the first known chapel at Livonia, operative during 1893-1907 as stated above, the area's next church building was not constructed until 1920. This was St. Joan of Arc Chapel, built through a $500 Catholic Extension Society donation in 1920, and located on the west bank of Bayou Grosse Tete, on property donated by merchant Humbert Major. It served as a mission of St. Joseph of Grosse Tete until 1945, when it was destroyed by a fire of unknown origin. Holy Mass was thereafter held on Sundays and one day of the week in the Livonia High School gymnasium, across the bridge, and on the east bank of Bayou Grosse tete.

While continuing to be part of St. Joseph church parish of Grosse Tete, property was purchased from Olivier Vallet immediately north of Livonia in 1951, and from Leo Doiron in Fordoche in 1952. At the latter place, St. Catherine of Siena Chapel was completed in 1953. At Livonia, St. Frances Xavier Cabrini Church, designed in early Romanesque style by noted architect A. Hays Town of Baton Rouge, and built by Horace Rickey of Lafayette Louisiana for $80,000, was completed in 1954. Its name honors the American saint who ministered to Italian immigrants earlier in the century.

In 1955, St. Frances Xavier Cabrini was elevated to independent status parish, with St. Catherine at Fordoche in its jurisdiction as mission chapel. Owing to the limited number of priestly ordinations, these two churches were combined with St. Joseph of Grosse Tete and Immaculate Heart of Mary of Maringouin, the latter two in adjacent Iberville civil parish, as the "Tri-Parish" churches of the Diocese of Baton Rouge in 2004.

Notably, the best-known and most-esteemed Jewish merchant family of Pointe Coupée Parish, the Dreyfuses of Livonia, were generous supporters of the building of Catholic churches in the area. Patriarch Theodore Dreyfus, native of Mannheim, Baden, donated toward the construction of St. Joan of

FIGURE 87: ST. FRANCIS XAVIER CABRINI AT LIVONIA

Arc Church on the west bank of the bayou, and his daughter and son-in-law Rosina Dreyfus and Alphonse Weil contributed toward the building of St. Frances Cabrini Church.

The Weils' daughter-in-law, gracious and joyful educator and humanitarian Ray Weill Weil, wife of Simon Weil, is gratefully recalled as helping her Catholic special-needs students at nearby Livonia High School prepare for their First Communion, in cooperation with then-pastor Rev. Francis Lamendola. The sight of her leading her little charges by the hand to the altar of St. Frances Cabrini is one remembered by area residents with particular fondness.

Distinguished and tireless Simon Weil, while president of the Pointe Coupée Parish School Board, was the only member of the body to vote for integration of the public schools of the parish, for which a burning cross was placed on the family's lawn and the Livonia High School set afire.

The Dreyfus-Weil relationship with the larger Catholic community echoes that of other Jewish families throughout Pointe Coupée for nearly 200 years, and bears testimony to the mutual respect and affection between the two oldest lines of the Abrahamic tradition. Particularly endearing to Simon Weil and his first cousin Sidney Dreyfus of Krotz Springs, Louisiana were the Catholic regular patrons and return visitors to the iconic Dreyfus Department Store in Livonia, who told of their First Communion and wedding clothing as being bought there, back in the early and mid-20th century.

New Orleans Archbishop Francis Rummel sent Dominican Rural Missionaries to serve the Bayou Grosse Tete area in 1953, alas in 1955 tragedy struck and three of the Sisters died in the collision of the car in which they were riding with a train in Slidell, Louisiana. The two surviving Sisters were relocated to Abbeville, Louisiana, where they had previously founded a community.

FATHER GUTTON'S CHAPELS

Owing to the physical incapacity of old St. Francis Church pastor, Rev. Pierre Berthet, New Orleans Archbishop Francois X. Leray in 1885 appointed St. Mary pastor Rev. J.P. Gutton as administrator of St. Francis. As he was also ministering to chapels he established on the Mississippi River northwest of New Roads and below town on False River, the overworked Fr. Gutton was assisted as needed in the liturgical and sacramental services at St. Francis by the pastors of Our Lady of Seven Dolors Church, upriver at New Texas Landing.

The chapel Fr. Gutton established on False River, about midway the west bank, at what would subsequently be known as Mix Post Office, Louisiana, was named for his patron saint. St. Philibert Chapel. In announcing that Mass would be celebrated there on the feast of Corpus Christi, the 23 May 1885 *Pointe Coupée Banner* described the chapel as being on (sic) the plantation of Louis Villeneuve Gosserand, but the Pointe Coupée Parish Clerk of Court conveyance records indicate it as actually adjacent to and on the south side of the Gosserand property.

The immediate neighborhood of St. Philibert, known in early days as *La Corne de Chevreuil* (buckhorn) for the nearby bayou of the name, was referred to as "Mulattoville" in an 1893 *Pointe Coupée Banner* article and as "Mulatto Bend" in title description of an adjacent property as early as 1920. These appellations refer to the large number of *Créole de couleur* landholdings and residences at that point since early antebellum times.

In Fr. Gutton's ledgers, St. Philibert Chapel first appears in 1884, when he noted that he blessed "a corpse" there. In 1892, he recorded paying taxes of $9.70 on the chapel, which likely indicates it was no longer operative, as lots and buildings used for religious or educational purposes are tax exempt.

Interestingly, a transfer of the lot was made in the following year, when Joseph Richy donated it to Archbishop Francis A.A.J. Janssens, in the name of the Archdiocese of New Orleans, "for the use and establishment of a Catholic church."

The attached plat indicated the lot as being nearly triangular in shape, owing to the bend of False River Road from northwest to southeast. It fronted 152 feet on east side of False River Road, had a rear or eastern line of 120 feet on False River, a north boundary of 92 feet, and south line of an undecipherable but much shorter depth than the north. The remainder of Richy's river frontage, some 40 feet, bounded the tract on the north and the south, likely 20 feet on each side of the chapel lot allowing him access to the river.

The plat includes on the northern part of the lot a "Church" measuring 22 feet front toward the road by a depth of 49 feet toward the river, and, adjoining its southeastern extremity, a "Vestry Room" of 22 feet front by 33 feet in depth. On the southern part of the lot is the sketched figure of a tree.

Fr. Gutton, per Archbishop Janssens' authority given on a small note attached to the deed and plat, received the property on His Grace's behalf. Subsequent to the incorporation of the Roman Catholic Church of St. Mary, the St. Philibert property was deeded in 1896 to the Corporation by the Archbishop, along with the other church properties in St. Mary church parish.

No record has been located attesting to St. Mary's disposal of the property, and it apparently reverted to Joseph Richy's successor in title. As such, the former church lot was acquired along with acreage across the road in 1920 by Francois Bonaventure, and his descendants continued to own it in the 21st century.

Pointe Coupée Banner articles of 1885 attest to periodic Holy Mass and annual Rogation Days, the latter highlighted by the Blessing of the Crops, at St. Philibert as well as at old St. Francis Church on the Mississippi River and at the Hopkins Chapel on the Lanaux (subsequently named Stonewall) plantation, about five miles west and upriver of St. Francis. Nothing else is known regarding the apparently short-lived Hopkins Chapel.

ST. CLAUDE

In addition to those listed above, two other chapels, established in adjoining church parishes in postbellum Pointe Coupée, came under the ministration of St. Mary of False River. In 1871, St. Claude Chapel was built in the Mississippi River port town of Waterloo and named for the patron saint of its benefactor, planter Claude Favre. It was established as a "parochial duty" of St. Francis of Pointe Coupée but subsequent to the dissolution of St. Francis church parish, St. Claude and its attendant hall were served by Fr. Gutton from St. Mary. Fr. Pierre Berthet, pastor of old Immaculate Conception, assisted in the ministrations at St. Claude during 1890-1892.

Like other churches and chapels of the period, St. Claude relied on various sources of income in addition to collections of those attending Holy Mass and receiving the sacraments. The St. Mary Parish Hall retains among its framed historical images and mementoes a handbill for a "Grand Entertainment" to be held for the benefit of the "Catholic Chapel at Waterloo" in the St. Claude Hall on the evening of 3 September 1878. The programme included three plays, featuring local actors, and a grand ball, with refreshments served by the ladies of the congregation.

Among the actors was Adalbert Démourelle, who would six years later meet a heroic death by drowning while attempting to save the main, state levee at Waterloo as it broke in the flood of 1884. One of the several Jewish merchants of the town, Abraham Michel, likewise appeared in the program, as a doorkeeper, floor committee member and actor. He and wife, née Victoria Singer, of another local Jewish merchant family, moved to New Orleans, where Abraham operated for many years on Carondelet Street the Michel Hotel, which gained considerable media attention during the years of legalized prostitution and prohibition.

The property on which St. Claude Chapel stood as donated in 1889 by Pamela Favre, widow of Ernest Robin, and daughter of the late Claude Favre, to Archbishop Janssens on behalf of the Archdiocese of New Orleans. The lot measured 100 feet front on the south side of False River Street, by a depth of 140 feet, and was bounded on the west by the (main, State-maintained) levee, and east and south by the remainder of Widow Robin's property.

In 1891, St. Claude, as well as other buildings in Waterloo, was raised considerably, owing to frequent levee failures and disastrous floods of the Mississippi. It was described by Catherine Cole, *nom de plume* of pioneer female journalist Martha R. Field, during her visit to Pointe Coupée that year, and published in the Sunday, 29 November 1891 New Orleans *Daily Picayune* thus: "A little church at the right had been lifted high in the air on slender trestles. It is perched there like a white stork."

Only three years later in 1894, St. Claude Chapel and the adjacent residence of the Cyrille Pourciau family were destroyed by fire originating in the latter. Only the organ was saved from the chapel, and the mission was abandoned by St. Mary. Curiously, St. Claude continued to be listed as a mission of St. Mary for the next several years in the annual Catholic directories of churches, institutions and clergy.

In 1896, a year after the incorporation of the Congregation of St. Mary Roman Catholic Church, Archbishop Janssens donated the St. Claude lot at Waterloo and other New Roads area church and cemetery properties to the Congregation of St. Mary.

St. Claude's sacramental records of baptisms and marriages are located in the St. Mary and Immaculate Conception registers, depending on which parish was ministering to the chapel at the time.

ST. GEORGE

Though many of the faithful of the Island of False River crossed the lake by boat, and beginning in 1847, by ferry to old St. Mary Church in New Roads, the need for a church on the Island was pronounced by clergy and parishioners alike.

In 1840, Rev. Jean Martin, then pastor, wrote to Bishop Antoine Blanc in New Orleans that a property owner had offered an arpent (.85 acre) of land on the Island opposite Benjamin Poydras' False River residence (present-day intersection of False River Drive and Major (Parkway), in what came to be called Ventress, Louisiana, for establishment of a church and school. Fr. Martin advised the bishop that, "in order to avoid difficulties," the land should be deeded to the Bishop.

Decades elapsed with no church being built on the Island until Rev. Marcelin Broquere, then pastor of old Immaculate Conception of Chenal, began St. George Mission at present-day Jarreau, Louisiana in 1881. On 27 April, he administered the first baptism there, to Francois Rosélius Aguillard, son of Paul and Celina St. Romain Aguillard, with godparents being siblings Francois Oréste LeBeau and Corinne Rosalie LeBeau.

FIGURE 88: ST. GEORGE CHAPEL

Fr. Broquere moved his residence from Chenal to St. George in 1882, and had a frame church with small steeple built on a three-acre lot in 1883. That same year, he blessed the cemetery of St. George Church, alas no records have been found indicating burials there. With Fr. Broquere's departure in 1884, St. George became a mission of old Immaculate

Conception of Chenal, though it was ministered to in 1888 by the tireless Fr. Gutton of St. Mary in New Roads.

St. George continued as a mission of old Immaculate Conception until closure at the turn of the century by pastor Rev. Louis Savouré. In 1907, the building was purchased and moved to Chenal by general merchant Joseph Lange David, and eventually dismantled. The sacramental records of baptisms and marriages are located in those of Immaculate Conception in the Baton Rouge Diocesan Archives.

The bell of St. George Church had originally hung at the old Pointe Coupée Parish Courthouse in New Roads. In 1896, It was donated by the parish's governing body, the Police Jury, to the faithful of the Island of False River. It was blessed in the following year by Fr. Savouré in a celebration which included the playing of the first-known musical phonograph on the Island.

After discontinuance of the chapel, St. George's historic bell was moved to a succession of locations: first, to North Bend Plantation at Oscar, Louisiana, site of early Immaculate Conception fairs; next, to a church in Denham Springs; and, ultimately, retrieved by Immaculate Conception of Lakeland pastor Rev. Hubert Brou and placed in the tower of the church at Lakeland, where two other bells also hang.

ST. JOSEPH, ON THE LOWER CHENAL

In 1849, during the pastorate of Rev. Jean Rogalle, one of the leading *Créoles de couleur* of Pointe Coupée Parish, Leufroy Decuir, donated a five-arpent-square lot on his plantation on the Lower Chenal of False River, near present-day Glynn, Louisiana, to the Diocese of New Orleans for construction of a chapel.

Owing to ongoing difficulties with the *marguilliers* of St. Francis church parish, Fr. Rogalle intended the Chenal mission to be independent of their control. They responded by reducing the pastor's salary, but he continued with his plans. Most of the materials for a brick building had arrived in the spring of 1850, when levee failures along the Mississippi River to the east inundated the region and work halted.

Construction resumed on the Chenal chapel, and the walls had been built to a height of 12 feet when another levee failure occurred on the Mississippi, at the Van Wickle plantation at Hermitage. The project was abandoned.

In December 1865, Rev. Gutton, pastor of recently-erected St. Mary parish in New Roads, wrote Archbishop Odin in New Orleans that he (Gutton) had visited what was begun of the chapel on the Lower Chenal, stating its distance as 18 miles from St. Mary.

Donor Leufroy Decuir lost the property on which the church was to be established at Sheriff's Sale in 1855. It was purchased at auction by Auguste Provosty II, who sold it shortly thereafter to Francoise Leufroy, "free woman of color," who later became Decuir's second wife.

It is possible the Diocese of New Orleans had not accepted Leufroy Decuir's donation of 1849, as in 1872, Francoise Leufroy Decuir repeated the donation, specifying that the site be used only for church and school purposes.

Leufroy Decuir died in 1876, and the sacramental entry of his burial, in the register of nearby Immaculate Conception Church of Chenal, states "he was buried in the Chapel of St. Joseph," by which he intended for the proposed chapel to be known, in honor of the patron saint of his white father, largescale planter, Joseph Decuir.

In 1881, Leufroy Decuir's remains were transferred to Immaculate Conception Cemetery at Chenal, three miles distant, and by the time Archdiocesan visitation reports commenced in 1890, there was no further mention of the proposed mission.

In her autobiographical manuscript "The Story of My Life As Far as I Can Remember," Decuir's granddaughter Lélia Decuir Lejeune recalled "walking on" the bricks of what were to be the walls of the building in circa 1880, which were, apparently, removed sometime later.

IMMACULATE CONCEPTION

Meanwhile, planter Jean Baptiste Bergeron II and others on the opposite, "Island," side of the Lower Chenal had seen to fruition the establishment of a church and cemetery named in honor of the newly- declared doctrine of the Immaculate Conception.

In preparation for the Jubilee of 1854, Rev. Hubert Thirion, then pastor of St. Francis of Pointe Coupée, wrote Archbishop Antoine Blanc in New Orleans of the necessity for stations in addition to St. Francis and St. Mary churches to enable as many as possible of the faithful to benefit from the special graces of the Jubilee.

Fr. Thirion pointed out the need for a station a Waterloo; two along the Mississippi River between the Bouis plantation and the Raccourci; two on (the south bank of) the Lower Chenal, near where Fr. Rogalle and Leufroy Decuir had attempted to build a chapel; two at Chenal proper (on the "Island side" or north bank of the Lower Chenal); and one on False River, distant from and independent of St. Mary.

Two years later, in 1856, Fr. Thirion wrote Archbishop Blanc of planned Confirmation services in the parish, obviously at either or both St. Francis and St. Mary, noting the distance of many who could be confirmed. Thirion remarked that residents of the (Grand) Bay on the Island side of the Lower Chenal claimed they had no transportation to church, the prelate adding "although they have it for dances."

In the following year, 1857, part of Fr. Thirion's vision came to fruition, when he baptized a large number of children, white and free colored, on the Island side of the Lower Chenal, likely at the home of Jean Baptiste Bergeron, II, as the sacramental entry of the latter's burial in 1864 identities him as

FIGURE 89: INTERIOR VIEW OF CHENAL CHURCH

the "principal founder" of the local church. It was originally named "Our Lady of the Immaculate Conception."

FIGURE 90: ORIGINAL IMMACULATE CONCEPTION CHURCH AT CHENAL

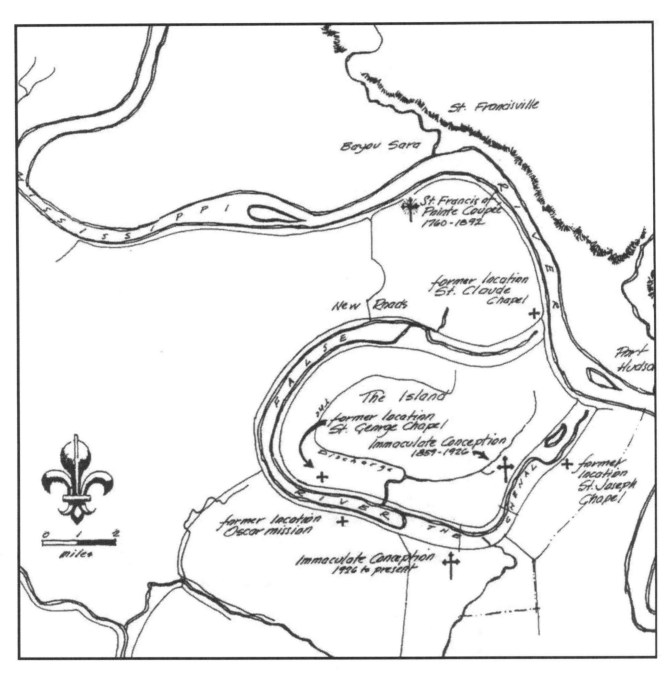

FIGURE 91: IMMACULATE CONCEPTION PARISH SHOWING LOCATION OF FORMER MISSIONS

Toward the end of 1857, Frs. Thirion and Mittelbronn purchased at their own expense a tract of land at Chenal from Sélicourt André. Fr. Thirion informed Archbishop Blanc in the following year that "an unfinished house" was serving as a chapel.

During the subsequent pastorate of Fr. Mittelbronn in 1861, Immaculate Conception was elevated to independent parish status, and its newly-completed house of worship served until 1927 when it was succeeded by the present Immaculate Conception Church at Lakeland, on the south bank of the Lower Chenal. The old cemetery at Chenal as well as the newer one at Lakeland continue to serve as final resting places for many of the area's faithful.

NEW IMMACULATE CONCEPTION, AT LAKELAND

The move of Immaculate Conception Church from Chenal to Lakeland during the pastorate of Rev. Louis Savouré was a highly contentious one, dividing some families. Parishioners on the Island of False River, including Chenal proper, wanted a new church built on the site of the existing one. While residents on the opposite side of the Lower Chenal wanted it built in the Lakeland area. Fr. Savouré reasoned that the majority of parishioners lived on the south side, in the communities of Hermitage, Glynn, Rougon, Lakeland, Oscar on False River, and Erwinville to the south, on Bayou Poydras. Moreover the road on that side was graveled, whereas the one on the Island continued to be of dirt.

Edward Cadbert Lorio, owner of the adjacent Celina and Fan sugar plantations, donated a five-acre lot at Lakeland for a new church, but oral history contends that when the first load of lumber was delivered to the site, it was burned by disgruntled parties, as was the workshop containing the tools of contractor Gérard Ricard. Séptime Evariste "S.E." or "Pat" Bertoniere headed a long list of Immaculate Conception plaintiffs, mainly from the Island, in suing Fr. Savouré, but the Archdiocese supported the latter.

The church was built at Lakeland, in brick, in Romanesque revival style, with parishioner Ricard as contractor. Completed in 1927, at a cost of $27,100, it was dedicated by Archbishop John Shaw on 27 June. Stained glass windows, depicting favorite saints of the congregants were, like those in the lateral walls of St. Mary in New Roads, produced by Emil Frei of St. Louis, Missouri.

FIGURE 92: LAKELAND CHURCH SHORTLY AFTER COMPLETION

FATHER SAVOURÉ

Of the pastors of 20th century Pointe Coupée Parish, Fr. Louis Savouré was particularly remembered as being demanding in catechetical instruction and as back-hand striking or kicking children who made incorrect, incomplete, or no response to his questioning. An adult woman, who apparently was attired in a dress of décolleté design was recalled to have been passed twice by the aged prelate, as she attempted to receive Holy Communion and struck back-hand by him as he passed a third time.

Germain Daniel, a *Créole de couleur* of legendary renown, served as Fr. Savouré's organist, housekeeper, and chauffeur for decades. He is remembered by older Immaculate Conception parishioners as having donned the pastor's vestments and reading the Mass and even sitting in the confessional, unbeknown to penitents. Of impeccable character was Daniel's successor, Harris "Ma Ya" Bizette, who is recalled with much respect.

Fr. Savouré died in 1948, at the age of 75, having served as a priest for 54 years, 52 of which were as pastor of Immaculate Conception. Active in temporal affairs, he represented the Sixth Ward of Pointe Coupée on the Parish Police Jury, and president of the body during 1904-1908, and was a board member of the First National Bank and the New Roads Oil Mill.

He showed the depth of his humanity during the evacuation of Morganza during the frightful flood of 1912. The New Orleans *Times-Democrat* found him waist-deep in water, assisting the flood

154

sufferers, and leaving Morganza only when compelled to by army evacuation officials. He then worked on the rations, clothing, and medicine distribution committees and was among those who helped round up 1,200 marooned cattle on the levees of Upper Pointe Coupée. In a humorous episode of the evacuation of Morganza, the *Times-Democrat* reported an aged evacuee informing a bewildered Savouré as having lost "both" of his (the evacuee's) wives in the chaos of leaving.

Fr. Savouré was honored during his lifetime through the naming of a public school in Bigman Lane south of Oscar, Louisiana as the "Savouré School," a new road built in 1939 to connect the church at Lakeland with the Island of False River as "Father Savouré Road" (now part of Louisiana Highway 413), and a community-wide celebration of his diamond jubilee as pastor of Immaculate Conception in 1946.

The last chapel to be built on the Island of False River was similarly controversial and involved Fr. Savouré, and its existence was short-lived. Surviving correspondence between St. Mary pastor Rev. John Hoes and Fr. Louis Savouré in the early 20th century suggest a mutually-hostile relationship, largely due to fees received by Fr. Savouré when he officiated at marriages and funerals of St. Mary parishioners conducted by him (Fr. Savouré) at Immaculate Conception.

The hostilities had begun earlier, however, when the newly-arrived Fr. Hoes established in 1914 a chapel at Dupont, on the Island, in a former store building on the land of Mrs. Noel Major (née Rosalie Miller). In a letter peppered with Latin phrases and claims as to his own physical strength, Savouré boldly informed the younger Hoes that the building was owned by Savouré and its location was within the limits of Immaculate Conception church parish. He ordered the St. Mary pastor to have the parties who "ruined the interior of my store at Dupont" to remit to him (Savouré) the sum of $20 for damages and remove therefrom "the pews, confessional, and altars."

FIGURE 93: FATHER SAVOURÉ

Historical ephemera of the churches of Pointe Coupée Parish held in the Baton Rouge Diocesan Archives includes an unidentified photograph of what appears to be a church or chapel interior in disarray, with chairs piled in confusion. While it may be an image of a destroyed church of the period of the First World War in German-occupied France or Belgium, it is not unreasonable to surmise that it may be of Fr. Hoes' contemporary, short-lived chapel at Dupont.

As regards missions, Fr. Savouré wrote at another time of his desire to establish a mission at Erwinville, on the border of Pointe Coupée and West Baton Rouge Parish, and within the territory of Immaculate Conception. Nothing came of the idea, but the prelate did for some time offer occasional Holy Mass at the Wooden of the World pavilion on North Bend Plantation at Oscar, for many years the site of the annual Immaculate Conception fundraising fair. After the move to the fair, an autumn tradition since 1922, to the Lakeland church grounds, the pavilion was moved near the church, enclosed, and served as the Parish Hall for many years.

FIGURE 94: LAKELAND CHURCH INTERIOR DURING FATHER SAVOURÉ'S PASTORATE

TWENTIETH CENTURY CHAPELS

Institutional chapels served by the pastors of St. Mary of False River in the 20th century included those of the St. Joseph Academy and Convent; the Sisters of St. Joseph Hospital; and the Sisters' subsequent freestanding chapel at Pointe Coupée General Hospital, all in New Roads.

Holy Mass has also been offered in recent decades, by the clergy of St. Mary and sister parishes in the various nursing homes in New Roads and in the Pointe Coupée Parish Detention Center northeast of town.

Weekly Masses are offered for the elementary and high school divisions of Catholic of Pointe Coupée in St. Mary Church, though special commemorative Masses are also held in the school gymnasium.

"ST. PAUL" RAILROAD CHAPEL CAR

The Catholic Church Extension Society provided sacramental and catechetical ministry to outlying areas of Pointe Coupée Parish in an interesting as well as effectual manner during 1917-1918. The Society's railroad chapel car "St. Paul" made its fifth missionary journey during that winter, traveling the main and branch lines of the Texas & Pacific Railroad and the main line of the Gulf Coast (formerly Frisco) Railroad. With Redemptorist Fathers as chaplains, five- to 12-day stops were made in various communities, where adult, young adult and children's missions were preached, converts received, catechetical instruction offered, and sacraments administered.

A daily review of the journey appeared in "The Chapel Car Manuscript," compiled by noted New Orleans journalist Roger Baudier, K.S.G., in 1956. It was edited by Charles E. Nolan, longtime Archivist of the Archdiocese of New Orleans, for inclusion in the work *Cross, Crozier and Crucible: A Volume Celebrating the Bicentennial of A Catholic Diocese in Louisiana.*, published in 1993.

The above article described the "St. Paul" as one of three cars employed by the Extension Society, the other two being the "St. Anthony" and the "St. Peter." The "St. Paul" was built by the Smith Company shops in Dayton Ohio. It was 86 feet in length, with an interior finishing in Cuban mahogany, and boasted both heating and electric lighting. The larger, "chapel," section of the car had an altar, pews and 75 individual seats. The remainder of the car was fitted as living compartments for a chaplain, manager and porter, and a kitchenette.

During October-November 1917, Rev. Bernard Kalvelage, C.SS.R. was aboard as chaplain, bound east on the Gulf Coast Railroad, and stops were made at Lottie, Blanks, Livonia, Erwinville, and Oscar Crossing (later Torbert Post Office). Notable events included a Baptist minister going aboard at Lottie, to apologize that his revival was coinciding with the visit of the chapel car and, therefore, attracting devotees who might have gone to the train for ministry. A Catholic member of the Fordoche Masonic Lodge renounced Freemasonry, owing to Fr. Kalvelage's explanation of the fraternity's first through third oaths.

At Blanks, the Episcopalian manager of a local sawmill provided a warm welcome and convenient location for the car to stop, thereby allowing the millworkers east access to ministration. Sugar cane cutting and grinding was in full swing when the "St. Paul" stopped in Livonia, resulting in less-than-expected attendance, but Rev. J. Murge, pastor of St. Joseph of Grosse Tete, in which jurisdiction the area was a part, was promised there the sum of $400 by the Society toward the construction of a church (St. Joan of Arc, which was completed in 1920), and a non-Catholic sawmill owner promised a supply of lumber for its construction.

Rev. Joseph A Girven, C.SS.R., assumed the office of chaplain of the "St. Paul" at Livonia, and at the next the next stop, Erwinville, he and personnel were repeatedly called upon by Catholics and non- Catholics, who also brought food. The train turned back to Oscar Crossing (subsequently Torbert Post Office), where Fr. Girven administered to a predominantly monolingual Italian population, then went north on the main line of the Texas & Pacific Railroad to minister in several communities of St. Landry Parish, on the west side of the Atchafalaya River.

Returning to Pointe Coupée Parish in January 1918, the "St. Paul" stopped at Fordoche, coincident with the coldest weather the community would experience that century, accompanied by snowfall. On the 13th of the month, the temperature dropped to four degrees Fahrenheit, resulting in few attendees at the last night of the mission there. Proceeding to Addis, the train left the main line of the Texas & Pacific and turned north along the branch line, which roughly paralleled the Mississippi River, with Rev. James H. Dreis, C.SS.R., as chaplain.

On the 30th of January, the train reached and a mission was begun at Torras, in extreme northeastern Pointe Coupée Parish, a community moderately rebuilt after the levee failure there and resultant deathly flood of 1912. Returning south, the train stopped at Lettsworth and Batchelor, thence back into West Baton Rouge Parish for similar ministry.

The number of sacraments administered from the "St. Paul" railroad chapel car at its various stops in Pointe Coupée Parish during 1917-1918 totaled: two children's and one adult baptisms; 135 first communions of children and adults; 674 communions; 399 confessions; and seven marriage revalidations.

CHURCH BELLS

Though largely hidden from view, church bells rank among the most treasured artifacts of 21st century Pointe Coupée Parish, having announced events of celebration, joy, warning and sorrow for three centuries. Few of the oldest bells are in their original locations, however, testimony of shifts in population and purpose, and their individual histories mirror that of Pointe Coupée in general.

1719 BELL AT ST. FRANCIS

The oldest known bell in Pointe Coupée Parish is the small ship's bell bearing *fleurs de lys* and the date 1719, suspended from the choir loft in St. Francis Chapel. This house of worship, dating from 1895, is the third church of St. Francis of Pointe Coupée, preceded by those of 1738 and 1760 downriver. The origin of this bell is uncertain, but might be one of the three recorded as having been in the first church, i.e., two small bells blessed on Holy Saturday 1738 or a third donated in 1741 by Claude Trénonay de Chanfret.

A lovely custom of the blessing of church bells in generations past was to name godparents, usually leading supporters of the church community. In the case of the 1741 bell of the first St. Francis, the godparents were Albert Decuir, Jean Baptiste Decuir, Pierre Germain, Pierre Haussy, Anne Decoux, Anne Gilan and Marie Augustine Haussy, among who were some of the first settlers of Pointe Coupée in 1720.

The bell in the belfry of the present St. Francis Chapel is of indefinite provenance, but may be any of the 1738 or 1741 bells listed above. Anticipated renovation work at the chapel may yield the opportunity for a closer inspection of the bell and analysis of its origin.

BOUÉ BROTHERS' BELL OF 1825

Having served three locations, the Boué Brothers bell of 1825 occupied successively the first St. Mary of False River church in New Roads, the original Immaculate Conception church at Chenal, and the present Immaculate Conception at Lakeland.

Two years after the establishment of St. Mary by Lyon native Fr. Antoine Blanc (subsequently fourth Bishop and first Archbishop of New Orleans) at New Roads in 1823, two priests of the Diocese of Lyon, brothers J. and L. Boué, presented St. Mary with a bell. It hung in the belfry of old St. Mary until being replaced in 1877 by the bell known as *Maria Seraphina Clara*. St. Mary's pastor at that time, Rev. Joseph Philibert Gutton, sold the bell of 1825 for $60 to the congregation of Immaculate Conception church at Chenal.

Immaculate Conception at Chenal was succeeded as parish church by the present Immaculate Conception at Lakeland in 1927, but the old church at Chenal was not dismantled until the 1950s.

The 1825 bell was then placed on a scaffold in Old Immaculate Cemetery and tolled during burials and on All Saints' Day until ultimately being relocated to the tower of the present church at Lakeland.

OLD COURTHOUSE BELL

For some years, a bell was located in the yard of the original Pointe Coupée Parish Courthouse in New Roads, which building was completed in 1848. Through a resolution of the Pointe Coupée Parish Police Jury on 9 December 1896, this bell was donated to the congregation of St. George Chapel on the Island of False River.

At its blessing at St. George on 10 May 1897, parishioners Eustache Bueche and Mme. Aristide Jarreau, née Noémie Sicard, served as godparents of the old courthouse bell. Several attendees paid 10 cents each to ring the bell, and another highlight of the occasion was the presence of a gramophone by which music could be heard through a receiver.

The pastors of old Immaculate Conception at Chenal ministered to St. George Chapel during most of its history, until St. George's discontinuance in 1907. The Old Courthouse - St. George bell was then moved to North Bend Plantation at Oscar, site of annual fairs for the benefit of Immaculate Conception and for a few years beginning in 1922 the occasional celebration of Mass.

After the move of the Hubert Bizette family, longtime residents of the North Bend house and caretakers of the bell, to Maringouin, the bell was given to a church in Denham Springs. Rev. Hubert Brou, when pastor of Immaculate Conception, retrieved the bell, had the crack found therein repaired by Roy Brothers welders in New Roads, and placed the much-traveled artifact in its current location in the Immaculate Conception church tower at Lakeland.

The Ladies' Altar Society of Immaculate Conception financed the electric wiring of the two old bells as well as the third, which had been commissioned specifically for the present church.

MARIA SERAPHINA CLARA

For generations the most familiar sound in New Roads—also immortalized in a 19th century poem—has been the bell in the tower of the present St. Mary of False River church. Commissioned for the original St. Mary which stood closer to the corner of West Main and St. Mary Streets by pastor Rev. Joseph Philibert Gutton, it weighs 580 pounds and was cast on 21 November 1876 by the Meneely & Kimberly foundry in Troy, New York and transported down the Mississippi River aboard the famed steamboat *Robert E. Lee*. The total cost of $228.70, including casting, mounting, freight and carriage, was paid through collections and donations.

The inscription on the east side of the bell reads:

MARIA SERAPHINA
DIE XXI
NOVEMBRIS
ANNO DI MDCCCLXXVI

On the west side of the bell is inscribed:

SPONSORS
CLAIR CAZAYOUX SERAPHINE RICHY
J.P. GUTTON PASTOR

In ceremonies on the Feast of St. Michael the Archangel, 29 September 1877, the bell was christened *Maria Seraphina Clara* in honor of the Virgin Mary, patroness of the church and town, and the bell's godparents, Mme. Joseph Richy, née Séraphine Boisdoré, and Jean Clair Cazayoux. The *Feliciana Sentinel* newspaper of St. Francisville, Louisiana subsequently reported more than 1,200 persons in attendance for the ceremony.

Presiding was His Grace Napoléon Joseph Perché, "Archbishop of New Orleans, Assistant to the Pontifical Throne, Roman Count, and Grand Cross of the Order of the Holy Sepulchre." Assisting were Revs. Joseph Anstaett, the Archbishop's private secretary; Francois Mittelbronn, pastor of St. Rose de Lima church in New Orleans, canon of St. Louis Cathedral, and former pastor of St. Francis of Pointe Coupée and St. Mary of False River; Patrick R. Glendon, pastor of Our Lady of Seven Dolors, New Texas Landing; Horace Cajone of Mississippi, occasional assistant at Our Lady of Mount Carmel, St. Francisville; T.A. Smith, pastor of Our Lady of Mount Carmel, St. Francisville; Fr. Marcelin Broquere, pastor of Immaculate Conception, Chenal; and St. Mary pastor *Pére* Gutton. Several of the above clergy posed with Archbishop Perché for a rare photograph commemorating the occasion.

In addition to sounding for church services, St. Mary's bells functioned as fire alarms in the 19th and early 20th centuries. In 1906, the town was divided into two fire districts, with St. Mary's bell serving American Company No. 1, whose cart, hose and horse were located at the foot of Poydras Avenue, immediately behind the church property, and which company was responsible for that part of town west of New Roads Street.

Meanwhile, the bell of First United Methodist Church on Pennsylvania Avenue was the alarm of Bouanchaud Company No. 2, headquartered on the bank of False River, with its own cart, hose and horse, west of the foot of North Carolina Avenue and which served the part of town east of New Roads Street. Upon completion of the present St. Mary church and dismantling of its predecessor in 1907, *Maria Seraphina Clara* was moved into its present location. Later in the 20th century, the bell was modified to be sounded by a striker while stationary. It was subsequently restored to its rocking motion through a donation in memory of late Ventress, Louisiana general merchant, Bobbie David.

FRANCIS FABIAN

The dedication of Our Lady of Seven Dolors church at New Texas Landing, upriver of Morganza, on 8 September 1892 consisted of a three hour-long program, during which the choir of St. Mary Cathedral of Natchez, Mississippi performed and Rev. Fabian A.B. Laforest, pastor of Seven Dolors, and attendees celebrated the blessing of a 1,500 pound bell named *Francis Fabian*. It was apparently named for the patron saints of Rev. Laforest and Archbishop Francis Janssens.

A large number of Seven Dolors parishioners as well as faithful from New Roads faithful served as godparents:

Joseph Torras and Mrs. Fanny Batto, Dr. and Mrs. Charles Marie Menville, Dr. Rigney and Miss Donna Smith, Dr. Frederick Gaulden and Miss Emma Vignes, Horace P. Ledoux and Miss Mary Ledoux, Mrs. and Mrs. Joseph Philibert Gosserand, Harry Demouy, James Lynch and Mrs. Lynch, James Tircuit and Mrs. Muse, Mr. and Mrs. Edgar Lacour, Mr. and Mrs. Nathanial Phillips, Mr. and Mrs. Jules Ledoux, Numa Tircuit and Miss Lizzy Tircuit, Mr. and Mrs. Elltringham, Hon. Olivier O. Provosty, Mrs. Ida Conard Bourgeois, Mr. and Mrs. J.D. Austin, and Mrs. and Mrs. Michael O'Connell.

The construction of the Morganza Floodway necessitated the closing of Our Lady of Seven Dolors, by then a mission of St. Ann church of Morganza, in 1939. Seven Dolors was dismantled in the following year and its bell placed in one of the towers of St. Ann.

POETIC TRIBUTE

Though many bells have served congregations, institutions and communities of Pointe Coupée Parish, one – *Maria Seraphina Clara* – was immortalized by 19th century False River educator and authoress Mary Frances Seibert in the close of her poem "Sunrise on False River":

… And from afar the muffled drone,
Of a bell,
Comes in monotones across the way.
'Tis the angelus of Saint Mary,
Once again,
Solemnly rising in the air,
With its sweet angelic prayer.

Relics of the Saints

Of the three altar stones at St. Mary of False River, one for each of the three altars, only the Main altar stone – largest of the three – contains a receptacle for relics. During the 1977-1979 renovation of the church, the removal of the Main altar mensa, and removal of the two side-altar mensas in order that the latter two could be joined back-to-back as a mandated Altar of Sacrifice, all three altar stones were taken out.

Neither the old altar stone nor a successor was set in the mensa of the Altar of Sacrifice, but, instead, the parish's religious education students were directed to print blessings for which they were thankful on slips of paper and place them in an opening in the new mensa, after which it was sealed.

The fate of the three old altar stones was largely forgotten until the renovation work of 2016, when they were found along with a silver processional cross and six metal and glass catafalque lamps mounted atop wooden staffs. All were found between a wooden vestment closet and the eastern wall of the sacristy.

Meanwhile, local artisan and parishioner, Kerry Callegan, who was fashioning a new mensa for the Altar of Sacrifice to replace the original which had deteriorated, was authorized by Monsignor Robert Berggreen, then pastor, to have the Main altar stone set in the new mensa. Callegan stated that while polishing the stone, the small, square covering of the relic cavity "popped out," revealing a small gold reliquary. Monsignor Berggreen had him return the covering in place, and the identities of those whose relics were contained in the stone – long a source of speculation among parishioners and scholars – remained unknown.

STS. FELISSIMUS AND JUCUNDIAN

In 2022, Rev. Christopher Decker reverently examined St. Mary's altar stone reliquary, a small, gold, round compact-like container, holding two small parchment packets, each sealed with red wax. From the Latin inscriptions printed thereon, he identified the contents to be bone fragments of two early martyrs for the Faith, namely Sts. Felissimus and Jucundian.

The *Roman Breviary* of 1908 identified Felissimus as one of the six deacons of Pope Sixtus II who were martyred by beheading with him in August of the year 258, during the persecution of Roman Emperor Valerian. The Pope, Felissimus and Agapitus were martyred on 6 August, and the day is observed in the Church calendar as the Feast of Sts. Felissimus and Agapitus. The best-known of Sixtus' deacons, Lawrence, was martyred on and commemorated in the calendar four days later, on 10 August.

The same edition of the *Breviary* related that Jucundian, of whom less is known, was martyred for Christ by being thrown into the sea off the coast of Africa. His feast day is 4 July.

It is unknown at present if the altar stones and relics were installed during the completion of the present St. Mary church in 1907 or had been transferred from an original setting in the preceding church of 1823.

Nonetheless, the Holy Sacrifice of Mass continued to be offered in the 21st century at St. Mary of False River above the relics of martyrs, thus continuing the venerable tradition of early Christians celebrating the liturgy on the resting places of the holy ones in the catacombs in which they had been entombed.

FIGURE 95: THE MARTYRDOM OF SAINT SIXTUS II AND HIS DEACONS (MARTYRE DE SAINT SIXTE II ET DE SES DIACRES), COTE: FRANÇAIS 185, FOL. 96V., VIES DE SAINTS (LIVES OF THE SAINTS), FRANCE, PARIS

STS. DIONYSUS, FLORENCE, AND GORDIANUS

At least one other church in 21st century Pointe Coupée Parish has an altar stone with documented relics: Immaculate Conception at Lakeland. The church was completed in 1927, and the Main altar therein had formerly served in St. Maurice Church, in the Lower Ninth Ward of New Orleans. The relics are those of Sts. Dionysus, Bishop and Martyr; Florence, Virgin; and Gordianus, Martyr.

According to the 1910 edition of *Butler's Lives of the Saints* by E.C. Donnelly and published by Benziger Brothers, St. Florence, whose feast day is 20 June, was the daughter of Duke Severian of Cartagena by his wife Theodora, and was of a family of saints: Sts. Leander, Fulgentius and Theodore were her brothers, and St. Hermingild, sovereign prince of the Visigoths, was their nephew. St. Florence died circa 633.

Per "The Life of St. Gordian" in *The Golden Legend*, published in the 13th century, Gordianus was a Roman pagan and judge who converted to Christianity during the reign of Julian the Apostate. He was tortured and beheaded for Christ in the year 362, and his feast day is observed 10 May.

There were several Bishop-Martyrs named Dionysus, including the well-known one of Paris, known in French as "St. Denis," alas it is not known of which Dionysus the relic at Immaculate Conception is related.

ST. ANNE

St. Ann Church in Morganza has under glass, to the right of the sanctuary, a small golden reliquary holding bone fragments of a most venerated saint: Anne, Mother of the Virgin Mary.

RELIC OF THE TRUE CROSS
LOST TO RECORD

The origin of St. Mary's most precious artifact, described as a Relic of the True Cross, remains unknown, as does its whereabouts in the 21st century. The Parochial Visitation Reports of 1919 through 1958 attest to its usual location as being the church sacristy, behind lock and key. Only the report of 1923 mentions the relic as having been exposed for veneration, and solely on Good Friday. The preceding report of 1919 and succeeding ones of 1935 through 1958 state that the relic was not exposed during those respective years.

As to documentation, the 1919-1935 Visitation Reports attest to the relic having no supporting documentation, and those of 1948-1958 contend that documentation had been lost.

No clergy, religious or lay persons who would have been alive in and before 1958 and were interviewed in 2023 had any recollection of the relic. Similarly, no document in St. Mary's on-site holdings has been found to mention it, and a search for same by Diocesan Archival Staff in Baton Rouge proved fruitless as well.

Relics kept in small crosses or reliquaries have been owned by a number of persons in St. Mary church parish. The pectoral cross of dear Rev. J.P. Gutton, which contains a relic, was presented after his death to local businessman George Pourciau, one of two orphaned boys whom Fr. Gutton reared.

Pourciau's descendants presented the cross and relic it contained to Rev. Frank Uter, another esteemed pastor of St. Mary, in a gesture of appreciation for his ministry. Fr. Uter, in turn, presented *Pére* Gutton's pectoral cross in 2022 to Rev. Andrew Merrick, a False River native and Catholic of Pointe Coupée graduate.

As an historical note, *The Pointe Coupée Banner*, ever vigilant in the exaltation of the Faith and welfare of the faithful, posted a cautionary note in its issue of 9 July 1881: "Two swindlers, a man and a woman, have been doing up this parish lately by selling pretended relics or blessed articles from Lourdes."

FIGURE 96: IMAGES OF ST. KATHARINE DREXEL

ST. KATHARINE DREXEL

St. Mary of False River was for more than a century, until remitting for safekeeping to the Diocesan Archives in Baton Rouge in 2021, the location of a second-class relic of St. Katharine Drexel. The second canonized American and the first as a native-born citizen of the country, Mother Katherine Drexel was foundress of the Sisters of the Blessed Sacrament and did much to aid the Native American and African American communities of her time.

Rev. John Hoes, as pastor of St. Mary in 1917, corresponded with Mother Drexel three times in requesting that she send Sisters to assist in the education of the children of African American parishioners in and around New Roads.

Her reply of 6 August that year, in which she regretted she had no Sisters to spare for the ministry but assured the prelate of their prayers, was a typed one. The signature and addressing of the envelope, however, are in ink and apparently of the same hand. The letter is signed "M.M. Katherine," and is therefore a second-class relic.

Among the subsequently-canonized individuals who visited and ministered in Pointe Coupée Parish was St. Frances Xavier Cabrini. As Mother Cabrini of the Missionary Sisters of the Sacred Heart of Jesus, this native of Italy visited southern Pointe Coupée Parish in the early 20th century during her ministry to the poor, particularly of Italian ancestry.

The Antoine Albéric Lorio family, owners of Ingleside Plantation near Lakeland, relate oral history of Mother and Sisters visiting for the collection of alms for the poor, singly joyfully as they entered the Ingleside gates via horse-drawn carriage. Her work was also commemorated in the naming of St. Frances Xavier Cabrini church parish, seated at Livonia. The church bears the full name of the saint while the adjacent parish hall is known as the Cabrini Center.

SHEPHERDS OF THE FLOCK

The following compilation of pastoral and administrative appointments and missionary activity in Pointe Coupée is based on contemporary correspondence now housed in the University of Notre Dame Archives, the exhaustive research of Roger Baudier, K.S.G. as presented in his monumental work *The Catholic Church in Louisiana* (1939), and primary sources in the Archives of the Catholic Diocese of Baton Rouge.

It is restated as a reminder here that missionary work began in the community in 1722, the first pastor assigned in 1728, St. Francis of Pointe Coupée being the mother parish, and St. Mary of False River established as a mission of St. Francis in 1823 and elevated to independent parish status in 1865.

All clergy not indicated as members of religious orders were secular priests. Abbreviations for orders are: O.F.M.Cap (Franciscan Capuchin), S.J. (Jesuit), O.Carm. (Carmelite), C.M. (Congregation of the Mission a.k.a. Lazarists), P.S.S. (Society of Saint Sulpice a.k.a. Sulpicians), and S.M. (Society of Mary a.k.a. Marists).

PASTORS AND ADMINISTRATORS OF ST. FRANCIS

- Philippe de Vianden, O.F.M.Cap., occasionally visited 1722-1723
- Raphael, O.F.M.Cap. Superior, visited 1726
- Paul Du Poisson, S.J., visited and made the first known sacramental entries 1727
- Maximin, O.F.M.Cap., designated first pastor 1728
- Pierre Vitry, S.J., occasionally visited during 1728-1735, making entries of baptisms, marriages he performed on *feuilles volantes* (loose sheets), which were inserted into a permanent register by Pierre de Luxembourg, O.F.M.Cap., in 1755
- Pierre, O.F.M.Cap., pastor 1735, who in 1738 dedicated first church of St. Francis of Pointe Coupée
- Pierre Vitry, S.J., visited again 1737
- Anselm de Langres, O.F.M.Cap., pastor 1738, assisted in his first year by Agnan de Chaumont, O.F.M.Cap.
- Charles de Rambervilliers, O.F.M.Cap., 1741
- Rémy, O.F.M.Cap., 1743
- Dagobert de Longuy, O.F.M.Cap., 1747
- Pierre de Luxembourg, O.F.M.Cap., 1753
- Denis, S.J., visited 1753 but left no records
- Ame, O.F.M.Cap., pastor 1753
- Barnabé, O.F.M.Cap., 1755

- Matherne, O.F.M.Cap., 1755
- Irenée, O.F.M.Cap., 1755-1764, under whom the second St. Francis of Pointe Coupée church was dedicated 1760 and cemetery blessed 1764
- Pierre de Luxembourg, O.F.M.Cap., again, and alternately with Irenée, O.F.M.Cap., 1763-1764
- Valentin, O.F.M.Cap., 1764
- Archange, O.F.M.Cap., 1765
- Irenée, O.F.M.Cap. again, 1767, during which time in 1774 he welcomed visiting Jesuits
- Valentin, O.F.M.Cap., again, Angelus a Revillagodos, O.F.M.Cap., and Stanislaus, alternately, 1774-1775
- Luis de Quintanilla, O.F.M.Cap., 1775
- Valentin, O.F.M.Cap., again, 1777
- Luis de Quintanilla, O.F.M.Cap., again, 1777
- Louis de Ste. Sépulchre, O.F.M.Cap., 1778
- Hilaire de Génévaux, O.F.M.Cap., 1780
- Luis de Quintanilla, O.F.M.Cap., again, 1780
- Bernard von Lempach, O.F.M.Cap., 1791
- Carlos Burke, O.F.M.Cap., 1796
- Claude Nicolas Gerboy, O.F.M.Cap., 1796
- Francisco Lennon, O.F.M.Cap., 1799
- Paul de St. Pierre, O.F.M.Cap., 1800
- Francisco Lennon, O.F.M.Cap., again, 1804
- François Pierre de L'Epinasse, O.F.M.Cap., 1807
- Francisco Lennon, O.F.M.Cap., again, as administrator, 1810
- Juan Brady, O.Carm., 1812
- Francisco Lennon, O.F.M.Cap., again, 1813
- Louis Guillaume Valentin DuBourg, P.S.S., Administrator Apostolic of the Diocese of New Orleans, as administrator, 1814
- Juan Brady, O.Carm., again, 1814
- __ DeCrugy, "Vicar General," as administrator, 1818
- Antoine Blanc, pastor, 1820, assisted during 1822-1827 by his brother Jean Baptiste Blanc, one of the first priest ordained in Louisiana, during which time Antoine Blanc founded the mission chapel of St. Mary of False River in 1823. Antoine Blanc was subsequently the Fourth Bishop and ultimately First Archbishop of New Orleans.
- Jean Baptiste Barnabé, 1831
- Louis de L'Hoste, Vicar General of the Diocese, pastor in 1832
- Jacques Marie Auguste Bonniot, 1833
- Jean Martin, 1834,
- Pierre J. Doutréluingne, C.M., visited 1842
- Pierre François Beauprez, 1842,
- Victor Jamey, pastor, 1846, assisted during 1847-1848 by Claude Antoine Tholomier

- Auguste Simon Paris, 1848
- Jean Rogalle, 1848
- Hubert Thirion, pastor, 1853, assisted by François C. Mittelbronn, and they also directed Poydras College during 1854-1857
- Francois Christophe Mittelbronn, pastor, 1858
- Jean Arthur Poyet, 1866
- Constantin Van de Moere, 1872
- Pierre Berthet, 1876, during whose pastorate in 1880 Amable Doutré boarded with him at St. Francis prior to the latter assuming pastorate of Our Lady of Seven Dolors at New Texas Landing
- Joseph Philibert Gutton, pastor of St. Mary, made administrator of St. Francis of Pointe Coupée in 1885, with occasional assistance of pastors of Our Lady of Seven Dolors of New Texas Landing
- St. Francis lost independent parish status in 1890, and became a mission of Our Lady of Seven Dolors church of New Texas Landing.

A new St. Francis, a mission chapel of Seven Dolors, was built four miles up the Mississippi River in 1895, and it continued as a mission of Seven Dolors and its successor parish of St. Ann of Morganza until becoming a mission of St. Mary of False River in New Roads in 1962.

PASTORS AND ADMINISTRATORS
OF ST. MARY

- Joseph Philibert Gutton, 1865
- Francis Cools, 1896
- Francois Laroche, 1899, during whose pastorate construction began on the present St. Mary Church in 1904
- Alfred Ottavien Bacciochi, 1906, during whose pastorate the present St. Mary Church was completed in 1907
- John Francis Hoes, 1913
- John William Anthony Janssen, 1942
- Arthur J. LeBlanc, Jr., 1962
- Christopher Springer, 1974
- Francis M. "Frank" Uter, 1976
- Victor G. Messina, 1984
- Miles D, Walsh, 1987
- Mark A. Alise, 1994
- Michael J. Schatzle, 1996
- Robert Stein, 2005
- Mons. Robert F. Berggreen, 2011
- Patrick Broussard, Jr., 2018

- Michael J. Schatzle, again, as administrator, 2020
- Christopher J. Decker, 2021

ASSOCIATE PASTORS AT ST. MARY

- Antoine Pompallier, S.M., 1882
- Alfred Ottavien Bacciochi, 1890, later pastor
- Francis Cools, 1891, later pastor
- Auguste M. Rochard, 1893, who also founded that year New Roads' first Catholic school, for African American children on site
- Wenceslaus Geens, in 1900 living with pastor, Francis Laroche
- Henry L. Pinard, 1901
- Eugene Royer, 1904
- Eugene Cabanel, 1905
- Joseph B. Pooley, 1952
- William Koninckx, 1955
- Louis Generes, 1956
- John Barrios, 1958
- Peter Jenniskens, 1959
- Lawrence Hecker, 1960
- Hubert Brou, 1961
- Gerard Lefebvre, 1963
- Rodolfo Ibanez, 1964
- Jerome Dugas, 1965, who simultaneously served as athletic coach at Catholic High School of Pointe Coupée
- Michael Moroney, 1971
- Andrew Joffrion, 1972
- Zenon Merino, 1974
- Kenneth Laird, 1977
- Thomas Duhé, 1980
- Miles D. Walsh, 1981, later pastor
- Cleo J. Milano, 1984
- Randy Cuevas, 1987
- Dean Martin, 1988
- Joseph Nguyen, 1992
- Peter A. Dang, 2014
- Nicholas J. "Jack" Nutter III, 2015

St. Mary's has experienced significant droughts in associate pastor assignments through the years. Most notably, no associates were assigned to St. Mary between 1905 and 1952. Reaching its peak in 1980, a maximum number of three associate pastors assisted the pastor of St. Mary. Due to the decline in ordinations, no associates have been assigned to the church since the retirement of Rev. Nutter in 2017.

ACCEPTING THE CALL

Throughout the history of the Catholic Church in Pointe Coupée, the sons and daughters of the faithful have generously devoted their lives in response to the call to religious vocations.

The first known parish vocation was a parishioner of old St. Francis Church, Sister Alexandrine Hélene Labry (born 1843), a Sister of Mercy, daughter of Alexandre II and Hélene Séverine Porche Labry of Morganza.

Another parishioner of old St. Francis' who entered the religious life was Sister Louise Delphine, a Sister of St. Joseph, who was born Emma Ledoux, daughter of Henri Ledoux and Indienna, née Ledoux, of the Pointe Coupée "coast."

Sister Louise Delphine marks the beginning of a long line of vocations to the Sisters of St. Joseph from among the parishioners of St. Mary of False River. This line stretched from the 19th to the 21st century.

LeBEAU FAMILY SET RECORD FOR VOCATIONS

No other family in Pointe Coupée Parish history has responded so generously as that of an Immaculate Conception couple of the 19th century, Alexis Octave LeBeau, and his second wife, Elizabeth Bergeron. Two of their children, Pierre Oscar and Marie Corinne, devoted themselves to religious vocations.

Pierre Oscar "P.O." LeBeau, known as "Oscar" in the family (1870-1915) was the first priest known to be ordained from Pointe Coupée. The first Josephite Father ordained in the United States, he made his profession of vows in Baltimore, Maryland in 1905, and offered his first and second Masses at his native Immaculate Conception in Chenal and St. Mary in New Roads, respectively. He established a church for the *Créole de couleur* Catholics around Bayou Petite Prairie in St. Landry Parish, Louisiana, and appropriately named it "Immaculate Conception."

Fr. LeBeau, in addition to serving his own, vast church parish, visited Pointe Coupée monthly beginning in 1898 to minister to African American Catholics. He was also among the priests serving St. Mary Church in New Roads in the absence of Rev. Francois Laroche, the pastor, in 1904. Ultimately assigned pastor of St. Katharine Church in New Orleans, Fr. LeBeau's sudden illness and death at age 45 in New Orleans, was met with widespread mourning. He is buried next to the church he founded, Immaculate Conception, in the community whose post office would bear his named as "LeBeau, Louisiana."

Fr. LeBeau's sister, Marie Corinne LeBeau, who was stationed in Bardstown, Kentucky, was known in religious life as Sister Clotilde, a Sister of Charity of Nazareth, and is buried in the cemetery of the order in Bardstown, Kentucky.

In the next generation, three grandchildren of M. and Mme. A.O. LeBeau accepted the call as Sisters of St. Joseph: Elizabeth "Ti Doo" LeBeau, daughter of Albéard and Léa Major LeBeau, as Sister Mary Bernard; and Sisters Mary Agnes and Anne Marie Lorio, daughters of Théodore Richard and Louisa LeBeau Lorio. Ada Lorio, another daughter of T.R. and Louisa LeBeau Lorio, was an Ursuline and took the name Sister St. Vincent de Paul. Considered a martyr, Sister St. Vincent de Paul died after tending to victims of the 1918 Spanish Flu Pandemic in New Orleans and succumbing to the illness herself.

The third generation of this devout family produced two St. Joseph Sisters: Beth and Rita Ann Lieux, who became Sisters Beth and Bertrand, respectively, daughters of Bertrand and Azéma Lorio Lieux.

The fourth generation was represented by Lynne Lieux, a Sister of the Sacred Heart, daughter of Theodore and Mary Alice Marionneaux Lieux.

The fifth generation was represented by Scott L. Smith, Jr. , grandson of John Charles and Magda Lieux Bonnette and son of Scott L. and Mary Frances Bonnette Smith. Smith entered the Jesuit Order, but later left religious life and returned to New Roads, where he became an attorney, author, and publisher – publisher, in fact, of this volume. Smith hopes that, among his six young children, there will be a representative for the sixth generation of vocations among the Lieux and LeBeau families.

A collateral LeBeau descendant, Fr. Andrew Merrick, also helps represent the fifth generation of vocations, lest the line of LeBeau vocations dies out. Fr. Merrick is a descendant of A.A. LeBeau, the brother of A.O. LeBeau.

Of the A.O. LeBeau descendants listed above, Sister Mary Bernard was an Immaculate Conception parishioner, while those of the Lorio and Lieux families were St. Mary parishioners.

PRIESTLY VOCATIONS

Rev. John Plantevigne, son of Justin and Cécile Bonnefoi Plantevigne, was a native of Immaculate Conception parish, the second native Pointe Coupéean to be ordained a priest, and the first Josephite of color to be ordained in the United States.

Ordained men from St. Mary church parish included Rev. Arthur Lieux, son of Arthur, Sr. and Nathalie Langlois Lieux; Rev. Allen Roy, son of A.J. and Lucy Roy; Rev. Maynard "Tippy" Hurst, Jr., son of Maynard and Helen Delores LaCour Hurst (Fr. Hurst is buried in St. Mary Cemetery); Rev. Larry Roy, son of Clément Eli and Stella Roy; Rev. Darryl Ducote, son of Alton "Billy" and Elaine Dufour Ducote; Rev. John H. Ricard, subsequently Auxiliary Bishop of Baltimore, Maryland, son of Macéo and Albanie St. Amant Ricard; Bro. Michael Langlois, a Benedictine monk, son of Ferdinand and Ruth Baum Langlois; and Rev. Andrew Merrick, son of Edward "Sandy" and Carolyn "Capi" Bergeron Merrick, who was Director of Seminarians for the Diocese of Baton Route in 2023.

Fr. Jamin David, son of Randy and Susan Reine David, is a native of St. Ann parish in Morganza. In the year 2023 he was serving as Vicar General, Moderator for the Curia, and Judge of the Diocesan Tribunal, among other assignments in the Diocese of Baton Rouge.

Men responding to the call from St. Augustine church parish included Rev. Conway Rodney. Jr., a Josephite Father, son of Conway and Rosalie Gaudin Rodney; Rev. Samuel Daisy, Jr., a Josephite, son of Samuel, Sr. and Lena Warr Daisy; Rev. Shelton Fabre, son of Luke and Theresa Vallet Fabre; Rev. John C. Gauthier, son of Joseph and Rosalie Polar Gauthier; and Rev. Cyprian Devold, a Benedictine, son of Douglas and Elizabeth Terrance Devold.

Shelton Fabre, a 1981 graduate of Catholic High of Pointe Coupée, is the highest-ranking prelate born in Pointe Coupée Parish, Louisiana. He was ordained a priest of the Diocese of Baton Rouge in 1989, appointed Titular Bishop of Prudentiana and Auxiliary Bishop of the Archdiocese of New Orleans in 2006, Bishop of the Diocese of Houma-Thibodaux in 2013, and Archbishop of Louisville in 2022.

RELIGIOUS SISTERS

Among the early vocations to the religious life from Pointe Coupée Parish was longtime educator Sister Claire Saizan, a Sister of the Sacred Heart, and daughter of Paul Sarazin Saizan and Amélie Demourelle of the Island of False River and New Orleans. Another Sister of the Sacred Heart from Pointe Coupée Parish, Sister Lynne Lieux, is discussed in the LeBeau Family section of this chapter.

Sisters of St. Joseph who were native St. Mary parishioners, in addition to those of the Lorio and Lieux families listed above, counted among their number Sister Ignatius, née Lélia Morel, daughter of William and Rosélla Pourciau Morel; Sister Isabelle Gosserand, daughter of Jacques Aristide and Harriet Seibert Gosserand; Sister Mary Bernard, née Emma Pourciau, daughter of George and Anna Vignes Pourciau; Sister Marie Adele, née Cydalise Labatut, daughter of Albert and Valéntine Dayries Labatut; Sister Claude Loupe, daughter of Elie and Dorothy Ybos Loupe; Sister Theresa Ann Cazayoux, daughter of Jules and Ida Glynn Cazayoux; Sister Agnes Jewell, daughter of Joseph Philibert and Olympe Mix Jewell; Sister Mary John, née Theresa Hotard, daughter of Sidney and Olympe Chauvin Hotard; and Sister Felix, née Cecile Loup, daughter of Paul F. and Ursula Rodrigue Loup.

Immaculate Conception parishioners taking vows included: Sister Mary Acquin, a Dominican, née Laura Lorio, daughter of Ferdinand and Marguerite Guérin Lorio; Sister Mary Clara, a Dominican, née Eloise Lorio, daughter of Albéric Antoine and Clara Moss Lorio; Sister Mary Timothy, a sister of St. Joseph, née Mary Smith, daughter of Alma Olinde David; Sister Mary Bridget, a Dominican, née Frances Major, daughter of Victor and Lucrétia Rougon Major; Sister Mary Gerard, of the Sisters of the Holy Family, née Sylvia Vallet, daughter of Théophile and Marie Lillian Michel Vallet; Sister Mary Luke, a Dominican, née Dorothy Dawes, daughter of Richard and Addie McKay Dawes; and Addie Burleigh, a Carmelite, daughter of Stephen and Mary Virginia Bass Burleigh.

Sisters of St. Joseph from St. Ann's church parish included Sister Mildred, née Céleste Dayries, daughter of Léon and Aurore Villeret Dayries; Sister Anne Michelle, née Myra Ramagos, daughter of Gilbert and Elmire LeBlanc Ramagos; Sister Anita Tircuit, daughter of Numa and Camille Dayries Tircuit; Sister Stephanie, née Wanda Bourgeois, daughter of Clarence and Delores Nash Bourgeois; Sister Barbara Hughes, daughter of William C. and Philoméne LeBlanc Hughes; and Sister Frances Landry, daughter of Richard and Eleonore Babin Landry.

Dominican Sisters from St. Mary parish included Sister Yvonne Cazayoux, daughter of Dr. Francis Eugene and Charlésia Mix Cazayoux; and Sister Jewell Rose Lorio, daughter of Samuel and Udell Jewell Lorio.

Sisters who were natives of St. Augustine parish included Sister Mary Thérèse, née Mary Gloria St. Amant, daughter of Marshall and Thésia Jean Pierre St. Amant; and Sister Mary Magdalene, née Bernadette Antoine, daughter of Earl and Cecilia Hébert Antoine.

Pointe Coupée youth discerning the call to priestly and religious life but ultimately committing to lay charisms included two with longtime dedication to the education of local youth: Joseph Octave LeBeau, twin brother of Rev. Pierre Oscar LeBeau, S.S.J., who returned home from seminary to become the longtime professor of the Chenal School; and Claire Cazayoux, daughter of Dr. Francis Eugene, D.D.S., and Charlésia Mix Cazayoux, who as "Miss Claire" likewise remained lay and was a teacher at Poydras High School and False River Academy for generations.

Prof. LeBeau, noted above, was united in marriage to kindly Isaure Gúerin of North Bend Plantation at Oscar, Louisiana, and they had one child, J.O. LeBeau, Jr., The latter remained single, and was recalled by cousin Murray G. LeBeau as able to recite the Latin Mass in its entirety, without need of text. Upon J.O., Jr.'s death, he bequeathed the family property at Chenal to the Josephite Fathers, of whom his uncle Rev. P.O. LeBeau was the first to be ordained in Louisiana.

FIGURE 97: PICTURED LEFT TO RIGHT ARE ST. MARY OF FALSE RIVER'S SISTERS OF ST. JOSEPH: THE LATE SISTER AGNES JEWELL, SISTER RITA LAMBERT, AND THE LATE SISTER MARILYN SALTAMACHIA

DEACONS

The declining number of ordinations at the turn of the 20th-21st centuries resulted in the discernment of a number of men toward the diaconate, and the churches of Pointe Coupée have been blessed to be served by a number of deacons.

Among the natives of the parish who were ordained to the diaconate were Norman Christophe, of St. Augustine parish, and Patrick Witty, native of St. Ann parish, Morganza, and subsequently longtime parishioner of St. Mary of False River in New Roads.

TERTIARIES

During the 20th and 21st centuries, at least three native Pointe Coupéeans made promises as tertiaries, or lay members, of religious orders, helping extend the charism of these orders according to individual states of life, in the Archdiocese of New Orleans and Diocese of Baton Rouge: late French professor and chemist Lafayette Jarreau, native of Immaculate Conception Parish and subsequent resident of Baton Rouge, in the Franciscan Order of Penance; the late Hon. Corinne "Lindy" Claiborne Boggs, native of St. Mary church parish, and subsequently resident of New

Orleans, Washington, D.C., and Rome, Italy, as a Redemptorist Oblate; and this author, also a native of St. Mary church parish, in the Mercedarian Order.

"Responding to the Call"

FIGURE 98: FATHER P. O. LEBEAU AND FATHER JOHN PLANTEVIGNE

CATHOLIC EDUCATION

Pointe Coupée Parish is noted as the cradle of public education in the state of Louisiana. The community's most famous citizen, Julien Poydras, provided for the erection of Louisiana's first public schools in the parish in 1808, and his will provided for a succession of schools named in his honor as well as funding for education in general.

Catholic education was long sought, but relatively slow in coming to Pointe Coupée. In 1816, Dr. Auguste Provosty, on behalf of the Corporation of the Congregation wrote the Regent of the College of Orleans in New Orleans, requesting "a good school master… of French origin, of mature age, sober, a Roman Catholic and to have good manners." Provosty continued, "The father of a family would be preferable to a bachelor, so that his wife could teach the young ladies."

Candidates were requested to have a thorough knowledge of the French and English languages "by the analytic method," as well as arithmetic, geography and history. In return, the Congregation would provide the teacher with a "spacious and comfortable" home with yard and garden. A copy of the letter was entered into the Minutes of the Corporation, alas no reference is made to a reply.

CATECHISM IN PUBLIC SCHOOLS

Pointe Coupée Parish has historically been called "The Cradle of Public Education in Louisiana," owing to the dedication of its most outstanding citizen, Julien Poydras. In 1806, the legislative council governing Louisiana at the time passed "An Act to provide for the establishment of public free schools in several counties of the Territory." Only two years later, in 1808, Julien Poydras and colleagues saw to fruition the "Establishment of Public Schools" in Pointe Coupée.

Five schools were to be opened: one on the Pointe Coupée Coast on the Mississippi River, two on False River, and two on the Island of False River. Pointe Coupée's governing body, the Police Jury was to provide $300 for each school; $25 to the family of each indigent student; establish a curriculum of writing, grammar, morality, Catechism, and arithmetic; and collect a tax of four *escalins* (a coin worth 12.5 cents) on each enslaved person of the parish from their respective masters.

Public schools known to have existed during 1808-1820 included those on the land of Baptiste Porche in the *Quartier du Poulailler*, or "chicken house neighborhood," east of New Roads; another on the nearby plantation of Narcisse Carmouche; and a third on Charles Stewart's plantation near old St. Francis Church.

Though documented record of the above schools is limited, it is known that the instruction of the Catechism was one offered to the faithful of the parish throughout the 19th century. One of the oldest items in the possession of St. Mary of False River, now in the safekeeping of the Archives of the Diocese of Baton Rouge, is a sewn, leather-bound *Catéchism Pour Les Enfants De M. Edmond Capdevielle, Recopié Le 26me Janvier* 1855. The French text includes sections on The Mysteries of the Incarnation, The Sacraments, Preparations for Holy Communion, The Commandments of God, and

The Commandments of the Church. Such hand-copied guides as well as professionally bound and published Catechisms were used by clergy and laity in the instruction of all ages and ethnicities in preparation for the sacraments of First Holy Communion and Confirmation. Among those recalled in oral history as being Catechism instructors of the time was Eustache Bueche, a native of Toulon, France and a planter on the Island of False River.

Parents of means who were desirous of their children receiving extensive scholastic as well as religious education in the antebellum period sent them to boys' and girls' colleges and academies in such places as Convent and Grand Coteau, Louisiana; Mobile, Alabama; Bardstown and Nazareth, Kentucky; St. Mary's, Kansas; and Georgetown, D.C.

POYDRAS COLLEGE

During the antebellum period, Poydras College, an endowment of Julien Poydras, operated on False River, three miles below downtown New Roads. It offered education for local as well as boarding boys, through several changes of administration, from 1833 until closing in 1867.

In 1852, the resignation of Poydras' director, Rev. Frederick Dean, a pioneer Episcopal minister to assume another assignment, inspired Rev. Jean Rogalle, then pastor of St. Francis of Pointe Coupée, that Poydras could became a Catholic school. He informed New Orleans Archbishop Antoine Blanc by letter that the institution had $3,000, and that he was conferring with the administrators.

Fr. Rogalle surmised that with the establishment of another priest in the parish, one could be stationed at the college and another attend to the churches: St. Francis, St. Mary and, when completed, the intended chapel on property donated by free man of color Leufroy Decuir on the Lower Chenal.

One of the Poydras administrators, Auguste Provosty II, an attorney and onetime *marguillier* of St. Francis, informed Archbishop Blanc of his own desire to see the idea to fruition, countering, however, that Julien Poydras' endowment was to the people of Pointe Coupée, who were of different faiths, and Poydras College, therefore, could not be an exclusively Catholic school. Rogalle's proposal was soon moot, as ill health and difficulties with the *marguilliers* resulted in his move from Pointe Coupée.

Fr. Rogalle's successor as pastor, Rev. Hubert Thirion, in 1854 renewed the move to establish a Catholic school in the community. He informed Archbishop Blanc that the house of the former cantor as well as the former Pointe Coupée Parish Courthouse could be used for the purpose, and Poydras College was offering its facility as well.

The parishioners, he continued, were urging him to accept Poydras College, and they had gone so far as to announce an opening date for classes there via the *(Pointe Coupée) Echo* newspaper. Shortly thereafter, Thirion wrote Rev. Stephen Rousselon in New Orleans, requesting that the latter send him from 50 to 70 catechisms to be used at Poydras, the payment for which Thirion would send "on the next occasion."

At the end of the 1854-1855 term, Thirion wrote Blanc that the session had been a success and had been publicized in New Orleans newspapers, complete with the "liberty" of inclusion of the archbishop's name as reference.

EARLY RECRUITMENT OF SISTERS OF ST. JOSEPH

In 1856, writing on Poydras College stationery, Rev. Hubert Thirion asked Archbishop Blanc of the possibly of a convent being located in the parish, ostensibly for the education of young ladies. Soon after, Thirion wrote the Archbishop again, stating that the former residence of (the late) Benjamin Poydras, a fine two-story structure four to five miles west of St. Francis Church on the Mississippi River, would be suitable as a convent. He said five fathers of families were in favor of the project, and he imagined renting it at $200 to $250, for four or five years.

Thirion identified the prospective occupants and educators as being the Sisters of St. Joseph of Bourg, who had been established at "the Bay," i.e., Bay St. Louis, Mississippi. Despite the ideal situation of the Poydras residence, Thirion stated he would leave the decision of where to establish the convent, and knowing the wishes of the parishioners, a place on False River would likely be chosen.

Archbishop Blanc visited the Sisters at Bay St. Louis that summer, offering to be their patron, and returning to New Orleans, he received a letter from their superior, Mother Eulalie, S.S.J. She requested the transfer of all but three of their number, religious and a young laywoman discerning a vocation with them, to Pointe Coupée Parish. Rev. Thirion received a similar request from her, and referred the matter to the archbishop for approval.

As to their location, Thirion stated that they could move into a house near St. Mary Church in New Roads. It stood on 100 acres, he continued, and the property had been offered to him for $3,500 on long-term credit.

Meanwhile, Fr. Thirion's assistant, Rev. Francois Mittelbronn, informed Archbishop Blanc of Thirion's ongoing illness (they both had suffered from the 1853 yellow fever epidemic), adding that Thirion was likewise "failing in mind." In early 1858, Mittelbronn wrote the Archbishop again, this time telling him that he had been forced to close Poydras College, as he was having to manage it in addition to physically caring for Fr. Thirion.

Fr. Mittelbronn was subsequently named pastor by Archbishop Blanc of St. Francis, with its attendant chapel of St. Mary in New Roads. Poydras College changed focus with new management, being advertised as "Poydras Military Academy." Mittelbronn continued in the role of educator, however, giving "instructions," likely religious, one day of the week at St. Francis and another at St. Mary.

No religious Sisters, either of St. Joseph or any other order, were established in Pointe Coupée Parish for decades thereafter. As providence had it, however, when an order did arrive for educational ministry in New Roads, in 1904, it was that of the Sisters of St. Joseph.

Poydras College closed in 1864, due to the Civil War. Its campus was occupied that summer, according to *The Official Records of the Civil War*, as a camp for 234 men of the Second Veteran Cavalry, New York Volunteers, and 75 men of the First Texas Cavalry Volunteers, Federal Army.

Rev. Francois Mittelbronn had been arrested by Federal troops while ministering on the Lower Chenal, and was imprisoned in Baton Rouge. Upon release, he returned to Pointe Coupée, but in 1866 transferred to New Orleans, where he ultimately founded St. Rose de Lima church parish. Testifying in his case against the United States government for material losses suffered at the hands of the Union occupation, Mittelbronn said that the Poydras College building had been used by the Federal troops as a hospital.

He further deposed that he had acquired "the remains of Poydras college library... about 800 volumes, and "bedding for fifty beds, which I had obtained from the Poydras college," only to have them stolen or destroyed by the Union sailors of the *U.S. Albatross* who ransacked the presbytery at

St. Francis on the Mississippi River in April 1863. Others testified in the case, however, that the students of Poydras had provided their own bedding.

Among the damaged books were the works of St. Jerome, St. Augustine and St. Thomas Aquinas, *La Revolution Francaise* by Thiers, the *Histoire Universelle de l'Eglise* by Rohrbacher, and the complete works of Corneille, Moliere, Racine, Rousseau and Voltaire, as well as general texts on philosophy, history, and mathematics.

CHRISTIAN BROTHERS REQUESTED

In 1867, the Poydras College directors, headed by Prosper Echelard, offered the institution for a seven- year term to whoever wished to operate it. St. Mary pastor Fr. J.P. Gutton recommended to New Orleans Archbishop Jean Marie Odin that the latter send Brothers of the Christian Schools to conduct the school, adding that the Poydras Fund would present a sum each year to assist some poor scholars.

This proposal did not come to fruition, however, and the college reopened, still as a non-sectarian institution, only to close again in seven months' time, "on account of expediency," college president and principal Hypolite Didier stated.

In 1868, the Freedmen's Bureau New Roads field office indicated in its reports that Company K, 70th United States Infantry, apparently serving as occupation troops for the area, established quarters in the former "Seminary," i.e. Poydras College, buildings.

ARCHDIOCESAN CONTRACT FOR GIRLS' SCHOOL ABROGATED

Still envisioning a Catholic school in the parish, the Poydras College Board of Directors were successful in 1873 in contracting with New Orleans Archbishop Napoléon Joseph Perché for the Catholic Church to conduct a white girls' school in the Poydras College building, and to provide for African American girls' education in an adjacent building on the campus.

The incoming Pointe Coupée Parish Police Jury, all but one of whom were African American, abrogated the contract, as their spokesperson, African American William Smith, who promoted segregation, feared interracial conflict if the girls were to mingle socially.

Two years later, in 1874, Mississippi River levee crevasses and disastrous flooding forced stricken Pointe Coupéeans to take refuge in the former Poydras College. Rev. Gutton encountered there sick and destitute women and children, practically naked and starving. Going to New Orleans, he delivered an emotional and successful plea for their rescue and financial assistance. As had the Freedmen's Bureau a few years earlier, the *Morning Star and Catholic Messenger* of New Orleans referred to the former college as the "old seminary" in its news accounts.

Poydras College served as a primary school for the neighborhood in 1878, and following its closing, as the home of former director Hypolite Didier, farmer Jean Baptiste Chustz and their families. In 1881, ironically one month after the Poydras College Board met to plan for reopening the institution, the building was accidentally destroyed by fire. Thus ended the history of one of the state's earliest boys' aca-demies.

Late antiquarian Donald Didier, descent of Prof. Hypolite Didier, related that a trunk said to contain papers and other ephemera from Poydras College had supposedly been retained by the family until a certain "daughter-in-law," for whatever reason, burned both trunk and treasures.

From 1865 through 1892, Pointe Coupée Parish suffered from numerous failures in the Mississippi, Raccourci-Old River, and Atchafalaya Rivers, flooding and causing flooding, destruction of improvements and crops, and loss of life to humans and livestock. Amidst the privations, education, both public and private, was frequently hampered.

SCHOOL AT OUR LADY OF SEVEN DOLORS

In July of 1888, Rev. Charles Clark, pastor of Our Lady of Seven Dolors Church at New Texas Landing, upriver of Morganza, saw to fruition the establishment of a Catholic school in his parish. A building was constructed at the cost of $1,475. As he was unable to procure religious Sisters or Brothers to conduct it, Fr. Clark employed two lay instructors. Enrollment numbered 18 boys and 17 girls, all white, in the first session.

Fr. Clark's successor as pastor of Seven Dolors, Rev. J.J. Ferguson, continued the Catholic school for white children and established a second one, for African American children. Insufficient funding caused the closure of the latter in 1902, though the white children's school continued for a few more years, until the establishment of the Texas & Pacific railroad through and a shift in population and infrastructure to Morganza, resulted in the demise of the port community of New Texas.

In 1916, Fr. Father Dominic Perino, as pastor, sold the half-acre lot containing the former school at New Texas Landing to the Pointe Coupée Parish School Board for $600, to help finance a new church in Morganza. From that time, the faithful of Upper Pointe Coupée desiring a Catholic education for their children have sent them to the schools in New Roads.

FIRST CATHOLIC SCHOOL IN NEW ROADS

The arrival of Rev. Auguste Rochard as assistant to Rev. J.P. Gutton at St. Mary of False River in 1893 resulted in the opening of a Catholic school, for African American children, with archdiocesan assistance, in the parish seat. A house was acquired, moved to the church property, and fitted for classroom purposes. In a letter to New Orleans Archbishop Francis A.A.J. Janssens, Fr. Rochard described the school, funds received and disbursed as follows:

New Roads, the 30 October 1893
To His Excellency
Monsignor Archbishop

Monsignor,

I am a little late in rendering an account of 500 dollars which I received from you, but I had to wait until the last work was completed.

I paid for the house	$250.00
To transport it to the property of the Church	40.00
For transporting the bricks	3.00
For making the pillars	5.00
A desk for the professor	3.00
For the benches, tables, doors and field fence	37.00

Paid to Mssrs. Lebeau & Co. [sic, Lebeau & St. Dizier intended] for wood and other supplies	54.50
[subtotal]	332.50
Insurance for 3 years (insurance in the name of Your Excellency)	20.25
Paint	6.00
For painting and whitewashing	5.25
An easel and blackboard	5.50
For the fireplace	2.00
A bill for wood to Mr. [Joseph] Richy	3.25
To same, for paper for [illegible]	0.25
Bromine and lime	1.25
Hooks for the doors, black paint, nails, oil	0.35
A footboard for the desk	2.50
A trip to Baton Rouge	5.00
A stove and its transport	6.10
Broom, water bucket, [illegible]	0.20
Nails for the fence	0.20
Chain for the big gate	0.50
For the fence of the animals' pasture	1.00
Feed for the horses	5.00
To Mr. Delage	1.55
[subtotal]	459.35
A book for rendering accounts and formulas for the receipts	4.10
A curtain, a table rug	2.55
Clock and its transport	9.25
Chairs for the school and their transport	6.00
Seltzer Water, for the professor	1.50
Total	483.35
I have received	$500.00
I have disbursed	$483.35
Remains on deposit	$16.65

The school has been open for fourteen days, twenty students have been admitted. I think that the number will rise well over fifty. I received $20.00 per month, from the [Public] School Board, and it is agreed that each child will pay 5 dollars per year.

Sincerely, Monsignor, with the homage of my deep respect and recognition,
Auguste Rochard

Interestingly, during 1866-1867, the New Roads Field Office of the Freedmen's Bureau conducted a school, open to white as well as African American children, on the lot immediately to the rear or north, then owned by Octave Lecoq and presently the site of St. Mary Parish Hall and parking lot.

Contemporary Church directories indicate that 20 students were enrolled in the first Catholic school at St. Mary in its third year, 1895. There is no mention of the school after the year 1904, and it is probable that it had been discontinued by that time.

The 1907 Sanborn Fire Insurance Map of New Roads indicates a small, Créole-style building at the extreme southeast corner of the St. Mary property, between the church and St. Mary Street. The 1905 Sanborn Map, however, shows no building on this corner, but does indicate both the old St. Mary Church and the present one, the latter under construction. It is possible that the little building shown on the 1907 Sanborn, but neither those of 1905 nor 1909, had been the school established by Fr. Rochard for African American students, and that it had been omitted on the 1905 map as it was intended to be moved at some future time.

SISTERS OF ST. JOSEPH ESTABLISH SCHOOL

Oral tradition transmitted through the Sisters of St. Joseph contends that white ladies of St. Mary of False River parish provided Catholic instruction for children at the turn of the 19th-20th centuries. Through the invitation of Rev. Francois Laroche, the Sisters of St. Joseph of Bourg, a half-century after expressing their own desire to open a school in New Roads, arrived in the town in 1904 and immediately opened St. Joseph School and Convent

Under the direction of Mother Marie Angelle, the Sisters employed a four-room Créole cottage in the second block of Richy Street for use as convent and school. A year later, they had 90 pupils enrolled in "St. Joseph's School."

FIGURE 99: ST. JOSEPH'S SCHOOL, ESTABLISHED BY THE SISTERS OF ST. JOSEPH

Civic leader Joseph Richy donated land in 1906 for the erection of a more suitable convent and school in the same block. The school built at that time was a three-room frame structure elevated on high brick pillars, and the convent a two-story frame building with lower and upper galleries and located immediately to the south of the school.

Purchases of surrounding lots made by the Sisters, with help of dedicated parishioners, in 1907, 1908 and 1909 resulted in the Sisters' acquisition of an entire city block, bounded by Richy Street on

FIGURE 101: ST. JOSEPH ACADEMY AT NEW ROADS, 1905-1928

FIGURE 100: THIRD ST. JOSEPH'S ACADEMY, BUILT IN 1929

the east or front, St. Mary Street on the west or rear, First Street on the south, and West Second Street on the north.

In the archival Mortgage volumes of the Pointe Coupée Parish Clerk of Court is a charter entered in 1911 by six Sisters of St. Joseph for an institution to be known as "St. Joseph's Academy for Young Ladies." The corporation term was to begin on 1 May 1911 and last for 99 years, domiciled in the Town of New Roads, Louisiana. It stated purpose was "to establish and maintain a school for the instruction of young ladies in literary and scientific studies."

The incorporators, signing under their birth and religious names, were: Mary Josephine Sutherland / Sr. Raphael Katie Uriacke / Sr. M. Regina Theresa Hall / Sr. Lorette Eugenie Chateaux / Sr. M. Rosalie Nora Cleary / Sr. Stephanie Myrthée Thiberville / Sr. St. Rose.

It is unknown at present if this charter was revoked, but it is clear that St. Joseph's enrollment was largely female for several decades. Girls from families of means were likely to be sent to St. Joseph, while boys of families were typically sent to Poydras Academy and its successor, Poydras High School, which offered football and other sports.

On 19 December 28, 1928, St. Joseph school, convent and auxiliary buildings were all destroyed by fire, which had begun in one of the classrooms. Fr. Hoes estimated the loss at $25,000.

The Sisters accepted the hospitality of the Pourciau family who offered their house (in 2023, the home of Dr. Alvin Fabre) as temporary living quarters. The school year resumed for the while in the Livonia Lodge Masonic Temple at Poydras Avenue and West Second Street, the Masons removing their paraphernalia from the second floor for the accommodation of classes. The students referred to their temporary quarters there as "St. Mason's."

Meanwhile, a block to the east, on the site of the destroyed convent and school, a new St. Joseph Academy rose. Parishioner and merchant Ernest Morgan, of Morgan's Department Store and New Roads Wholesale Grocery Company facilitated the financing of a convent and school under a single roof, a three-story structure with brick ground floor and two stories of frame construction above.

ST. JOSEPH ACADEMY AND CONVENT OF 1929

The new St. Joseph Academy and Convent was dedicated with great solemnity in conjunction with the celebration of the completion of the bell tower of St. Mary Church, by Rt. Rev. Francis L.R. Gassler, Dean of Baton Rouge, on 19 September 1929, as related elsewhere in this volume.

With enlarged facilities and an expanded curriculum, St. Joseph attracted students from throughout Pointe Coupée and surrounding parishes. Boarding was available for out-of-town students, the most notable one being Corinne "Lindy" Claiborne, ultimately the Hon. Mrs. Hale Boggs, a United States Representative and Ambassador to the Holy See.

The individual church parishes of Pointe Coupée offered their support for St. Joseph Academy. St. Ann's Church Parish, for example, purchased a used bus for $1,300 in 1945 to transport the children of its parish to school in New Roads. By 1947, 32 children from St. Ann's were enrolled at St. Joseph's.

Increasing enrollment at St. Joseph Academy resulted in the acquisition of the former George Pourciau family home, a block to the east and fronting New Roads Street, for the accommodation of the middle school grades in the 1950s.

In 1958, the Congregation of St. Mary Church purchased the following: (1) from Josephine Currieri "Madam Joe" Tuminello, a 10.6-acre tract and Lots 21 and 22 of the Tuminello Addition to the Town of New Roads, fronting on Napoleon Street; and (2) from Ferd C. Claiborne, Lots 1, 2 and

3 of the Claiborne Addition, likewise fronting on Napoleon. The Napoleon Street campus the entire block, between Louisiana Avenue on the east and Claiborne Street on the west.

The former Tuminello tract was one of the historic properties of Pointe Coupée Parish, having been the plantation of Marie Pourciau Robillard Olinde, benefactress of St. Mary Church, and upon which occurred the rebellion of her enslaved laborers of Mina ethnicity in 1791.

Successively it was part of the plantation of Michel Olinde, Auguste LeCoq, Joseph Richy (as his "Home Place" plantation), and Richy's nephew Simeon Parent, from whose succession Madam Joe had bought it.

Significantly, in 1869, the first-known Protestant congregation in New Roads, St. Paul Methodist, comprised of formerly enslaved people, leased from Auguste LeCoq, then owner of the above tract, a building and one-half-acre lot for their worship purposes. It appears to have been in the area of Napoleon Street.

ST. MARY ELEMENTARY SCHOOL

During 1958-1959, construction proceeded on the front of the properties acquired by the Congregation of St. Mary, at the address of 302 Napoleon Street, of a brick, single story school building. Containing 11 classrooms, a library, and a cafeteria for grades 1 through 8, it was completed at a cost of $226,000.

Doors opened to students on 31 August 1959, and the facility was dedicated as "St. Mary Elementary Parochial School" on 20 September, with Archbishop Francis Rummel presiding.

A statue of Our Lady of Beauraing was installed on the front campus in 1962, with Mons. Patrick Gillespie, Vicar General of the new-erected Diocese of Baton Rouge providing a blessing, and Rev. J.W.A. Janssen assisting in what was one of his last official acts of pastor of St. Mary.

With the establishment of St. Mary Elementary in 1959, the old St. Joseph Academy at 183 Richy Street accommodated grades 9 through 12 and was rechristened "St. Joseph High School."

CATHOLIC HIGH SCHOOL OF POINTE COUPÉE

Within a few years, however, the need was realized for more spacious, modern facilities for the high school division. A new school, named "Catholic High School of Pointe Coupée," was built on the Napoleon Street tract, to the north of St. Mary Elementary School and having 504 Fourth Street as its address.

Conveniently located in the center of the large church-owned tract, the school had an entrance via West Fifth Street and exit on Fourth Street. Costing $224,633 the two-story, ultra-modern brick building was designed by J. Roy Haase of Baton Rouge Construction and built by Buquet & LeBlanc construction company, also of Baton Rouge built.

FIGURE 102: CURRENT LOGO (CREST) OF CATHOLIC OF POINTE COUPÉE

Catholic High School was built largely with the proceeds of the sale of a portion of Austerlitz Plantation at Oscar by Miss Marie Bathilde, one of the six celibate children of Joseph Aubin and Marie Louise Isméne Bergeron Rougon. Bathilde willed the property for the establishment of a Catholic high school to serve all of Pointe Coupée Parish.

As originally built, Catholic High School in New Roads included seven classrooms, a library, chemistry laboratory, commerce department, lecture room, faculty lounges and offices. Sister Adrian, S.S.J. who had been principal of St. Joseph High School on Richy Street, continued as principal of the new Catholic High.

Catholic High School of Pointe Coupée opened for the 1964-1965 term as the first integrated school in the Diocese of Baton Rouge. The facility was dedicated at the end of the first school year, on 30 May 1965, with Baton Rouge Bishop Robert Tracy presiding.

END OF OLD ST. JOSEPH CONVENT

The former St. Joseph Academy/High School on Richy Street continued to serve as the convent for the Sisters of St. Joseph, until its aging condition resulted in its demolition in 1978 and the Sisters moved to a new, single-story, brick convent at the corner of Napoleon Street and Louisiana Avenue, immediately east of St. Mary Elementary School.

Among the artifacts of old St. Joseph Academy/Convent which remained in the year 2023 were the large wooden cross formerly topping the structure, which was mounted on a pedestal and forms the focal point of St. Mary Parish Hall.

A large statue of Jesus with the Sacred Heart, distinctive in that that He is depicted as drawing open His robe to display the Heart within, was found and returned to the community by Catholic of Pointe Coupée alumnus Lisa Poché David in 2022.

St. Joseph Academy alumnus Magda Lieux Bonnette recalled the life-size artwork to have been located in the vestibule of the main floor of St. Joseph. In the year 2023, it was located in the visitors' waiting room of the St. Mary Parish Office.

Also preserved in the Parish Office is a portion of a Communion rail, executed in a columned and arched style, which is believed to have salvaged from the Sisters' private chapel in the old St. Joseph Academy / Convent.

Lost to record, however, is the large statue of St. Joseph formerly located in an arched glass shrine on the old school campus, of which a postcard image exists.

CATHOLIC MIDDLE SCHOOL

In 1971, the St. Augustine School on New Roads Street was incorporated into a Catholic of Pointe Coupée school system. Grades 1 – 6 were taught in the former St. Mary Elementary School on Napoleon Street, grades 7 and 8 in the former St. Augustine School on New Roads Street, and grades 9 – 12 in the Catholic high school building with address of Fourth Street.

A decade later, a new, single-story brick Catholic middle school was built between the Catholic elementary and high school buildings, financed in part in memory of Joseph Costello. The former St. Augustine school was closed, and all Catholic education combined as Catholic Interparochial School of Pointe Coupée, while Fr. Uter was pastor of St. Mary.

A new gymnasium was built on the campus, north of the high school building contemporary with the demolition of the old St. Joseph/Catholic High gymnasium on First Street behind St. Mary Church to make way for the new St. Mary Parish Hall.

Following the discontinuance of the school for African American children adjacent to St. Mary Church circa 1904, nearly three decades elapsed before the opening of a successor facility. Beginning in 1917, Rev. John Hoes, then pastor of St. Mary, requested three times via correspondence with Mother Katherine Drexel that she send Sisters of the Blessed Sacrament for the education of African American children. As previously related, she replied each time, regretfully, that she had no Sisters to spare. in New Roads.

Chenal native Rev. Pierre Oscar LeBeau, first Josephite Father to be ordained in the United States, journeyed from his parish of Immaculate Conception in St. Landry monthly beginning in 1898 to administer to African American and *Créole de couleur* Catholics in Pointe Coupée, alas neither church nor school was established for several years.

ST. AUGUSTINE CHURCH AND SCHOOL

In October 1922, the Society of St. Joseph of the Sacred Heart, commonly called the Josephite Fathers, began a congregation in New Roads, and rented the former Simon Parent general store at

the northeast corner of Richy Street and the Texas & Pacific Railroad right of way as a temporary church, ministered by Rev. Thomas Slatery, S.S.J. Interestingly, this structure had been built in 1905 by an African American Baptist congregation for a short-lived church. A "twin" in appearance of the Fazende general store at the opposite corner of Richy, the Parent Building was subsequently location of the Crescent Saloon and Central Night Club stood until demolition at the turn of the 20th-21st centuries.

St. Augustine Church was completed in 1923, during the pastorate of Rev. Edward Hartnett, S.S.J., on an eight-arpent tract on the east side of New Roads Street donated by the Congregation of St. Mary. The classical revival structure was built by the Barbay Construction Co. of Baton Rouge, at a cost of $8,900, which the Congregation of St. Augustine borrowed from the Josephite

FIGURE 103: ST. AUGUSTINE CHURCH (1996)

Fathers. A statue of Jesus with the Sacred Heart placed in a nice above the columned entrance was donated by Mrs. Albin Major, née Marie Langlois, an extensive landowner and St. Mary parishioner.

Fr. Hartnett lived with Fr. Hoes in the St. Mary Church rectory from the time of his (Hartnett's) arrival in New Roads in 1922 until acquisition of a house opposite New Roads Street from St. Augustine as a rectory for the latter church parish in 1923

St. Augustine's parochial report for the year 1923 indicated 1,500 congregants living in a 10-mile radius of the church. As regards the number who had transferred from St. Mary church parish, Rev. John Hoes, pastor of the latter, estimated 2,000 members at St. Mary in the Parochial Visitation Reports of 1919 and 1923 (prior to the completion of St. Augustine Church), but 1,600 in the 1935 Report, from which it may be deduced that 400 transferred from St. Mary to St. Augustine.

Parishioners of St. Augustine Church continued to use St. Mary Cemetery for burials until the establishment of St. Augustine Cemetery, north of the church, in 1951, and some families continued to bury in St. Mary for generations thereafter.

Only four years after completion of St. Augustine Church, it was threatened by floodwater advocating from the last levee failure of the 1927 Flood, at McCrea, on the Atchafalaya River, in Upper Pointe Coupée. Though the water reached the church, no material damage was reported, and the majority of the town of New Roads remained dry.

The establishment of St. Augustine Church provided the impetus for the opening of a Catholic school for African American children. During the pastorate of Father Thomas McNamara, S.S.J., the first St. Augustine School, a four-room facility located immediately south of the church on New Roads Street, was dedicated on 27 December 1932. Graduates of Xavier University in New Orleans served as instructors there until 1951, when the ministry was assumed by the Sisters of the Holy Ghost.

Approximately 200 children enrolled for the first school year at St. Augustine, and pioneer educator Junius Hurst served as first principal at a salary of $30 a month. He was assisted in his labors by three teachers whose salaries, like that of the principal, were provided by a mission fund and Mother Drexel.

A 1925-model school bus was purchased for $50 in which to transport students to the new St. Augustine School. Running a daily circuit of approximately 50 miles, the bus transported approximately 85 students from the New Roads and Oscar areas and the Island of False River.

By 1943 the nine-grade school was being conducted by seven lay teachers in seven classrooms. Some 250 children used the services of a Dodge model bus which was purchased in 1947. The bus travelled 110 miles each school day on its circuit of the greater New Roads area.

The Sisters of the Holy Ghost, the second order of female religious to be established in Pointe Coupée Parish, arrived at St. Augustine to assume the administration of the school in September 1951. A two- story convent, located just north of the church, was constructed with the help of a $15,000 grant.

During the pastorate of Fr. Daniel Cassidy, S.S.J., who took up residence at St. Augustine in 1951, the Pointe Coupée Parish School Board began to offer free transportation for students attending St. Augustine School.

In 1952 a school lunch program was instituted, and the Sisters moved into their newly-completed convent. By 1956. three nuns and six lay teachers were teaching some 456 children at a growing St. Augustine School.

In 1971 the school was integrated into the Catholic of Pointe Coupée school system. The former St. Augustine School facilities were used to house grades 7 and 8. A year later, there were only 142 children from St. Augustine Parish enrolled in the inter-parochial school system.

CATHOLIC SCHOOLS OF NEW ROADS CONSOLIDATED

The Sisters of the Holy Ghost withdrew from their educational ministry in New Roads in 1973, and focused on the religious education of those parishioners in the public schools. In 1979, the St. Augustine campus was closed, and all Catholic school children in grades K-12 began to attend classes on the 10-acre Catholic Interparochial campus in St. Mary church parish.

In the 2022-2023 school year, Catholic of Pointe Coupée numbered approximately 600 students in grades Pre K3 through 12 and 60 faculty members, per school secretary Amy André. Enrollment is from throughout Pointe Coupée and adjacent civil parishes, and all faculty are laypersons. The Pre-K3 facility, known as "Hornets' Haven" for the school mascot, is located in the former 1978-vintage Sisters of St. Joseph Convent at Napoleon Street and Louisiana Avenue.

FIGURE 104: FORMER ST. AUGUSTINE SCHOOL, LATER INCORPORATED INTO THE CATHOLIC OF POINTE COUPEE SYSTEM AS THE MIDDLE SCHOOL

MARDI GRAS AND MOTHER'S DAY

The annual New Roads Mardi Gras celebration is the state's oldest outside of New Orleans, with parades recorded as early as 1880 and it has been an annual event since 1922. Estimated attendance tops 100,000 persons in years marked by ideal weather conditions.

Unlike exclusive krewe parades in New Orleans and other cities and towns, New Roads' duo of parades are civic events, open to public participation, and the first-known to be staged as charitable fundraisers. The Catholic schools and lay associations in St. Mary and St. Augustine church parishes have participated by having elaborate floats in the parades for generations in a manifestation of juvenile talent and community affirmation.

"Bible Stories" was the theme of the 1977 New Roads Lions Carnival parade, and it was customary for the current pastor or associate at St. Mary to ride as a character on the C.Y.O. (Catholic Youth Organization) float. The Community Center Carnival parade has throughout its century-long history featured floats with titles such as Our Lady of Fatima, The Execution of St. Dorothy, Christ is Born, The Last Supper, and Peace.

Music is an essential part of Mardi Gras and other traditional celebrations in New Roads, and youthful musicians from the Catholic schools of St. Mary church parish participated from the early years. The first school band in Pointe Coupée Parish was the Melody Makers' unit founded in 1940. The New Roads Lions Carnival succeeded the Mothers Culture Club Children's Carnival parade in 1941 in order to provide full scale floats, and bands, for the spectators. Successful fundraising that year enabled the purchase of uniforms, and the unit was renamed the Pointe Coupée Parish Band.

All white public schools were able to send musicians to participate in the band, the size of which necessitated its separation into the main, Senior, and Elementary or Junior bands. In 1961, the band was divided into No. 1 and No. 2 units, with St. Mary Elementary School joining Poydras and Livonia High Schools to comprise the No. 2 band.

The wrapped, miniature loaves of bread tossed by the Holsum baking company of Baton Rouge in the Lions Carnivals parades during 1966-1984 are fondly recalled by the faithful as their collation on the following, fast day of Ash Wednesday, often with a teaspoon of peanut butter.

A unique and lovely event was the Mother's Day parade staged by St. Augustine Elementary School in 1961. Following the principal streets of New Roads, the profession included a statue of the Virgin Mary borne by school children, two floats, one of which carried a King, Queen and four Dukes and Duchesses, and the crack Rosenwald and Batchelor High School bands.

ST. MARY'S SCHOOL AT ROUGON

An early attempt to establish a Catholic school in Immaculate Conception church parish was thwarted. In 1908, Chenal native Rev. John Plantevigne, the third Josephite to be ordained in the United States, spearheaded a drive to open a school for the children of Immaculate Conception's Africa American and *Créole de couleur* parishioners.

A citizens' committee selected a site, and money was raised for its acquisition. Fr. Plantevigne wrote to Archbishop Hubert Blenk for permission to build the school and to Mother Katherine Drexel for funds to finance its construction as well as a teacher's salary. A history of the Josephite order states that Rev. Louis Savouré, then Chenal pastor and of strong personality, apparently convinced the archbishop to deny permission, and the school was never built.

A school did open in Immaculate Conception Parish, nearly 30 years later, but its duration was short- lived. In 1937, a group of men known as the Fathers' Organization, descendants of early *Créoles de couleur*, opened St. Mary's Private School on property of the Decuir family near Rougon, Louisiana.

Miss Hazel Mathis served as first teacher, and the subjects offered were secular and religious. Subsequent instructors, according to former student Donald Fuselier, longtime usher at St. Mary in New Roads, included Mrs. Jesse Decuir, née Nola Darensbourg, and Mrs. Alfred Ricard, née Trina Chustz.

St. Mary's School at Rougon operated until 1958 when improvements in the parish's public school system and the migration of many members of the Fathers' Organization from Pointe Coupée resulted in its closing.

FIGURE 105: RELIGION CLASS AT ST. FRANCIS CHAPEL, CA. 1939

THE JOSEPHITES' MARY IMMACUALTE NOVITIATE

In 2016, the Josephite Order established its American novitiate in St. Augustine church parish in New Roads. The former Sisters of the Holy Ghost convent, it was named "Mary Immaculate Novitiate" and subsequently called the Father Conway Rodney Center. The novitiate building is located immediately north of the church and was converted into chapel, classroom, and living space. The first novice master was longtime educator Rev. Joseph Doyle, S.S.J.

Through the years, several Josephite aspirants proceeded through the novitiate before returning to Baltimore, Maryland, seat of the Josephite Fathers, for ordination. The Mary Immaculate Novitiate offered the highest degree of education in Pointe Coupée and surrounding civil parishes while in operation. Owing to declining health, Fr. Doyle was succeeded as novice master by Rev. Roderick Coates, S.S.J. in 2021. The novitiate was relocated to New Orleans later that year.

CATHOLICISM IN OTHER SCHOOLS

Owing to the predominance of the Catholic faith, however, which stood at 80 percent of the 60 percent of Pointe Coupéeans reported to belong to any religious congregation in the year 2023, the public and private schools are respectful of the Catholic majority. These schools, including private, non-sectarian False River Academy, and those of the Pointe Coupée Parish Public School system, have traditionally suspended classes on Holy Days of Obligation as well as the Christmas season and either during Holy Week or Easter Week. Catholic students have likewise been allowed to attend required religious instruction that occurs within the regular school hours, including preparation for First Communion and Confirmation.

Poydras Academy and its successor schools of Poydras High School and Poydras Elementary consistently had a strong relationship with the adjacent, old and present St. Mary churches. Poydras and Fr. J.P. Gutton shared a special bond, and the school heartily mourned his passing and honored his memory.

Poydras Academy's day scholars and boarding students sponsored at least one entertainment, with refreshments, for the benefit of the present St. Mary Church. The 25 June 1904 *Pointe Coupée Banner* related that the program netted $100.50, and the raffle of a cake donated by "Mr. Laurent" (likely Clay Laurent, of the New Roads Bakery a couple blocks west) brought in $20, and additional donations totaled $229.50. A material legacy of the school and church's relationship is the Ninth Station of the Cross mural in the present church, installed in 1915 and blessed in the following year. The brass plaque thereon states it was donated by "The Pupils of Poydras Academy."

Significantly, Poydras was the last of the public high schools in the parish to erect an on-campus gymnasium, this occurring in 1957. Prior to that time, Poydras' athletic events and graduation ceremonies were held in the old St. Joseph Academy Gymnasium at First and St. Mary Streets, at the rear of the church lot. This was a former military barracks which was dismantled, moved to the site and reassembled though the generosity of area fathers, under the direction of Mother Frances, C.S.J., in 1949.

In the 2022-2023 school year, Pointe Coupée Parish schools, in addition to Catholic in New Roads, included the following: STEM Magnet Academy (northwest of New Roads), Livonia High School, and Rosenwald (in New Roads), Rougon, Valverda and Upper Pointe Coupée (at Batchelor) Elementary Schools, all in the Pointe Coupée Parish Public School System; and False River Academy and John Robert Lewis Multicultural STAR Academy, non-sectarian private schools located in New Roads.

RELIGIOUS INSTRUCTION
OUTSIDE OF THE CATHOLIC SCHOOLS

Religious instruction outside of the Catholic school system, for students of public and private schools in Pointe Coupée Parish, has been provided by trained laity through the generations. Into the mid-1900s, pastors of the churches were often instructors as well. The introduction of the Confraternity of Christian Doctrine (C.C.D.) at St. Mary of False River during the 1950s set a standard of instruction and sacramental participation for parish youth from pre-First Communion to Confirmation by religious and lay teachers.

Though some instruction was and continues to be offered in St. Mary Church proper, nearby facilities have served the purposes of the classes, which have progressively been referred to as Catechism, Religion, C.C.D., and Parish School of Religion (P.S.R.). Circa 1920, one of the "two old houses" standing on the rectory lot adjacent to the church served for Catechism classes, per the late Virginia Costello. Mid-century, the Knights of Columbus Hall on the bank of False River, opposite Poydras High School, was the venue for C.C.D. classes as well as other church and community functions.

Beginning in the 1970s, St. Mary, later Catholic, Elementary School on Napoleon Street was the location of C.C.D. instruction, initially on weekday afternoons and later on Saturday mornings, and during the latter era the church provided bus transport for out-of-town students on both sides of False River. In the early 21st century, the St. Mary's Parish School of Religion was located in the various rooms of the St. Joseph Center as well as in the Parish Hall on the church grounds. A total of 73 students were enrolled for the 2022-2023 term with 13 certified lay instructors.

LAY ASSOCIATIONS

The long history of lay associations in St. Mary of False River and sister parishes of Pointe Coupée attest to the respect for tradition and the support of Holy Mother Church and its ministries by the laity. The Society for the Propagation of the Faith, founded at Lyon, France by Blessed Pauline-Marie Jaricot in 1822, provided religious materials and other assistance to the faithful of Pointe Coupée and counted a number of members in St. Mary church parish. It continues a century later as the oldest Pontifical Mission Society of the Church active in the United States of America.

Similarly, Blessed Pauline-Marie's devotion to the intercession of St. Philomena, Virgin and Martyr of the era of Diocletian, spread in Louisiana, and generations of Pointe Coupéeans have had a veneration to the young saint. The Universal Archconfraternity of Saint Philomena, an apostolate of prayer and works of mercy seated at her shrine in Mugnano, Avellino, Italy, established Louisiana Centre 43 of Philomenian Devotion at New Roads, Louisiana in 2014.

Numbering approximately 150 members in the year 2023, its territory encompasses all of the State of Louisiana outside of the city of New Orleans. Rev. Brent Maher, when and subsequent to his pastorate at St. Ann Church in Morganza, has been chaplain of the Centre and annually celebrates the feast with Holy Mass in the Latin form.

Two other venerable apostolates placed by the Holy Fathers of the 19th century under the patronage of St. Philomena are the Children of Mary (*Enfants de Marie* in French) and the Universal Living Rosary Association of Saint Philomena. A chapter of the Children of Mary was established by Rev. J.J. Ferguson during his pastorate of Our Lady of Seven Dolors church at New Texas Landing in the 1890s, and subsequently another was established at Immaculate Conception Church of Chenal-Lakeland.

Scores of faithful from Pointe Coupée and parishes beyond have been enrolled individually in the Children and Mary and Living Rosary apostolates since the establishment of New Roads Centre 43 of Philomenian Devotion in 2004. The Catholics Daughters of the America and Holy Name Society at St. Mary Church had as one of their goals in early 2023 the establishment of a chapter of the Children of Mary in the parish.

EARLY SCAPULAR INVESTEES

The custom of wearing devotional scapulars, most popularly the "brown scapular" of Our Lady of Mount Carmel, is one that has continued through generations of the faithful, by the clergy, religious and laity in Pointe Coupée Parish. In the Archives of the Diocese of Baton Rouge, there is a remarkable document, in French, entitled *"Personnes qui sont membres de la Confrérie du scapulaire de Marie"* (Names of Persons who are Members of the Confraternity of the Scapular of Mary), dated 5 May 1853, Pointe Coupée.

The record does not state which particular one it was of the four approved scapulars of the Virgin Mary existing at that time: Our Lady of Ransom (Mercedarian), Our Lady of Mount Carmel, the

Seven Dolors of Mary, or the Blue Scapular of the Immaculate Conception. Likely, it was the last-named, owing to the proclamation of that mystery as dogma by Blessed Pope Pius IX shortly before, on 8 December 1854.

The list of the members of the confraternity is illuminating in that of the 60 members listed, two have been identified as male, the remainder female, at least 17 were free people of color, and one an enslaved person. Many of the members have descendants among the Catholic community of Pointe Coupée in the 21st century.

The "*Mme. Charlemagne* [sic]" listed was actually Mme. Charamel, a free colored parishioner on False River, and ancestress of television commentator and sportscaster Bryant Gumbel (who is likewise of local Jewish descent).

The postbellum period was marked by the establishment of many organizations throughout the nation, some of which were national or regional associations of a fraternal nature, while many more were of local origin and predominantly religious or benevolent in character. Most of them collected dues from their membership and offered, in return, some form of insurance benefits.

BENEVOLENT SOCIETIES

Rev. Joseph Philibert Gutton, who assumed the newly-erected pastorate of St. Mary of False River in 1865, spearheaded or supported the establishment of both national and local organizations of the faithful of all ethnicities in New Roads. These were exclusively men's organizations and owing to the legalized segregation of the time, composed of either "white" or "colored" members, though the latter were under the special patronage of Rev. Gutton and heartily supported by the white community.

The African American associations, similar to organizations in the city of New Orleans and other Louisiana communities, were religious, social and beneficent in character. In each, nominal monthly dues and periodic special assessments were paid into a treasury, from which medical and funeral expenses were paid for the ill and deceased of the organization. Similar "benevolent" societies existed into the turn of the 20th and 21st centuries, particularly among the American Baptist population, long after the govern-mental institution of social programs.

The societies in St. Mary church parish, as in other communities, held annual celebrations or "festivals," usually on their anniversary or the feast of their patron saint. These included processions complete with floating banners, uniforms and brass band music, communal High Mass and reception of Holy Communion in the church, and an *al fresco* banquet. The latter were held under the lateral galleries of the church, or in the "Olinde Grove" a few properties to the west. The ceremonies and meals were open to white as well as African American attendees.

The oldest-known of the societies in St. Mary church parish was the Benevolent Association of Saint Vincent de Paul of False River, established in 1870 among African American faithful of the neighborhood ultimately known as Mix, Louisiana. It was commonly known as the St. Vincent de Paul Society, and is not to confused with the international ministry of that patronage.

The St. Vincent de Paul Society of False River in 1870 erected one of the first and largest tombs in St. Mary Cemetery, located on the second aisle from the main entrance on New Roads Street. It has 20 vaults, and its name was engraved on a tablet set in the uppermost façade, but this slab had apparently fallen and was standing at ground level by All Saints' Day 1938, when the cemetery's burial places and mourners were strikingly captured in photographic form by Works Project Administration photographer Russell Lee. See photographic feature below.

IMAGES OF NEW ROADS AND VICINITY ON ALL SAINTS DAY 1938 BY W.P.A. PHOTOGRAPHER RUSSELL LEE

FIGURE 106: ST. VINCENT DE PAUL TOMB, PRESENTLY INDIGENT TOMB

These photographs, as well as agricultural scenes around New Roads in the preceding days are housed in the Library of Congress and available for viewing on its online internet website. Additional examples of Russell Lee's photographs for the Works Project Administration are featured in this section.

FIGURE 107: ALTAR SERVERS ASSISTING DURING ALL SAINTS DAY LITURGY

FIGURE 108: WHITE-WASHING THE GRAVESTONES AND CEMETERY FEATURES PRIOR TO ALL SAINTS DAY

Figure 109: Graves decorated for All Saints Day festivities

Figure III: Adorning the Seibert vault at St. Mary's Cemetery for All Saints

Figure IIO: White-washing headstones and grave markers is a common preparation for All Saints Day

FIGURE 113: KNEELING BESIDE GRAVES DURING BLESSING OF THE GRAVES

FIGURE 112: GRAVES DECORATED FOR ALL SAINTS

FIGURE 114: LIKELY DEPICTION OF A BLESSING OF THE GRAVES CEREMONY

FIGURE 115: CHILDREN AT ALL SAINTS DAY

Figure 117: "Man Resting on Sacks"

Figure 116: Photograph from the Sugar Cane Harvest

FIGURE 118: POIGNANT PHOTOGRAPH OF MAN KNEELING IN PROFILE AT ALL SAINTS DAY CELEBRATION, FEATURED IN 1941 WPA VOLUME, *LOUISIANA: A GUIDE TO THE STATE*

FIGURE 119: MEN PRAYING THE ROSARY, ALL SAINTS DAY

FIGURE 120: CROSS WITH VINTAGE WIRE IMMORTELLE WREATH

ST. VINCENT DE PAUL, CONTINUED

In 1890, the Benevolent Association of St. Vincent de Paul of False River purchased a tract of 176.80 acres in the wooded "interior," behind the former St. Cyr plantation, from which members procured firewood for home use. Following the dissolution of the society, about the time of the First World War, the Paul family, who had been among the stalwarts of the society, acquired the property.

During the renovation of St. Mary Cemetery and dismantling of deteriorating and unclaimed tombs in the late 1970s, the St. Vincent de Paul mausoleum was acquired by the church parish, repaired, and has since been employed for the respectful entombment of indigent deceased.

SOCIETY OF ST. JOSEPH

A similar organization founded under Fr. Gutton was the Society of St. Joseph, active by 1890. When it held its annual festival in 1896, the St. Vincent de Paul societies of False River and St. Francis Chapel attended, and the subsequent *Pointe Coupée Banner* of 3 October 1896 reported: "these societies are composed of the best element of our colored population," further elaborating:

> These organizations are of long standing in our community, and are regarded with much favor by the whites, who extend to them every possible encouragement; for while they are religious in character, they are organized on principles of mutual benevolence and hence our [sic] conducive to the temporal welfare and moral improvement of their members as well as to the cultivation of their religious tendencies.

Soon after Hélene Richy, widow of Francois Voirin and sister of Joseph Richy, subdivided her property north of West Second Street and between New Roads and St. Mary Streets into streets, blocks, and lots, the St. Joseph Society in 1900 purchased a 96 foot square lot at the southeast corner of St. Mary and Fourth Streets. They built thereupon a hall facing St. Mary Street for their as well as public use. In 1903, the New Roads Town Council ordered the closure of a dance hall which had been established in the building, owing to complaints of the "loud music" and "foul language" associated with the dances.

The property remained in possession of the St. Joseph Society until 1919, when its membership sold it to contiguous lot owner to the east, devoted parishioner Hilary Vignes, whose residence fronted on Richy Street. The sale excepted the hall building, which the Society was to move from the site. The Society of St. Joseph acquired a lot at the southeast corner of Richy and Fazende Streets in the same year, 1919, and thereafter met in a new hall there for generations.

OTHER BENEVOLENT ASSOCIATIONS

Yet another society for African American men established under Fr. Gutton was the St. Lawrence Mutual Benevolent Association, comprised of parishioners of the Ventress area, on the Island of False River, opposite New Roads. This organization was officially chartered in the Mortgage records of the Pointe Coupée Parish Clerk of Court in 1900, four years after Fr. Gutton's death.

The fourth-known society for African American men in St. Mary Parish founded during the pastorate of Fr. Gutton was identified in the 1901 account of his reinterment ceremonies as the "Young Men of America." Likely, this was the Young Men Protected League Union, chartered in 1888, with the motto: "Love, Charity and Benevolence Towards Each Other." In 1906, the Young Men purchased a lot on the Island of False River for its meeting purposes.

One of the earliest-known associations for the female faithful in St. Mary church parish was the Ladies of the Rosary Society, which was active as early as 1907. In addition to communal recitation of the Holy Rosary, the Rosary Society provided material objects and funding for the interior ornamentation of the church, well into the pastorate of Rev. John Hoes. In the Parochial Visitation Reports, it was last noted in 1935.

The Rosary Society, as well as the Needlework Club of the same era, were succeeded in purpose by the St. Mary Altar Society, first mentioned in the 1948 Parochial Visitation Report. This organization helps provide the liturgical necessities for daily and weekend worship and assists in the beautification of the church. The St. Mary Altar Society was an all-female organization until circa 1990, when men, typically spouses of the existing membership, were welcomed into membership.

In early 2023, membership of the St. Mary Altar Society was the largest in the church parish, with approximately 200 female and male members, according to Keely Nickens Chustz. Of the number, she estimated 25 to be consistent participants and the remainder to be united in prayer and offering their services for feast day preparation and other activities.

In addition to the above, locally-based organizations, national and international associations which established chapters in St. Marcy church parish during the late 19th and early 20th centuries included the Catholic Knights of America, the Knights of Columbus, the Catholic Daughters of the Americas, and the Holy Name Society.

CATHOLIC KNIGHTS OF AMERICA (C.K.A.)

The Catholic Knights of America (C.K.A.) was founded in 1877 in Nashville, Tennessee, and offered life insurance to its members. It chartered two branches at St. Mary Church in New Roads during Rev. Gutton's pastorate: Branch No. 367 in 1884 for white men, and Branch No. 550 in 1889 for African American men. In 1892, Alphonse Lamartine Jewell, Clerk of Court of Pointe Coupée Parish, was recorder for Branch 367, while Gatien Decuir, who had been a Reconstruction-era Sheriff of Pointe Coupée, was recorder of Branch 550, per the *Biographical and Historical Memoirs of Louisiana* published that year.

New Roads Branch No. 367 C.K.A. erected a meeting hall at the southwest corner of the St. Mary rectory lawn, which, in addition to its purposes, served as a venue for community meetings and fundraisers. One of the entertainments offered by the C.K.A. in its hall was a "Panoramic display" on the evening of *Pointe Coupée Banner* press day, 22 June 1889. A striking and popular amusement of the time, a panorama was a circular representation of a historical location or event which enabled the viewer standing within to feel as if he or she was actually "there" in the place and time of the subject.

Next-door neighbor Poydras Academy held its first closing exercises in the Catholic Knights Hall on 1 July 1889, per the subsequent, 6 July, issue of the *Banner*. In the following decade, on 5 April 1897, the New Rhodes (sic) Town Council agreed to remit to the president of Branch 367 of the Catholic Knights the sum of $50 for rent of the hall by the "primary school of New Rhodes."

As did the independent benevolent societies of the community, both branches of the C.K.A. at St. Mary, received faithful and glowing coverage by the *Pointe Coupée Banner* through the years, in news articles as well as correspondence from readers. The June 1 1889 issue of the paper included a letter dated "New Texas, May 27 '89," in which the sender, who signed as "Freedom," complimented both branches in their "romantic town" and at whose "general communion" on the preceding day a number of ladies and men from New Texas were guests. The lengthy tribute included the following:

Oh! How edifying to behold such a band of Brothers, united in a God loving crusade, approaching the Dove of the Tabernacle to receive their Lord. A finer body of men in any rural district it would be impossible to find, in some of whose veins the best and oldest blood of Pointe Coupée flows, and as a reward of their merit, the highest offices within the gift of the people of the civil parish [Pointe Coupée] has been conferred on several members of this body… Judging from the moral appearance which seems to characterize St. Mary's congregation, it seems as if the serene waters of your crescent river (i.e., False River) has irrigated such a crop of virtue.

The account continued that the members of both branches were seated "Inside the altar railings," while Rev. J.P. Gutton offered a High Mass, with assistance from Rev. (Thomas) Larkin, (S.M. or Marist Father), from St. James (Parish). Dr. Charles Menville, St. Mary's organist at the time, and a choir provided music for the liturgy.

Afterward, Menville, as President of Branch 367, and Hon. O.O. Provosty offered toasts at a banquet in the C.K.A. Hall, attended by some 75 knights and guests. Typical of the lyrical prose of the time, the writer described the dining table as "fairly groaning with the choicest edibles of the season, and sparkling juice of California grape."

Branch 367 of the Catholic Knights of America was recorded in the St. Mary Church Parochial Visitation Reports as being active as late as 1923. Extant Reports begin with 1919, in which Branch 550 was not listed, and had apparently become inactive by that time.

KNIGHTS OF COLUMBUS (K. of C.)

The Knights of Columbus (K. of C.) was founded in 1882 in New Haven, Connecticut by Blessed Rev. Michael J. McGivney for Catholic men as an alternative to fraternal groups prejudiced against the Catholic Church and likewise offers life insurance to its membership. New Roads Knights of Columbus Council 1998, seated in St. Mary of False River church parish, was founded on 20 May 1919 by indefatigable parishioner Hilary "Rook" Vignes.

FIGURE 121: KNIGHTS OF COLUMBUS, 4TH DEGREE HONOR GUARD

Reports of the 28 June and 5 July 1919 *Pointe Coupée Banner* relate that 50 men were initiated on 29 June 1919. The inductees and 137 out-of-town knights met in the "hall" on the second floor of the landmark Graugnard-Richy Building at the northeast corner of West Main and Richy Streets, from which they were escorted by a brass band to St. Mary Church for High Mass. They returned to the hall, where the first and second degrees were conferred by a Baton Rouge K. of C. degree team, and the third degree by a New Orleans team.

All 187 knights proceeded up Richy Street to the St. Joseph Convent, where a dinner was served by ladies of the parish. Visiting K. of C. officials and Rev. John Hoes, St. Mary's pastor, offered remarks after the meal. The day concluded with a dance in the Graugnard-Richy Building hall, at which Butler's Orchestra of White Castle played for the knights and wives from New Roads, Baton Rouge, Plaquemine, Donaldsonville and New Orleans.

The local knights were chartered in the following year, 1920, as New Roads Council No. 1998, K. of C., with Hilary "Rook" Vignes as first Grand Knight. The council received its charter, thereby becoming a legal entity, on 19 June 1926, while George Pourciau was Grand Knight. Traditionally the largest men's organization at St. Mary, the K. of C. counted 100 members at the time of the 1935 Parochial Visitation.

Notable New Roads knights have included businessman, Pointe Coupée Deputy Sheriff, and foster son of Rev. Joseph Philibert Gutton, Joseph Philibert "J.P" Gosserand; George Pourciau, likewise a leading businessman and foster son of Fr. Gutton; District Attorney and former *Pointe Coupée Banner* owner and editor Albin Provosty; Pointe Coupée Clerk of Court Alphonse Lamartine "A.L." Jewell; Jacob H. "Jake" Morrison, a District Attorney and father of New Orleans Mayor deLesseps "Chep" Morrison; District Attorney and Louisiana Lieutenant Governor Hewitt Bouanchaud; Pointe Coupée Sheriff, New Roads Mayor and businessman Lamartine Bouanchaud; Joseph Thomas "Tom" Jewell Speaker of the Louisiana House of Representatives; Pointe Coupée Public Schools Superintendent Samuel P. Lorio; regional businessmen and financiers Humphrey T. Olinde, Sr. and Jr.; businessman J.C. Chenevert, who served as Secretary of the State Council for Louisiana of the K. of C.; New Roads Mayor and businessman Lionel J. "Lou" Langlois; Col. Henri A. Rougon, of Austerlitz Plantation and the Louisiana State Police; Pointe Coupée Sheriff Alcide J. "Bub" Bouanchaud; Pointe Coupée Police Jury Treasurer and lay retreat pioneer Ludovic T. Patin; Louisiana Legislative Auditor J. Bradford Lancaster; financier and Poydras Fund Commissioner Joseph Jeff David; and Maringouin attorney and Louisiana Legislator Samuel J. Cashio.

In 2023, the current Grand Knight is Scott L. Smith, Jr., an attorney, theologian, prolific author, and publisher, including publisher of this volume.

After initially meeting in the upper floor of the Graugnard-Richy Building,[9] K. of C. Council 1998 purchased, in succession, two lots and buildings on the bank of False River to serve their and community purposes: the former French Hotel Building at the southeast corner of West Main and St. Mary Streets in 1926, and following that landmark's dismantling in 1944, the former residence of Dr. Marie Olivier Becnel and family, opposite Poydras High School.

While the Knights of Columbus owned and met in the former French Hotel, one of its most active members and a leader in the civic, social and spiritual life of the state, Hon. Albin Provosty, accidentally fell to his death when seated on the upper balcony railing while a dance was in progress indoors in 1932.

After sale of their second hall, the former Becnel property, the Knights contributed substantially toward the construction of the present St. Mary Hall, built in 1980, and where they continue to meet.

In early 2023, New Roads Council 1998 of the Knights of Columbus numbered 78 members, of whom seven have achieved the Fourth Degree, according to Grand Knight Scott L. Smith, Jr.

Knights of Columbus councils established elsewhere in Pointe Coupée Parish included: Morganza Council No. 2150, founded in St. Ann church parish, Morganza, in 1920; Pope Paul VI Council 8030,

---

[9] The Graugnard-Richy Building had previously housed Livonia Lodge 270 F. & A.M. during 1901-1905, and the False River Telephone Line switchboard for a few years beginning in 1906

in St. Frances Xavier Cabrini church parish. Livonia – Fordoche, 1982; and Father Louis Savouré Council 8878, Immaculate Conception church parish, Lakeland, 1985. Growing rapidly, Father Louis Savouré is the largest K. of C. council in Pointe Coupée Parish, and assisted in its work by a Ladies' Auxiliary.

FIGURE 122: CORPUS CHRISTI EUCHARISTIC PROCESSION, 2022, LED IN PART BY THE KNIGHTS OF COLUMBUS, STILL FROM A FILM PRODUCED BY KC SUPREME COUNCIL

In the year 1951, some 31 knights of New Roads Council 1998 held the highest, Fourth degree of the K. of C., according to the "Historical Sketch of New Roads Council 1998" by Charles K. Jordan, owner and editor of the *Parish Courier Journal* newspaper during 1922-1927 and Grand Knight of the Council during 1920-1925.

Thirty-four years later, in 1985, Fourth Degree Knights of the various K. of C. councils in Pointe Coupée, West Feliciana and East Feliciana Parishes formed the appropriately-named Archbishop Antoine Blanc Assembly No. 2047, Fourth Degree Knights of Columbus. It is seated at St. Mary Church in New Roads, but has met and held activities at the various churches in its territory.

Most visibly, the Fourth Degree served for several years as the honor guard for participating clergy and religious in the annual Blessing of the Boats ceremony the Sunday afternoon preceding Memorial Day on Morrison Parkway West, opposite the church.

KNIGHTS OF PETER CLAVER AND AUXILIARY

The Knights of Peter Claver and Ladies Auxiliary was founded in 1909 in Mobile, Alabama. It is the oldest and largest African American lay organization in existence, and similar in organization to the Knights of Columbus and Ladies' Auxiliaries. Men of St. Augustine church parish in New Roads were chartered as Fr. Hartnett Council No. 41 on 16 December 1923, and its Ladies Auxiliary was chartered in 1934. Both continue in spiritual and charitable ministry in the 21st century.

CATHOLIC DAUGHTERS OF THE AMERICAS

The Catholic Daughters of the Americas (C.D.A.), founded in 1903 in Utica, New York, is likened as a female counterpart of the Knights of Columbus in its charitable ministrations. Court Maria Theresa Catholic Daughters No. 849, named for the devout Habsburg Holy Roman Empress, was established at St. Mary of False River in 1923, as recorded in then-pastor Rev. John Hoes' journal.

Three years later, in 1927, the Catholic Daughters, under their Grand Regent, Mrs. Hilary Vignes (née Elise Guérin), successfully worked to collect the $500 required for the installation of electric Gothic lanterns in the church. Fr. Hoes' journal attests that they staged a play, parties and raffles and contributed their own funds to the project.

This C.D.A. court was apparently short-lived, as it was not mentioned among the active parish societies in the subsequent, 1935, Parochial Visitation Report.

Nearly a century later, in 2022, during the pastorate of Rev. Christopher Decker, more than 50 of the faithful were chartered as St. Mary Court No. 2782 of the Catholic Daughters of the Americas,

FIGURE 123: CATHOLIC DAUGHTERS OF AMERICA, INDUCTION CEREMONY, 9 OCTOBER 2022

thus reviving a timeless charitable ministry in a significantly-changed world. By early 2023, some 75 ladies were members of the court, headed by Regent Megan "Meg" Moore of Baton Rouge.

Among the expressed goals of the local Catholic Daughters in 2023 was the establishment of a chapter of the universal Children of Mary apostolate, at St. Mary of False River, thus providing a base for spiritual formation through the ages.

Court Maria Isabella No. 809, Catholic Daughters of the Americas, named for the pious Queen of Spain and Servant of God, was founded on 20 May 1923 in St. Ann church parish, Morganza, with Mrs. Robert C. Dawson, née Dionysia De La Cruz, as first Grand Regent. The organization observed its 100th year of continuous ministry in the year 2023, as one of the oldest ladies' organizations in Pointe Coupée Parish.

HOLY NAME SOCIETY (H.N.S.)

One of the oldest universal associations of the faithful, the Confraternity of the Most Holy Name of God and Jesus, was founded in the 13th century by Dominican friars in Europe to counter blasphemy and oaths. Commonly known as the Society of the Holy Name Society or Holy Name Society (H.N.S.), the devotional apostolate numbered 500,000 male faithful in the United States alone by the early 20th century. The St. Mary Church Holy Name Society was chartered in 1936, under

FIGURE 124: BLESSING OF THE NEW STANDARD OF THE HOLY NAME SOCIETY, 23 APRIL 2023

the umbrella of the New Orleans Archdiocesan Union of Holy Name Societies, and counted 30-50 members during its history. One of its lasts documented undertakings was as coordinating committee for Rev. J.W.A. Janssen's retirement celebration in 1962.

The Holy Name Society, like several other Church societies, dwindled into discontinuance in the Vatican II era, but was reactivated under its original charter, with 18 male and female "disciples" or members, in 2022 during the vibrant pastorate of Fr. Decker. In early 2023, the chapter counted 28 members and three novices, and with the author serving as its re-activator.

SODALITIES AND OTHER ORGANIZATIONS

The League of the Sacred Heart originated through the Apostleship of Prayer which was founded in France in 1844 by Francois X. Gautrelet. It established a chapter at St. Mary of False River in 1921, under Rev. Francois J. Baissac, who was then serving the parish during Fr. Hoes' sojourn in Europe. The Sacred Heart League was last mentioned as being active at St. Mary in the Parochial Visitation report of 1948, when it was listed as having 89 members.

Also active during the pastorates of Revs. John Hoes and J.W.A. Janssen were the Sodality of the Blessed Virgin Mary for young ladies, active during the 1935 Parochial Visitation; the Society for the Propagation of the Faith; and the American Council of Catholic Women (A.C.C.W.), all listed in the Parochial Visitation of 1948; and the American Council of Catholic Men (A.C.C.M.), listed in the 1954 Visitation report.

Of the above-mentioned lay organizations, the Sodality of the Blessed Virgin Mary was for years the largest, having chapters at St. Joseph Academy and public Poydras High School, and a total of 143 members at the time of the 1948 Parochial Visitation. A decade later, however, the report of 1958 indicated that the apostolate had "died out" in the parish.

Since the inactivity of the Propagation of the Faith and the Sacred Heart League as established chapters at St. Mary, many of the faithful of it and sister parishes have been members of these movements on an individual basis. Similarly, the St. Jude League, founded in 1929 by the Claretian Fathers in honor of St. Jude Thaddeus and in support of their missionary work, has counted several individual members in St. Mary, church parish, owing to generations of local devotion to the "Patron Saint of the Impossible."

The Catholic Youth Organization (C.Y.O.) was introduced at St. Mary under Rev. Joseph B. Pooley, who was named Associate Pastor in 1952, but disbanded upon his transfer to another Archdiocesan assignment in 1955. The C.Y.O. movement was revived at St. Mary in the mid-1960s and active into the 1980s. Its mission was continued for years thereafter by the homegrown St. Mary Youth Group.

A local organization, the St. Mary Study Group, was founded in 1940 as a work of the A.C.C.W. Ladies of the parish. They were formed into four groups which met periodically for the purposes of study, social activity and community service. Through an article in the 2 October 1941 *Pointe Coupée Banner*, the Study Group cordially invited interested parties to join.

NEW ORGANIZATIONS

Among the newest organizations at St. Mary is the international Guild of St. Stephen, for altar servers, established in London in 1904. The local chapter was established by Rev. Decker in the apostolate-active year of 2022. At Easter 2023, of the 34 altar servers at St. Mary—men, boys and girls—16 were enrolled in the Guild.

In addition to the formal organizations listed above, a number of St. Mary parishioners have been active in Catholic Charismatic sharing groups, the Men of St. Mary's and similar Bible study and prayer groups which meet periodically, and Supper and Substance dinners with guest speakers. Some of the prayer groups originated as Lenten devotional circles at the turn of the 20th and 21st centuries, and their members elected to continue meeting through the calendar year.

Many New Roads area Catholics hold annual America Needs Fatima public Rosary rallies in October; participate in March for Life rallies; and make the "Passionate Walk With Christ" along False River between St. Mary Church in New Roads and Immaculate Conception in Lakeland, praying the Rosary and guiding a large cross on wheels each Good Friday.

Men and women have for decades received the blessing of directed and group retreats by clergy, religious and qualified laypersons. Many of the males have been among the "Men of Manresa," making annual retreats at the Jesuit Fathers' Manresa Retreat House on the former Jefferson College Campus at Convent, St. James Parish, Louisiana.

Ludovic T. Patin, longtime Secretary of the Pointe Coupée Parish Police Jury and accountant of Southern Cotton Oil mill in New Roads, was one of the most dedicated laymen in St. Mary Church history. A pioneer in the retreat movement, Mr. "Do Vic" was for generations, the captain of retreatants from St. Mary and adjacent church parishes who attended annual retreats at Manresa.

LUDOVIC PATIN

Figure 125: Model Layman and Manresa Retreat Captain, Ludovic Patin

INVESTED LAITY

Several Pointe Coupée Catholics of late 20th and 21st centuries were recognized for service to Church and community by investiture in Catholic and dynastic orders of merit and charitable chivalry. These included: the Pontifical Equestrian Order of St. Gregory the Great (bestowed by the Holy Father), the Equestrian Order of the Holy Sepulchre of Jerusalem (Holy See), the Royal Brotherhood of the Order of Saint Michael of the Wing (House of Bragança), and Military and Hospitaller Order of Saint Lazarus of Jerusalem (Melkite Patriarchal).

The most decorated native Pointe Coupéean was U.S. Congresswoman and Ambassador to the Holy See Corinne "Lindy" Claiborne Boggs. Hon. Dame Boggs was, while a resident of New Orleans and Washington, D.C., invested in five orders: the Order of Pius IX (or Pian Order, awarded by the reigning Pope), Order of the Holy Sepulchre, Order of Malta, Constantinian Order of St. George (presented by the Borbone House), and the Order of St. Lazarus. As a lay tertiary, she was a Redemptorist Oblate.

SECULAR LAY ORGANIZATIONS

The Knights of Honor (K. of H.) was founded in Kentucky in 1873 as a non-sectarian national organization offering insurance to its members, By the time its 10th anniversary, a lodge had been established in Pointe Coupée Parish. The 14 July 1883 *Pointe Coupée Banner* included a statement commemorating the 10th anniversary of the founding of the Knights, submitted by Waterloo Lodge No. 2628 K. of H. and signed by R. (Rosélius) Pourciau, who held the office of "Dictator," and L. (Lewis) Lindsly, the Secretary.

As the Knights of Honor continued to expand, Special Deputy A. A. Achée visited New Roads on the *Banner* press day of 13 June 1903, to determine interest in establishing a lodge in New Roads. The news item telling of such stated, "The Knights of Honor is a very strong fraternal organization and one of the few which the Catholic Church does not oppose."

Catholic men also joined other national organizations of a fraternal, patriotic and charitable nature active in New Roads in the late 19th and early 20th centuries, including the American Legion of Honor; Clay Camp 278 of the Woodmen of the World, who financed the Fourteenth Station of the Cross in St. Mary Church in 1915; False River Tent 165 of the Knights of the Maccabees, named for the Old Testament heroes; the Knights of Pythias; American Order of United Workmen; Chippewa Tribe 37 of the Independent Order of Red Men; and Herd 2 of the Benevolent Order of Buffaloes, the last four named being of brief duration. These organizations had predominantly Catholic membership, owing to the preponderance of the Faith in the region.

Masonic and Pythian fraternal organizations owned two of the 13-known two-story buildings featuring upper and lower galleries in 20th century New Roads, employing them for their own purposes as well as renting them out to other organizations and churches for meeting and entertainment purposes. The Livonia Lodge 270 Masonic Temple at the southeast corner of Poydras Avenue and West Second Street was built in 1905, and familiar by its castle-like turret at the corner. Its lower floor, considerably higher than the upper floor, was for decades the New Roads Opera House, scene of dramatic performances, early motion pictures, and fundraisers for St. Mary Church.

The upper floor, the Masons' meeting hall, served as temporary classroom for St. Joseph Academy students after the 1928 fire in the old school and until completion of its successor in the following year. The old Masonic Temple was replaced by the present building in 1951, incorporating materials of the old building.

The Knights of Pythias No. 56, for African American men, built a similar two-story, galleried building at the southwestern corner of Pennsylvania Avenue and the Texas & Pacific Railroad in 1907.

It was often employed for dances and other entertainments held by St. Augustine Church congregants into the 1930s.

The Sons of Columbus Society, active in New Roads during 1927-1940, was a patriotic association of men of Italian ethnicity and virtually all-Catholic in composition. A similar organization was the *Fratellanza Italiana di San Guiseppe* (Italian Fraternity of St. Joseph), seated at Valverda in southern Pointe Coupée Parish.

Catholic laywomen predominated in civic and social organizations of the early 1900s, including the Mothers Culture Club of New Roads, founded in 1914 and a periodic supporter of youth activities at St. Mary; *Les Mysterieuses*; the P.S. Circle; the Book Club; and the Reading Circle. The latter two are still in existence in the 21st century as is the Mothers Culture Club.

CATHOLICS AND FREEMASONRY

Despite at least 11 Holy Fathers' pronouncements about the incompatibility of the Church doctrine with Freemasonry, and that from 1738 until 1983 a Catholic joining a Masonic lodge incurred immediate excommunication from the Church, a number of Catholics have been members of both, into the 21st century.

In a particularly striking example, Gen. Jean Baptiste Labatut, veteran of the Battle of New Orleans and progenitor of a prominent merchant family of that city and Pointe Coupée, served in the early 19th century as Worshipful Master of Perfect Union Lodge No. 29 and a member of the 1811 Grand Consistory of Louisiana, as well as being a curator and marguillier of St. Louis Cathedral.

Moreover, in 1829, Labatut and Zenon Cavalier served as testamentary executors of the Estate of the late Fr. Antonio de Sedella, O.F.M.Cap., familiar as *Pére Antoine*, and Rector of the Cathedral.

One of Pointe Coupee Parish's most respected citizens, Alcide Bouanchaud, was also a practical Catholic and member of Livonia Lodge 270 F. & A.M., though there is little record of his activity as to the latter. Son of onetime Corporation of St. Francis marguillier and subsequent St. Mary council member Pierre Bouanchaud, Alcide was captain of the celebrated Company A or "Bouanchaud's Battery" of the Pointe Coupée Artillery Battalion. Cited for exceptional heroism in the Battle of Nashville

FIGURE 126: POPE LEO XIII WROTE INIMICA VIS (1892), AMONG THE MANY PAPAL ENCYCLICALS TO OPPOSE FREEMASONRY

in 1864, after the war the former Confederate became an agent of healing the political and social climate of the time.

Bouanchaud joined the Republican Party, to be assured of victory in his campaign for Parish Judge, explaining to former comrades that he would not have been able to help them, or the community, if he had remained in the Democrat Party of the defeated South. He likewise empowered formerly enslaved persons in new lives of their own by purchasing the former Charles Gremillion plantation on the Island of False River, divided it into nine farms and sold them exclusively to African-Americans.

Capt. Bouanchaud died on 7 August 1886, a few days shy of his 48th birthday, and his funeral was held at 5 p.m. on the following day in St. Mary Church. Bouanchaud's remains were conveyed to St. Mary Cemetery, where they were interred in the presence of the largest assembly of mourners to date, per the subsequent, 14 August *Pointe Coupée Banner*. The Livonia Lodge offered the final honors, and the following, 21 August, issue of the paper related that the lodge would "drape" its "jewels" and the members would wear badges of mourning for 30 days.

The LeBeau family was long recognized as one of the most *ultra-montane* and provided more religious vocations than any other in Pointe Coupée Parish. Nonetheless, several of the family were active Free-masons.

Second generation member Oréste LeBeau, a carpenter, brick mason and pioneer sugar planter of the Island of False River, was a member of Livonia Lodge No. 270, which was located successively at Livonia, Lakeland (where he served in the office of Tyler) and, ultimately, in New Roads.

LeBeau's burial entry in 1900, made by Rev. Louis Savouré, then pastor of old Immaculate Conception of Chenal, stated that the octogenarian had received the Last Rites of the Church, after having renounced Freemasonry, receiving First Holy Communion, and having his civil marriage (of 54 years, to Rosalie Gremillion) blessed while on his deathbed.

Interestingly, Oréste LeBeau was recorded in the St. Mary sacramental records to have been the godfather of at least two children. His ultimate embrace of the Faith may have been due to the persistence of a long-suffering wife, as Rosalie Gremillion LeBeau is documented as godmother of at least 10 godchildren.

In 1990, oral historian Murray G. LeBeau, a great-great-nephew of Oréste LeBeau, identified in a circa 1900 photograph of the Livonia Lodge membership three relatives, all False River merchants: his grandfather Charles Hazael LeBeau, a nephew of Oréste LeBeau, and a marshal in St. Mary's Corpus Christi procession of 1885; Joseph Leliot LeBeau, son of Charles Hazael, and Murray's half-uncle; and a cousin, Joseph Dano Samson.

FROM THE PEWS: ORAL HISTORY

Oral history, a valuable resource that helps fill in where the documented record cannot be found and puts a human touch to the chronicle of any institution or community, demonstrates that early Catholicism in Pointe Coupée, as in other rural communities, had its basis in the home. Before the establishments of hospitals and funeral homes, the "domestic church" was where children were born and reared and, in some instances, baptized, and where most people died and were waked prior to burial.

The home is also where the young, principally from the mother, learned the basics of the Catholic faith and a code of ethics for relationships within the family and wider community. Church attendance well into the mid-20th century was limited, principally, by those living within an hour or so ride on horseback, on an animal-drawn vehicle or on foot. Extreme weather conditions ruled out virtually any mode of transport.

HOME ALTARS AND SACRAMENTALS

Homes, then as now in many traditional families, included crucifixes, statues, holy images, and small bottles of holy water for use in daily prayer, as well as various forms of Viaticum or "sick call" sets. A fondly recalled custom was the family recitation of the Rosary between dinner and bedtime. Children, learning their first, basic prayers at home, usually recited them while kneeling with a parent immediately before bedtime.

Home altars, of varying scope and elaboration, were found in some homes, as were *pre-dieux*. False River Road saloon owner Philip D'Amico, native of Santo Stefano Quisquina, Sicily, had religious statues interspersed amongst the bottles of liquors and wines on his shelves, and in the adjacent family quarters had one of the best-known home altars. His daughters recalled him kneeling at prayer and reading the Mass for three hours each afternoon, and many of the faithful sought him for his charism of healing. The huge cross fronting the D'Amico saloon and residence was a familiar sight on False River Road for decades.

D'Amico, as did "Madam Joe" Tuminello in her downtown New Roads confectionery and apartment, and Mr. and Mrs. Mike Affronti on Poydras Avenue, often furnished St. Joseph Altars for public viewing on the hallowed 19 March feast day. They brought this tradition from their native Sicily, where the faithful who were saved from starvation in a drought offered altars of food to the needy as they had promised St. Joseph if he would successfully intercede for the sufferers.

The St. Joseph Altar tradition has continued for generations at St. Ann Church in Morganza, on a grand scale, through the San Giuseppe Ladies, many of whose ancestors were from the Sicilian seaport of Cefalú. St. Joseph Altars have been presented in recent years in Catholic Elementary School and St. Mary Parish Hall in New Roads. In addition to traditional fruits, Italian cakes and cookies, and bread loaves fashioned as lambs, sandals, monstrances and other symbols of the Faith, they inevitably include heirloom statues and holy pictures a century or more in age.

The respect for religious items was evident in early Pointe Coupée. In the legal affixing of seals to doors, windows and storage items prior to inventorying the estate of the late Claude Trénonar de Chanfret, murdered at this dinner table by his enslaved Ibo worker named LaTulipe in 1791, officials opened a door to a small room adjoining the *grand salon* (drawing room), and "seeing therein religious objects, closed the door." This may or may not be evidence of a home chapel, but clear evidence that blessed religious items in general were not assigned a monetary value as any potential sale of them would negate the blessing.

Among the rarest religious items in existence in 21st century Pointe Coupée is an exquisite porcelain figure of an angel holding a chalice while kneeling on a cloud. A touching witness to the Faith in the Parlange plantation home on False River, it dates from the early 1800s, and family tradition is that this holy water receptacle was used in baptisms on the plantation by visiting clergy of St. Francis and St. Mary. Many homes treasure heirloom family rosaries, small ivory-bound missals, Bibles, and old religious texts and hymnals. A large collection of 19th century leather-bound books in French as well as an early *Catholic Encyclopedia* were inherited by Pierre Eugéne Berthier, pioneer pharmacist and Pointe Coupée Parish Assessor, who had been reared at Chenal by Rev. Pierre Berthet. Some are inscribed, and the collection was donated to St. Mary Church circa 1990 by Berthier's granddaughter, the since-deceased Cornelia "Connie" Berthier.

THE CHURCH YEAR

Domestic life followed the Church calendar, beginning with Christmas, which was observed as a purely religious holiday, and New Year's Day being the time for receiving and exchanging small gifts. The Carnival season featured costume balls and cavalcades in New Roads and the rural eras, with organized street parades occurring as early as 1880. Lenten abstinence and fasting were generally observed, and generations of faithful have done so on every Friday and Wednesday, year 'round.

Way of the Cross devotions are noted since at least the 1870s at St. Mary, and some families attached extra practice to the Friday ceremony, including widower Henry Costello who escorted his children to the church on Fridays, three and a half miles each way, on foot, as an extra "penance."

Good Friday was observed by many as a form of deep contemplation, with neither food nor liquid, "not even coffee," as emphasized by older informants, until noon. That morning was reserved for prayer, and there was a general belief that if one gardened on the day, the earth would issue blood in sorrow for the Sacred Passion. The less devout, however, said mustard seed sown on the day were most likely to succeed.

Easter Sunday, and curiously, for some, Good Friday, was the day to wear new clothing to church, and children brought their decorated eggs to church on Easter Sunday, engaging in the *toquer* or egg-knocking play combat on the St. Mary parvis.

The faithful observed the Marian feasts of 15 August and 8 December at Holy Mass, though non-churchgoing men traditionally began the hay harvest on Assumption Day, St. Mary's patronal feast.

RECOLLECTIONS OF MURRAY LeBEAU AND CONTEMPORARIES

Pointe Coupée Parish's most familiar oral historian of the 20th century, Murray G. LeBeau, of False River Road, was born in 1909, and the source of considerable information regarding the community and Church of the early 1900s, particularly during the pastorates of Revs. Alfred Bacciochi and John Hoes at St. Mary of False River. Interviewed in 1990 by this author, LeBeau began with memories that demonstrated the importance of practical faith in the home:

> Each house had prayer beads, holy water in a little bottle, candles, and Christ on the Cross [i.e., a crucifix or holy image] … In those times religion was in the home because people couldn't get to church easily. There was little transportation. Baptism, confirmation, marriage and burial was in the church, though.

Regarding the familiar rite of receiving blessed palm fronds at Palm Sunday Mass, LeBeau and contemporaries recalled that attendees often brought their own palms, or the more readily available magnolia leaves, for the blessing. Though blessed candles could, and still can be, obtained from churches, it was the blessed leaves that the faithful at home burned while praying for deliverance during times of severe weather.

LeBeau pointed out how the pastor was usually viewed as the "father" of the community, stating, "You know, the priest was often the most educated man in the community. People went to him with family problems for advice."

Regarding family roles in religious instruction and Mass attendance, he continued:

> It was the women who taught their children the religion. On False River, few men went to church. It was the women… The Samson men at Poulailler [Patin Dyke Road] were very religious…. Father Hoes said it was a strange thing: all the men from Poulailler went to church, but the men from False River didn't go to church!

LeBeau recalled as particularly devout citizens of Patin Dyke Road the brothers Albin and Ernest Samson, who married, respectively sisters Bernadette and Laure Langlois. The ladies, whose mother, Laure Pourciau Langlois died and was entombed in St. Mary Cemetery during the 1882 flood, as related elsewhere in this work, vended Langlois' Cure for Dysentery and other herbal medicines in the tradition of their octogenarian paternal grandfather, Zenon Langlois. The latter, who married Dometilde Robillard, a daughter of St. Mary Church donor Marie Pourciau and Charles Robillard, is said to have learned of the healing properties of certain indigenous plant forms from the Native Americans of the parish at the turn of the 18th-19th centuries.

A striking exception to the rule of False River men being non-churchgoers, Paulin George, who lived on the riverbank opposite present-day Fairfield Avenue, was recalled by Murray LeBeau by the nickname "*Bon Dieu*," French for "the Good Lord." LeBeau remembered him to always being dressed in black, and to have gone to St. Mary Church for Mass in a black buggy drawn by a black horse. Mr. George spoke of *le Bon Dieu* so frequently in regular conversation that neighbors called him "Bon Dieu."

About church attendance in general, LeBeau stated:

> Phillip D'Amico used a jersey wagon to bring his family to church…. Old Raoul Langlois, closer to New Roads, was one of the last people to use a buggy. I remember him taking his family to church by buggy […]

It took people on False River about an hour to walk to church. Most people didn't have the [transportation] means to go to church. All along St. Mary Street were hitching ranks for the people from the country who went to church by buggy. The people in town walked to church. People with big families took turns going to church in the family buggy. The boys could go on horseback. Later, old man Phillip Jarreau had a big moss truck. During Lent, he would put seats in it and pick up people to go to Way of the Cross in New Roads.

There was always an early, early Mass and a later, High, Mass on Sundays. Father Hoes would keep people long at High Mass, usually because of a long letter from the archbishop, which was read after Mass, maybe five pages long that he could have summed up in a few sentences!

It was a custom for the men and women to stand on opposite sides, out in front of church, and talk before Mass started. Father Hoes didn't like that. He wanted them to go directly into church, even though most of them had reserved pews.

As regards seating, Murray LeBeau's lifelong neighbors on False River Road, Joseph, Sr. and Inez Aguillard Costello, related that most pews were rented annually by heads of families and, therefore, reserved for their use. However, if the pew was unoccupied, the general public was allowed to sit there. A few pews at the extreme rear of church were reserved by the pastors for persons unable to pay pew rents, and they were occupied on a first-come first-occupied basis. Mrs. Costello recalled that some mothers who brought their infants to church discretely nursed them in these "public" pews.

With the discontinuance of pew rentals in the 1950s, a box was installed inside, near the entrance into the nave, into which worshippers could deposit voluntary sums for the privilege of seating, Mr. Costello stated. This custom, however, was discontinued during the time of the Vatican II reforms, and seating open without discrimination, except in times of special ceremonies, in which participants sit in pews nearest the altar which are for the occasion marked off by ropes and "Reserved" signs.

The late Cornelia "Connie" Berthier, in 1987, recalled from the 1940s and 1950s that many of the males who went to church on Sundays often left during Holy Mass to smoke outdoors; stood in the main entrance, then closed off from the nave by swinging double doors, installed by Rev. J.W.A. Janssen; or never went into church at all, but stood outdoors or waited in their parked automobiles for their families attending Mass.

Ms. Berthier likewise recalled that at Christmas Midnight Mass and on the vigil of the Feast of the Circumcision (since renamed Solemnity of the Blessed Virgin Mary, Mother of God) on 31 December, males who had "imbibed" in the libations of seasonal festivity but managed to make it to Holy Mass sat in the curtained confessionals throughout the liturgy.

Of the 1910s and '20s, when Mass attendees donned their "Sunday best" attire, LeBeau recalled:

You know in those days, when you went to church, that's when you showed off your new clothes. My grandmother [Catherine Davisia Hurst LeBeau] came from church one Sunday morning, in the horse and buggy days, and she said to those assembled, "*J'ai vu Madame Charles Hebert. Elle avait une toilette encrasant.*" She had on a smashing outfit!

Mrs. Charles Hebert and her family lived just outside New Roads…. They had left New Roads and moved to New Orleans and she comes [sic] back to visit relatives and, naturally, she wanted to show the younger generation they moved to New Orleans and were successful. I'll never forget that!

Now, today, people go to church half-dressed, in short pants. In those days, a man didn't go to church without a suit, even in summer, hats and all. If he didn't have a suit, he didn't go to church. The women had to have gloves, good dresses, hats. If they didn't have that, but went to church, they sat in the back of church, not the front.

Their main point of assembly in those days was the church. Most of the entertainments and fairs were centered around the church, like fundraisers or dances for the church. Protestants looked down on that, but the French people didn't mind going to church early in the morning and get together in the afternoon to dance or have a party. That was a common custom. Of course, today, all of that is gone.

Glenn Morgan echoed LeBeau's memory of church attire from Morgan's childhood of the 1940s and 1950s, attesting to ladies and girls attired in dresses, stockings, gloves and either hats or veils. The males, he recalled almost universally came in suit and hat, doffing their hats upon entry and throughout Mass.

Even in the torrid months of summer, in those decades before an air conditioning system was installed in 1958, men arrived in suit or sport coats, but about the time of the homily removed them in an attempt to keep cool. An audible sound was emitted as heavily-starched skits which had adhered to the pew backs were loosed when the men stood up.

Also during liturgical celebrations of the era, Morgan recalled that the roar of large "typhoon" fans situated in the sanctuary for the benefit of clergy and servers often drowned out the celebrants' voices, and how in the days of total fast from midnight until reception of Communion, occasional thuds could be heard, as weakened female worshippers fainted, and had to be "carried out" by male attendees.

The latter situation occurred most noticeably at weddings during the hot months, Morgan continued, when the entire wedding party had fasted and were to receive the Sacrament, and bridesmaids, and occasionally brides, fainted.

All now-deceased parishioners interviewed on St. Mary church attendance of the early 1900s were unanimous in the general decorum of worshippers, who were respectfully silent in entering and exiting church, did not "look around" at others of the congregation, and participated silently either by reading the Mass prayers from missals brought from home or prayed the Rosary.

Murray LeBeau, transmitting the oral history of his elders, also spoke of St. George Chapel on the Island of False River, which administered to in the 1880s by Rev. J.P. Gutton, and in its latter years by the pastors of old Immaculate Conception Church of Chenal.

Of the little house of worship, and Immaculate Conception's most noted pastor, LeBeau stated: "Father [Louis] Savouré closed the chapel on the Island [in 1907] because he said the only people who went to Mass there were old ladies with spectacles!"

The practice of religion was, therefore, more of a female observance, though oral history, rendered in print by Roger Baudier, K.S.G. in his nearly three decades of feature articles in New Orleans' religious and secular journals.

These sources added, however, that regardless of men's church non-attendance and lack of sacramental participation, most carried a Rosary in their pockets and placed it under their pillows at night, often wore blessed medals or crosses, and fasted and abstained from meat on Fridays.

Rev. John Hoes, like his contemporary and in several instances nemesis, Rev. Louis Savouré of Chenal – Lakeland, had a loyal following of parishioners, alas his "strict" manner, and habit of "grinding his teeth," frightened many of his younger flock.

The late Mrs. Wade Lejeune of the popular Harbor Bar in the Mix community on False River, was born Alice Duvernet, one of many children of New Roads hoteliers Emile and Augustine Roy Duvernet. The elder Duvernets' first hotel was on Richy Street, likely on the second floor of the building whose lower floor housed the B. Olinde Wholesale Grocery concern. From 1909 until 1943, the Duvernet family operated the Lake View Hotel, formerly the American Legion of Honor hall and The Grand department store on the site of 113 West Main Street.

The Duvernets' hotel and the nearby French Hotel, owned by Casimir and Clotilde Gebhart Savignol, were popular with traveling salesman or "drummers," weekend visitors to the lakefront town, and hosted dinners for visiting archbishops and their retinue at Confirmation.

For years, Mr. and Mrs. Duvernet prepared a special lunch on a certain day of the week for Fr. Hoes, and their daughter, as Mrs. Lejeune, would follow in the tradition for the succession of pastors thereafter. Mrs. Lejeune recalled that it was she, as a girl, dispatched to the rectory with Fr. Hoes' weekly lunch.

She stated that she always awaited with trepidation for the prelate to answer her ring of the front door, and Hoes' greeting was always the same when he opened the door: "*Vell, vell, vell… Vut do ve have today?*"—his Dutch pronunciation of "Well, well, well…. What do we have [to eat] today?"

The late Mrs. William G. Haag, née Olinde Smith, recalled her and fellow parishioners' difficulty in understanding Fr. Hoes' accent, and following his death, looked forward to having a pastor who would speak English more clearly.

However, when his successor, Rev. J.W.A. Janssen, likewise a native of the Netherlands "opened his mouth" (i.e., began his homily, in English), a groan went up from the congregation, as he, too, had a decided accent.

RECALLING THE ST. JOSEPH SISTERS AND SCHOOLS

Another illuminating oral history session, conducted in 1995, addressed Catholic education and the Sisters of St. Joseph in early 20th century New Roads. Three St. Joseph Academy alumni, Miss Louise Laurent (identified as "Louise" in the text below), her sister Ida Laurent Schexnayder ("Ida"), and the latter's daughter Rose Marie "Posie" Schexnayder Jarreau ("Posie"), were interviewed by a fourth St. Joseph alum, Glenn Morgan ("Glenn"), and their conversation was transcribed by this author in 1997 as follows:

Ida Laurent Schexnayder: I finished [graduated] in 1931. At one point, there came a time when there were not enough students for two grades, so they combined them and I was among them. I think they had only two or three in two classes so they combined them and some students were able to skip a grade.

At this point of the conversation, Glenn Morgan explained how his artistic rendering in ink of the 1905 St. Joseph School for the Catholic school's 1979 anniversary programme was drawn from the recollections of Ida, her brother and sisters.

Ida: The [1905] school was right on the road [Richy Street]. This one burned. Then we went to school in the Masonic Hall. We had to climb a staircase to rough tables and chairs. There was a locked room where we could see light in there. We used to try to peek in to see.

The old school was shotgun [i.e., narrow but deep] style. The nuns must have lived downstairs. We were upstairs in school. They had all the grades there, but two or three grades in one room. We learned more by having more than one grade per class.

Glenn next told of the successor, 1929 St. Joseph Academy, the donation of False River planter, inventor and author Allan Wurtele, a non-Catholic, for a school library wing to the rear, a fire in bathroom facility, the enclosing of the exterior open galleries, and the dormitory on the third floor for girl boarders.

Miss Louise Laurent: In 1930, we were the first class to graduate in the new school. We had a ground basement, too.

Ida: Milton Laurent built an elevator on the stairs for Sister Stephanie [who was mobility limited]. The nuns stayed on the third floor. When the school burned, the sisters lived in [Vivian] "Vee Vee" Pourciau's house. The three people who had been in Vee Vee's house moved into Claire Cazayoux' house which was already full of people. The convent burned the day Vee Vee's mother was buried. Mr. [Ernest] "Sing" Morgan, was instrumental in getting the new building up.

I've written about my religious training ever since I started school. I started off at school, remembering most of all, Sister Stephanie chopping wood, raising chickens, milking cows and raising a garden while all the other Sisters were teaching. I think she was the most brilliant of the bunch, because she wrote beautiful poetry and was a mathematician.

They [the Sisters] were so poor when they were first here. She would have to go out on the road to beg for a few nickels to keep the school going. They might have charged $2 for tuition. Some people gave a sack of potatoes or onions, whatever they had.
Sister Stephanie used to tell me of those terrible years. She said she'd pray that God would let her
die in the night so she wouldn't have to go beg the next day; that's how hard it was.

Through the years she begged so much that when we started to have fairs, we would send Sister Stephanie out to get a calf to make hamburgers. She would come back with about 17 calves! So they sold the surplus.

Without Sister Stephanie there would have been no St. Joseph Academy. She was a Rock of Gibraltar. She was from Ireland and had very fine thoughts.

Glenn Morgan: My Aunt [Dorothy Morgan] "Dot" Jewell says that "Paw Paw Sing" [Ernest Morgan] would insist that a green cake be made for Sister Stephanie each year for her birthday. She's buried in the Sisters of St. Joseph tomb here [St. Mary Cemetery]. She is recorded as being called to the convent in Baton Rouge to show them how to do a Victory Garden.

I gather that when the Sisters first arrived in New Roads, the Becnels and Provostys arranged to keep them for a while there was talk of moving to a new house. During 1904-07, it seems as if the school was built.

Glenn then presented a drawing of a typical Créole cottage labelled "First Convent."

Glenn: I don't know where this comes from.

Ida: Me neither.

Note: Transcriber saw a copy of the image in the Sisters of St. Joseph Archives, then on Mirabeau Avenue in New Orleans, in 1995.

Ida: When Mother Frances came to New Roads, the boys started coming in greater numbers, and Leo Mougeot started a football team. Before that, it was mostly girls [enrolled]. You might have one boy in a class. We played basketball on the south side of the school. Nerida Dayries came from New Orleans where she was living with an aunt and introduced basketball to the school.

Concerning our religious instruction, we respected Mama [Marie Rodrigue Laurent] and didn't dare disobey her. She ruled with an iron hand. We went to Benediction, litanies and the Rosary every Sunday evening, regardless of the weather, and it was a least a mile to the church.

We were all teens and could have been doing other things on a Sunday afternoon, but Mama said we had to go to Benediction. For Mass, we walked almost every morning to Mass because Mama insisted.

I think religious training should start at home.

Every time we went into class or left for recess, we prayed at school. When the bell would ring, we prayed, when we went to recess, we prayed, when we came back in, we prayed, every time we went in or out of the classroom, we prayed. In October and May, the Blessed Mother's month, we would process quietly and say the Rosary.

It was prayer all the way through. We had the old blue *Baltimore Catechism*. Today, all you hear about is love, love, love as if you can do anything today and get forgiveness!

Glenn: How many Sisters were there when you were in school?

Ida: There were no lay teachers. There was only one lay teacher the year I graduated: Kate Allen. Father Hoes used to come with our report cards. We shook in our boots all the time because he was a very strict person.

Glenn: How was the building laid out?

Ida: There was no corridor, we went from room to room. The entire building could be opened up into one room. I'd say there were, maybe, three big rooms.

Louise: In the 10th and 11th grade we met in a cross room, under [i.e. instructed by] Sister Loretta. Some of the Sisters may never have gone to college.

Ida: Sister Patricia taught there, too.

Glenn: The nuns must have lived in another building.[10]

Ida: In those days, nuns were considered so sacred that you didn't even touch their habit. Today, it's different.

When we got into high school, we had a big religion book and we went deeper into religion.

Rose Marie "Posie" Schexnayder Jarreau: I think the teachers were inspirational then, just by the way they lived.

Ida: Now, almost all the teachers are lay teachers, and I'm sure they're not all Catholics.

Glenn: As early as 1816, they were writing letters, asking for someone to come teach here. There's a wonderful letter before Father [Antoine] Blanc came. We were without a pastor, even.

It's only after the Civil War, when St. Mary's was raised to a full parish, that they began to have regular religious here. All of the religious came from Europe.

Ida: Sister Dorothy was a Lanusse from New Orleans. She was a very popular figure in society before becoming a nun.

Glenn: She said, "I used to run with the best of them - the Monteleones and the Jahnckes!"

Ida: Shirley Andry, Alice and Hilda Schexnayder boarded at the school. They lived on Pointe Coupée Road and, of course, the roads were dirt. In the 1929 building there were a lot of boarders… [including] an Owens girl.

Louise: Mabel Porter [was another boarder].

Ida: Really, it's when Mother Frances came that the boys began to come, in the late '40s. Maybelle [Laurent, her sister] had just one boy in her class, C.E. Hebert [Jr.], and "Lou Lou" [i.e. Louise Laurent] had one boy.

Glenn: Did you go to church from school?

Ida: Oh yes. And when the Blessed Sacrament was exposed. We used to stay after Communion when we were children.

Another beautiful ceremony was First Communion when the little girls dressed like brides and the boys were all in white. I can remember old Mrs. [Susan] Brown [a practical nurse] go to the ceremony and think it was so beautiful she would cry.

We had a procession with flower girls who dropped rose petals in front of the First Communion class. They had gorgeous flowers, two bouquet girls, and two candle girls. The

---

[10] A two-story building immediately south

bouquet girls escorted them to Communion and the candle girls escorted them back to the pew after Communion.

Mother Gertrude, the Mother Superior, taught me in 7th grade. Mother St. John the Baptist was the Mother Superior when I graduated. Mother Gertrude died here. I remember Mother Regina before her.

Glenn: I saw the Sisters as very unworldly people who made great sacrifices. They were getting no support from the Parish [sic][11] run that school.

Ida: I remember being seven months' pregnant and going house to house on Pointe Coupée Road to collect live chickens for the fair. My oldest child, Rodney, had whooping cough. We had to raise money to keep the school going.

The [Pointe Coupée] Parish Fair was three days and we sold all three days there to raise money for the school. There were school fairs, too. It was hard work trying to keep that school open. It was $2 [monthly tuition] per person.

Glenn: It was $20 per month when I was in school [1950s].

FIGURE 127: GLENN MORGAN (RIGHT) PICTURED HERE WITH AUTHOR

---

[11] It is not known whether St. Mary church parish or Pointe Coupée Parish government was intended here.

APPENDIX: RESTING PLACES OF EARLIEST PARISHIONERS

Legend has it that the first European Pointe Coupéeans buried their dead across the Mississippi River, on the bluff upon which is now situated the town of St. Francisville, as the high ground was immune from the seasonal floods of the great river. No markers are known to have been found to substantiate this claim.

The burials from Pointe Coupée and establishment of a Spanish Capuchin Franciscan monastery on the high ground across the Mississippi from the old St. Francis churches had led to longtime oral tradition that the town of St. Francisville took its name from the Capuchin Franciscans and their patron.

PRIVATE CEMETERIES

The original St. Francis Church of Pointe Coupée was dedicated in 1738, reputedly above present-day Waterloo. It stands to reason that a burial ground would have been attached to the church. Owing to transportation difficulties, however, it is obvious that many internments were also made at homes for more than a century. A sacramental record, for example, states that George Chustz died in 1865 and was buried on his property in the present-day Frisco area.

The sacramental records of St. Mary of False River bear evidence of a private cemetery on Parlange Plantation, in which three burials were made in 1875: of two children of Jean Baptiste and Anna Barthiot, named Eugénie, age eight, on August 18, and John, age six, on 17 September; as well as Jean Baptiste Prosper III, 16-year-old son of Jean Baptiste II and Evélina Dumoulin Prosper, on 23 September.

Brandon G. Parlange, in 2016, related family oral history that the remains of those buried in this cemetery were subsequently transferred to Old Immaculate Conception Cemetery at Chenal.

Another private cemetery was that of Thomas Mix, on his first property on False River Road, owned in the year 2023 by the heirs of Dr. Bobby and Mrs. Tommie Joffrion Fulmer. Among the burials there, recorded in the sacramental records of St. Mary, was Antoinette Decuir, wife of Irenée Randall, *Créoles de couleur*, she having died in 1889.

West Baton Rouge Parish Museum caretaker Kirby Guérin, who grew up on the bank of False River, nearly opposite the former Mix property, related in the year 2020 that as an adult plowing the property for cultivation, he knew the location of the cemetery, as it was higher in elevation than the surrounding ground. Whether or not the remains of those buried there were transferred elsewhere at some time is indeterminate at present.[12]

According to his unpublished, circa 1892 manuscript of the history of the early Church in Pointe Coupée, St. Mary of False River pastor Rev. Joseph Philibert Gutton stated that the first St. Francis

---

[12] The children of the late Fulmers stated they had no knowledge of the cemetery.

Church, built in 1738, was destroyed in a storm. He did not state, nor has it been determined from other sources, if a cemetery was thereto attached.

ST. FRANCIS CEMETERY OF 1764

The second St. Francis Church was built in 1760 and stood until being dismantled in 1892. It was in what is now the bed of the Mississippi River, a quarter mile west of the old New Roads-St. Francisville ferry crossing. Much documented evidence and several illustrations survive of this church and its surrounding cemetery, the latter of which was blessed in 1764.

For nearly a century, "Old St. Francis," as the 1760 church is commonly called, served as the only official burial ground in Pointe Coupée Parish. Not until the 1850s were other cemeteries established: old Immaculate Conception Catholic at Chenal and St. Stephen's Episcopal at Williamsport.[13]

Old St. Francis was the final resting place of countless Pointe Coupéeans: French and Anglo-Saxon whites, Native Americans, African Americans, and persons of mixed ancestry. It also received the remains of the victims of the ghastly *Constitution* steamboat explosion which occurred nearby in 1817, and for whom a requiem High Mass was offered, as well as a Native American chief named Chikagon who died *en route* down the Mississippi River.

PYRAMIDAL AND WOODEN TOMBS

Some of the tombs at Old St. Francis were pyramidal in shape[14] and others were single above-ground vaults topped by identifying slabs, as evidenced in woodcuts and photographs from the 1880s. At least a few graves at Old St. Francis were topped by "wooden tombs," likely small house-like structures such as those still seen in the Istre Cemetery at Morse in Southwest Louisiana. The minutes of the *marguilliers* or wardens of St. Francis authorized one to be placed *gratis* above the grave of late altar server Nicholas Vensary in 1840.

An advertisement of the *marguilliers' Tarif* or interment fees at St. Francis effective 1842 set that for the placement of a wooden tomb at $10. That year, the wardens approved the request for exhumation of the remains of Charles Robillard and dismantling of his wooden tomb located near the front fence for reburial and erection of a new tomb in wood in the rear of the church.

The funeral register of the church for January 1849 notes on the 29th of the month that a wooden tomb was built by Henri Demouy over the grave of a child of Zenon Collins and on the following day another was built over the grave of Pamela Major, wife of Jean Pierre Major.

BURIALS UNDER CHURCH FLOOR

Sacramental entries and succession proceedings indicate that some influential citizens were buried under the floor of the Old St. Francis Church, among their number members of the Allain and Decoux families. Fees for internment beneath the church set in the above-mentioned *Tarif* of 1842 were $150 for within the area from the front door to the middle of the building and $200 from the middle to the altar.

---

[13] Above present-day Innis
[14] Owing to the contemporary interest in Ancient Egypt

Though the first St. Mary Church was built at New Roads as a mission of Old St. Francis in 1823, no attendant cemetery was established at the time. New Roads area residents continued to bury their dead at Old St. Francis until St. Mary Cemetery opened on the New Road[15] in 1865.

LOST TO THE RIVER

As much of the old "Pointe Coupée Coast" along the Mississippi was located on the recessive shore of the great river, all known colonial structures were lost - if not by other means - in the caving of the banks and resultant setbacks of levees and roads. Disastrous crevasses occurred near Old. St. Francis in 1865, 1867, 1882 and 1890, each of which spelled ruin for Pointe Coupée and numerous parishes to the south.

In his above-cited manuscript, Fr. Gutton stated that between 1865 and 1890, some six arpents[16] of land in front of the church were lost to the river, owing to caving banks and levee and road setbacks.

The 2 June 1888 *Pointe Coupée Banner* announced that a new levee – located in the rear of the aged church and cemetery – was nearing completion. It was evident that the ancient house of worship and its surrounding graves would soon fall into the river. On 27 October of that year, the *Banner* reported that the removal of bodies from Old St. Francis to St. Mary Cemetery in New Roads had begun, but that Mass would be celebrated at the old church on All Souls' Day, 2 November.

In at least one instance, an entire tomb at Old St. Francis was dismantled and moved to St. Mary's: the magnificent structure which had been erected at the front of Old St. Francis after the 1842 death of Vincent Ternant II, builder of Parlange Plantation Home. The intriguing and documented account of its move to New Roads is related elsewhere in this work, but it is noteworthy here that the death date of his father, Vincent Ternant I – 1818 – is the oldest date of Pointe Coupée Parish cemetery inscriptions.

Conditions at Old St. Francis continued to disintegrate, and on 8 February 1890 the *Banner* announced that a small, front levee recently built to protect the site, had fallen into the Mississippi and the bank was caving rapidly. Many "handsome tombs" containing the remains of pioneers of the community remained around the building, the article stated, adding that their descendants were helpless to save either church or tombs, owing to the diminished size of the congregation and its poverty.

COFFIN(S) FLOATING IN FALSE RIVER

It is likely from the time of the 1890 flood that oral traditions began of seeing a coffin or coffins from Old St. Francis Cemetery floating in False River. Late educator and oral historian Idolie Olinde David of the Island of False River, in her unpublished manuscript "Historical Sketch of Early Pointe Coupée," recalled elders of her community stating they had seen a coffin in the lake.

A few years earlier, the 15 August[17] 1885 *Pointe Coupée Banner* reported that a coffin had surfaced where a levee crew had been at work at Scott Lake. This site was adjacent to Old St. Francis, and was named for the Scott Levee, breaches in 1865, 1867 and 1882 having gouged out a crevasse channel which continued to hold water.

Paul Decoux, Magistrate of the 1st Precinct of the Fifth Ward of Pointe Coupée was summoned, and he found the coffin broken, with two-thirds of it in the water and the balance on the bank. He

---

[15] Present-day New Roads Street
[16] More than 1,100 linear feet
[17] Feast of the Assumption

was unable to ascertain an identity for the remains found therein, owing to their advanced decomposition, and he respectfully reburied it a safer distance from the lake.

NEWS ACCOUNTS OF DOOMED CEMETERY

Local as well as New Orleans newspapers ran feature articles, the latter with woodcuts of Old St. Francis Church and Cemetery, as the hallowed site caved into the Mississippi River. The city's 26 April 1891 *Daily Picayune*, in an especially long and illustrated article stated:

The old churchyard was the pride of the surrounding country, but presents to-day a very sad appearance. Many of the monuments and tombs have been removed, but some still remain. The river has destroyed the graveyard piecemeal, and there is nothing left but crumbling bricks and rubbish. The sight is a ghostly one, as in their sepulchral whiteness the tombs loom up above the waters. The bones of the dead are now being lashed and washed by the angry waves of the mighty river, and as the water recedes, they will sink deeper and deeper in the seething eddies unknown and forgotten.

The writer further commented that relatively few of the bodily remains had been removed, offering the following explanation:

Tradition tells that an epidemic of cholera visited this section of the state and that its many victims were buried in this little resting place. The events of those perilous times are still fresh in the memories of the oldest inhabitants, and although the period is quite remote the people still have a superstitious awe of the dreaded scourge. They therefore loathe to engage in the work of disentombing, and this, it is said, is one of the reasons why so few of the dead have been removed from the impending danger.

POYDRAS' REMAINS TRANSFERRED

As regards Pointe Coupée's most celebrated figure, Julien Poydras, a proposal had been made to move his remains from the front of Old St. Francis cemetery as early as 1870, according to that year's 27 August issue of the *Pointe Coupée Echo*. Apparently, no action was taken for many years, as the above-cited 26 April 1891 *Daily Picayune* article, elaborated by another in an 1903 edition of *The Gulf States Historical Magazine*, stated that his coffin had been recently moved from its original 1824 resting place next to the Ternant tomb in the front of the cemetery into the "chancel" of the doomed church, thence to a grave "without headstone or inscription" at the rear of the premises.

On 18 October 1891, the revered bones were buried beneath a slab and topped by the Poydras Monument on the campus of Poydras Academy in New Roads. In time, a tumulus or earthen mound was raised atop the grave and surmounted by the monument. Ultimately, in 1961, the tumulus was enclosed in the present octagonal vault upon which the monument stands.

Though little, if any, frame materials of the old St. Francis Church were salvageable, the bricks from abandoned and deteriorating tombs were offered for sale for months. On 3 October 1891, the *Pointe Coupée Banner* ran the first of several advertisements of 14,000 cleaned bricks for sale, at the price $6 per thousand. Buyers could contact either local brick mason Oscar Saizan or "call" at the site.

Despite the precarious conditions of the doomed cemetery, interments continued to be made there as late as 9 June 1892, when Fr. Gutton recorded the burial therein of 17-year-old Joseph Maurice.

A decade later, the rearmost part of its attendant cemetery remained, according to the 26 May 1902
New Orleans Daily Picayune:

> A little of the foundation of the ancient [1760] church yet remains in the river's caving bank, almost opposite Bayou Sara. A third, possibly, of the churchyard yet remains, but ruthless vandals have broken open the tombs and scattered the dust of the sleepers to the four winds. Some of the broken slabs bear inscriptions that were old when the nineteenth century began. In some of the tombs that are nearly a hundred years old, or quite, the metallic caskets are there, through corroded. Every one of them has been opened by ghouls in search of jewels.

Evidencing the latter, low water stage of the Mississippi River in the summer of 1903 revealed old jewelry at the cemetery location. The 12 September issue of that year's *Pointe Coupée Banner* related that Oscar Saizan, one of the last of the old families who remained in the area, discovered a pair of gold earrings, located "about twenty feet under the bank," while he was walking through the site. The *Banner* stated that the earrings were in the custody of (Chief Deputy) J.P. Gosserand and could be seen at the Sheriff's Office.

FROM OLD ST. FRANCIS TO ST. MARY

As previously noted, St. Mary Cemetery at New Roads was established in 1865. Sacramental records indicate the first burial there as being of little Amélina Olinde, on 7 February 1866. Markers in this cemetery predating 1866, therefore, are obviously those transferred from Old St. Francis Cemetery on the Mississippi. Most appear on tombs in the southwestern quadrant of the graveyard, i.e., near the corner of New Roads and East Fifth Streets. In several instances, the markers brought from Old St. Francis are located on the lateral and rear walls of the tombs. The visitor to St. Mary Cemetery in the year 2023 can note the following transfers from Old St. Francis:

On the Ternant tomb, located at the corner of the center aisle and first aisle in the northwest quadrant of the cemetery: (on the base of the since-demolished miniature sarcophagus above) Claude Vincent Ternant 1786-1842. Note: This tomb, transferred from Old St. Francis in 1888, was donated by its owners, the Parlange family, to St. Mary's Church to be used as an ossuary for remains retrieved from ruined and unclaimed tombs that were demolished by church authorities in the late 1970s. The original slabs of the Ternant tomb were removed, but bore the following inscriptions: Sainville Ternant, died 1820; Dorothée Legros, wife of Claude Vincent Ternant II, 1791-1835; Claude Vincent Ternant [I] 1757-1818, Constance Lacour, his wife, 1766-1837; Marius Claude Vincent Ternant, 1836-1861.

The present slabs, as well as those surrounding the tomb, bear the names of those whose remains were collected from condemned tombs and were transferred to the Ternant tomb after the Parlange donation. Since that time, the decorative iron fence which formerly surrounded the Ternant tomb was moved to St. Mary's Church and, in the 1980s, church authorities demolished the temple-like superstructure and ornamental miniature sarcophagus atop the burial chambers. This mutilation is lamented as one of the state's greatest architectural losses.

FIGURE 128: PHOTOGRAPHS OF THE TERNANT TOMB PRIOR TO THE DESTRUCTION
OF THE COLUMNED SUPERSTRUCTURE AND MINIATURE SARCOPHAGUS

On the Provosty tomb, on the east side of first aisle in northwest quadrant: (on three slabs on rear of tomb) Auguste Provosty 1818-1868, Elma Provosty 1845-1846, Anna Provosty 1846-1848, Valéntine Provosty 1849-1851, Auguste Provosty 1848-1873, Delphine Ledoux Provosty 1799-1838, Volma Provosty 1813-1821, Delphine Provosty 1822-1870, Adélaide Gosserand 1778-1848, Jean Laurans 1797-1849, Mathilde Laurans Provosty 1848-1879, Paul Decoux 1826-1888, Séverine Porche Labry 1823-1847, Anna Masterson Labry 1824-1859, Caroline Vignes 1800-1844, Emile Hubert 1837-1855, Otis Provosty 1880-1882, Frédéric Provosty 1887-1887, Alexandre Labry 1780-1840, Mélanie Vignes Labry 1794-1844, Emilie Labry Hubert 1812-1869, Mélanie Labry Laurans 1812-1851, Julie Labry Vamalle 1815-1880, Alexandre Labry 1819-1869, Adele Labry Decoux 1820-1864, Lucien Labry 1825-1857, Alexandrine Labry Plantevignes 1827- 1851; (on north side of tomb), Mrs. Alexandre Labry 1830-1859 and mother, Marguérite Lalla, widow of Henry Masterson, and an unmarked slab.

Vignes tomb, west side of second aisle in northwest quadrant: (on north side of tomb) Délphin Verges Vignes 1798-1853; his wife, Anna Vignes, died 1843; Pierre Alcide Bondy, no date but aged three years, 10 months; Anna Augustine Vignes 1853-1854.

Decoux-Cambre grave, east side of second aisle in southwest quadrant: twin sisters Blanche and Rose Decoux 1853-1861.

Mix tomb, east side of second aisle in southwest quadrant: Adélina Bergeron 1838-1855.

Hesley tomb, east side of second aisle in southwest quadrant: (on front of tomb) Evélina Hesley 1841- 1863; her husband, Omer Samson, 1839-1865; their children, Joseph Louis Aristide Samson 1860-1865 and Francois Mathieu Omer Samson 1859-1863; Mathieu Hesley, died 1878; Joséphine Janis 1839-1852; Joseph Eugéne Janis 1854-1863; (on north side of tomb) Eliza Hesley 1839-1844. Note: Four members of this extended family died in a single year, i.e., 1863.

Pourciau tomb, west side of second aisle in southwest quadrant: (on front) Antoine Gosserand 1770- 1834; (north side) Marie Anne Jarreau, wife of Antoine Gosserand, died 1828; (south side) Sévérin Gosserand 1801-1848 and Jacques Gosserand 1799-1853; (on rear) Joseph Boisdoré 1790-1829.

Cazayoux tomb, east side of fifth aisle in southwest quadrant: Perrine Jarreau, wife of Francois Samson, died 1829; Francois Samson II, died 1850; Virginie Gosserand, first wife of A.O. LeBeau, 1831-1853.

Samson tomb, west side of fifth aisle in southwest quadrant: St. Ville Gosserand 1807-1855, Francois Gosserand 1833-1865, Térence Samson 1798-1858, James Volsey St. Dizier 1852-1854, Auguste F. St. Dizier, died 1859.

It is apparent that other remains and markers were transferred from Old St. Francis to St. Mary Cemetery, but these the stones have been destroyed or otherwise removed through the years. Veneta De Graffenreid Morrison in her circa 1960 unpublished compilation "Catalog of Cemeteries of Pointe Coupée Parish, Louisiana," lists at least two names for whom markers no longer exist in St. Mary: Francois Lebeau, died 1847, and Cheri Anatole (Démourelle), son of Amélie Lebeau, 1847-1852. Their tomb, a relatively wide and low sepulcher located immediately south of the present Echelard tomb on the east side of the fourth aisle in the southwest quadrant, was demolished during the time of the 1970s cemetery renovation.

Of the markers not moved from Old St. Francis to St. Mary Cemetery, marble fragments may be found in the front yard of the home of Emily Merrick King on Fond de Lac Plantation, located near the Mississippi River and just southwest of the site of the colonial church and cemetery.

One grave slab from Old St. Francis found its way at some indeterminate time to the present St. Mary Church. It is like the horizontal slabs which appear atop single brick above-ground vaults in the old cemeteries of Natchitoches, Opelousas, St. Martinville, and other early communities.

Turned over upon its transfer to St. Mary, this slab's plain underneath surface served as a stepping stone for the church's northeast sacristy door.

When lifted to make way for a new sidewalk in the 1990s, the marker revealed the epitaph of Eusébie Tounoir, wife of Alexandre Leblanc de Villeneuve, whose dates were 1796-1831. Moved once again, the slab now rests beside the Ternant tomb in the church cemetery.

AT PRESENT ST. FRANCIS CHAPEL

The third St. Francis of Pointe Coupée, a mission chapel of St. Mary, was built in 1895 on land donated by Jules Labatut, at a site several miles upriver of its 1760 predecessor. The only remains and markers which appear to have been moved from Old St. Francis of Pointe Coupée to the present St. Francis Chapel grounds are those of the Labatut, Loupe, and Morrison families.

The Labatut tomb appears to have been built at the time of transfer, but the elaborate iron fence is obviously older and probably surrounded their earlier resting place at Old St. Francis. At present the only markers on the Labatut tomb are those of Mr. and Mrs. Jean Pierre Labatut. Mr. Labatut's stone, bearing the dates 1788-1827, is located in the front pediment. The marker for Mrs. Labatut, nee Euphémie Bara, bears the dates 1802-1838 and is located on the north face of the tomb. It is of the horizontal type which appears atop single brick above-ground vaults in Louisiana's old French communities as above listed.

Of the interments made at St. Francis Chapel since its 1895 construction, at least one is now under the church, owing to the building having been moved back (i.e., southward) to accommodate the building of the present levee and road. It is the grave of Mary Bouquet Ramagos, located near the front steps, according to 2019 testimony of late St. Francis sacristan Numa Loupe, Jr.

After the transfer of administration of St. Francis Chapel from St. Ann Parish to St. Mary Parish in 1962, some remains were moved to either of those parish's cemeteries, Mr. Loupe stated in 2019. He had the remains of his paternal grandmother, Elie Loupe, transferred to St. Mary Cemetery in New Roads, though the remains of Elie Loupe's mother-in-law and Numa Loupe's great-grandmother, Catherine Chardin Ybos, and other family members remain in the railed Loupe plot just southwest of St. Francis Chapel. Numa Loupe further deposed that other remains were located where the St. Francis kitchen and restroom building stands, but were transferred by family members to St. Ann Cemetery in Morganza.

AT ST. ANN

St. Ann Cemetery in Morganza contains one burial and marker that logically would have come from old St. Francis of Pointe Coupée, that of Bernard E. Dayries, 1800-1829. As St. Ann Cemetery was not established until 1918, it is most probable that Dayries' remains and marker would have been moved from old St. Francis at the time of its abandonment to Our Lady of Seven Sorrows Cemetery at New Texas Landing (established 1872), and, upon the abandonment of Seven Sorrows (circa 1940), they would have been moved to St. Ann.

TO ST. FRANCISVILLE

Remains located in the Lebret plot in Old St. Francis Cemetery were moved across the Mississippi River, to the Hearsey plot in the Catholic Cemetery of St. Francisville on 31 August 1892, according to the subsequent 3 September issue of the *Feliciana Sentinel* newspaper. The remains were identified as those of Pierre Lebret and children Stephanie, Albértine, Pierre, Jean, Periclés, Etienne and Isonne; John Lebret and mother; Mme. Francoise Martin and three children; and Albért and Annie Grisham.

From the above accounts and present-day location of burial markers, it is apparent that only 83 known persons or markers representing that number bear witness to transfer from Old St. Francis of Pointe Coupée. This is a relatively small number, indeed, since sacramental records and the 1891 *Daily Picayune* article testify to thousands of pioneers buried in the 130 years that Old St. Francis Cemetery existed. Moreover, evidence is clear that no known markers transferred to New Roads predate 1818, before which time nearly a century of lives, deaths and burials had elapsed in Pointe Coupée Parish.

BIBLIOGRAPHY

Personal Communication

Amy André
Gertie Marie Beauford
Mons. Robert Berggreen
Cornelia Berthier
Charlene E. Bonnette
Magda Lieux Bonnette
Ann Boltin
Kerry Callegan
Lisa Jarreau Chutz
Inez Aguillard Costello
Joseph Costello, Sr.
Virginia Costello
Cathie Hymel Crochet
Marguerite D'Amico
Rev. Christopher J. Decker
Mary Ann D'Amico
Denova Donald Didier

Gladys Broussard Didier
Sidney Dreyfus
Douglas Fulmer
Gene Fulmer
Donald Fuselier
Alton Gaudin
John Gauthier
Mary Guarisco
Kirby Guérin
Olinde Smith Haag
Barbara Mars Hébert
Posie Schexnayder Jarreau
Anna Lee Swindler Jewell
Patricia Lorio Langlois
Louise Laurent
Murray G. LeBeau
Numa Loupe, Jr.

Glenn C. Morgan
Humphrey T. Olinde, Jr.
Katie Oubre
Brandon G. Parlange
Lucy Brandon Parlange
Ludovic T. Patin
Renée Bergeron Richard
Jacqueline Major Saizan
Rena Schergen
Ida Laurent Schexnayder
Nora LeBlanc Serio
Amy Simone
Scott L. Smith, Jr.
Dinah Weil
Simon Dreyfus Weil
Cassandra Will

Official Records

The Bureau of Refugees, Freedmen, and Abandoned Lands, records of the Superintendent of Education, records of the Assistant Commissioner, and records of the Field Office [of New Roads, Pointe Coupée Parish, Louisiana]

Minutes, Town / City of New Roads, Louisiana, Historic Materials Collection, electronic format, Pointe Coupée Parish Library, New Roads, Louisiana

Minutes, Pointe Coupée Parish Police Jury, electronic format, Historic Materials Collection, Pointe Coupée Parish Library, New Roads, Louisiana

Minutes, Corporation of the Congregation of St. Francis Roman Catholic Church of Pointe Coupée, translated copy

Pointe Coupée Parish Clerk of Court conveyance, mortgage, incorporation, civil suit and marriage records, New Roads, Louisiana

Archdiocese of New Orleans sacramental records of baptism, marriage and burial

Diocese of Baton Rouge sacramental records of baptism, marriage and burial

French and American Claims Commission records, Library of Congress, Washington, D.C.

Parochial Visitation Reports, St. Mary Church, New Roads, Louisiana, 1919, 1923, 1935, 1948, 1954 and 1958, Catholic Diocese of Baton Rouge Archives

Sanborn Fire Insurance Maps of New Roads, Louisiana, 1905, 1907 and 1909 editions, L. Bouanchaud Insurance Collection, Historic Materials Collection, Pointe Coupée Parish Library, New Roads, Louisiana

United States Census Schedules, various

Newspapers & Journals

Annales de la Propagation de la Foi, Lyon,

France *Capitolian-Advocate*, Baton Rouge,

Louisiana *Acadiana Profile*, Lafayette,

Louisiana

Clarion Herald, New Orleans,

Louisiana *Daily Democrat*, New

Orleans, Louisiana *Daily Picayune,*

New Orleans, Louisiana *Dixie*

Magazine, New Orleans, Louisiana

Louisiana Sugar Planter and Manufacturer, New Orleans, Louisiana

Morning Star and Catholic Messenger, New Orleans, Louisiana

Démocrate de la Pointe Coupée / Pointe Coupée Democrat, New Roads, Louisiana

Pointe Coupée Banner, New Roads, Louisiana

Pointe Coupée Echo, Pointe Coupée Post Office, Louisiana

Josephite Harvest, Baltimore, Maryland

Books

Baron, Bill, editor. *Census of Pointe Coupée, 1745*, New Orleans, Louisiana: Polyanthos, Inc., 1978

Baudier, Roger, *The Catholic Church in Louisiana,* New Orleans, Louisiana, 1939

Biographical and Historical Memoirs of Louisiana, Volume II. Chicago, Illinois: The Goodspeed Publishing Company, 1892

Conrad, Glenn R., gen ed. *Cross, Crozier and Crucible: A Volume Celebrating the Bicentennial of A Catholic Diocese in Louisiana.* Archdiocese of New Orleans, in conjunction with University of Southwestern Louisiana, Center for Louisiana Studies, 1993

Costello, Brian J. *The Catholic Church in Pointe Coupée: A Faith Journey.* Marksville, Louisiana: Randy DeCuir and Associates, 1996

Costello, Brian J. *The Life, Family and Legacy of Julien Poydras.* New Roads, Louisiana: Ewing's, Inc., 2001

Costello, Brian J. *From Ternant to Parlange: A Créole Plantation Through Seven Generations*. New Roads, Louisiana: Ewing's, Inc., 2002,

Costello, Brian J. *From Porche to Labatut: Two Centuries on the Pointe Coupée Coast*. New Roads, Louisiana: Ewing's, Inc., 2002.

Costello, Brian J. *The House of Lejeune*. New Roads, Louisiana: Ewing's, Inc., 2002

Costello, Brian J. *A History of Pointe Coupée Parish Louisiana, The Murray G. LeBeau Memorial Edition*. Donaldsonville, Louisiana: Margaret Media, Inc., 2020

de Voragine, Jacobus. *The Golden Legend*. Thirteenth century Donnelly, E.C. editor. *Butler's Lives of the Saints*. New York, Cincinnati and Chicago: Benziger Brothers, 1910

Edmonds, David C. *The Guns of Port Hudson: Volume One, The River Campaign (February – May 1863)*. Lafayette, Louisiana: Acadiana Press, 1983

Eshelman-Lee, Julie. *Our Family History: A Louisiana Homecoming*. Roanoke, Indiana, 1996.

Fortier, Alcée. Louisiana: *Comprising Sketches of Counties, Towns, Events, Institutions, and Persons*. Volume II. Atlanta, Georgia: Century Historical Association, 1914

Greene, Glenn Lee. *Masonry in Louisiana*. New York, New York: Exposition Press, 1962

Hall, Gwendolyn Midlo. *Africans in Colonial Louisiana*. Baton Rouge, Louisiana: Louisiana State University Press, 1992

Haussy, André. *Du Hainaut au Mississippi*. Y. Robert, Union Europénne, 1996

Hoffman's Catholic Directory, Almanac, and Clergy Directory. Milwaukee and New York: Hoffman Bros.

Lamendola (Rev.) F.S. *The Catholic Church on the Grosse Tete Ridge*. No publisher listed, 1984.

Maduell, Charles, Jr., compiler and translator. *The Census Tables for the French Colony of Louisiana*. Baltimore, Maryland: The Genealogical Publishing Co., Inc., 1972

McWilliams, Richebourg Gaillard, translator and editor. *Iberville's Gulf Journals*. Tuscaloosa, Alabama: The University of Alabama Press, 1981

Ochs, Stephen J. *Desegregating the Altar: The Josephites and the Struggle for Black Priests, 1871-1960*. Baton Rouge, Louisiana: Louisiana State University, 1990

Paul Wilhelm, Duke of Wurttemburg *Travels in North America, 1822-1824*. Savoie Lottinville, editor. University of Oklahoma Press, 1979.

Sadlier's Catholic Directory, Almanac and Directory. New York: D. & J. Sadlier & Co.

Sanford, J.I. *Beautiful Pointe Coupée and Her Prominent Citizens*. New Orleans, Louisiana: American Printing Co., Ltd., 1906

The Roman Breviary, 1908

Thomas, LaVerne III. *LeDoux: A Pioneer Franco-American Family, With Sketches of Allied Families*. New Orleans, Louisiana: Polyanthos, Inc. 1982

War of the Rebellion: A Compilation of the Official Records of the Union and Confederate Armies. Washington, D.C.: Government Printing Office, 1880.

Winters, John D. *The Civil War in Louisiana*. Baton Rouge, Louisiana: Louisiana State University Press, 1963

Unpublished Manuscripts

David, Idolie O. "Historical Sketch of Early Pointe Coupée," 1976, copy in Historic Materials Collection, Pointe Coupée Parish Library, New Roads, Louisiana

Gutton, Joseph Philibert, untitled manuscript, circa 1892, Catholic Diocese of Baton Rouge Archives, xerox copy in Historic Materials Collection, Pointe Coupée Parish Library, New Roads, Louisiana

Jordan, Charles K., "Historical Sketch of New Roads Council 1998," circa 1951, xerox copy in Historic Materials Collection, Pointe Coupée Parish Library, New Roads, Louisiana

Lejeune, Lélia Decuir, "The Story of My Life as Far as I Can Remember," edited and copyrighted 2010 by great-granddaughter Julie Eshelman-Lee, New Roads, Louisiana

Olinde, Lillie Grace, and Mary J. Guarisco. "The History of our Parish: The Immaculate Conception of the Blessed Virgin Mary Catholic Church, Chenal – Lakeland, 1728-2010," 2020, copy in Historic Materials Collection, Pointe Coupée Parish Library, New Roads, Louisiana

"St. Mary Parish Bulletin," St. Mary of False River Church, New Roads, Louisiana, various issues

The Society of St. Joseph of the Sacred Heart. "The Josephites and the African American Community, State of Louisiana, 1897-1977," Baltimore, Maryland, 1997

Archival Correspondence

Archdiocese of New Orleans
Archdiocese of St. Louis
Diocese of Baton Rouge
University of Notre Dame

Additional Sources

Archives of the Archdiocese of New Orleans
Archives of the Diocese of Baton Rouge
Archives of Notre Dame University
Archives of the Sisters of St. Joseph, New Orleans, Louisiana
Pointe Coupée Parish Clerk of Court conveyance, mortgage, and civil suit records
Beautiful Pointe Coupée and Its Prominent Citizens by J.I. Sanford
1906 Minutes of the Marguilliers of St. Francis Church
The Guns of Port Hudson by David C. Edmonds, 1983, *Acadiana Press*
The Catholic Church in Louisiana by Roger Baudier, 1939
The Pointe Coupée Banner, official journal of Pointe Coupée Parish
New Orleans Daily Picayune
The Church on Bayou Grosse Tete by Father F. S. Lamendola
Desegregating the Altar by Stephen J. Ochs, 1990, *LSU Press*
LeDoux by LaVerne Thomas III, 1982, Polyanthos, Inc.
Cross, Crozier and Crucible, edited by Glenn R. Conrad, et al., 1993, Center for Louisiana Studies
Church histories and directories of St. Ann, St. Augustine, and St. Frances Xavier Cabrini church parishes

INDEX

ABOUT THE AUTHOR

BRIAN J. COSTELLO
KCHS, RISMA, SRI

Brian James Costello is an 11th generation Pointe Coupeean and a lay tertiary of the Mercedarian Order. He is a graduate of Louisiana State University; the author of 28 titles in Louisiana, European and spiritual studies; and founding historian of the Pointe Coupee Parish Library Historic Materials Collection. He has been a resource and active in international media in his areas of study for more than 35 years. Costello is a Knight Commander of the Equestrian Order of the Holy Sepulchre, Knight of the Order of St. Michael of the Wing, and Knight of the Association of the Nobility of the Holy Romain. A member of more than a dozen devotional and charitable apostolates, he is founding representative of Louisiana Centre 43 of St. Philomena Devotion, reactivator of St. Mary Church Holy Name Society, and an associate in the cause of Bl. Karl of Austria.

ABOUT THE PUBLISHER

SCOTT L. SMITH, JR.
J.D., M.T.S.

Scott L. Smith, Jr. is a Catholic author, attorney, theologian, publisher, and 13th generation Pointe Coupeean. He and his wife Ashton are the parents of six wild-eyed children and live in their hometown of New Roads, Louisiana.

Smith is currently serving as the Grand Knight of his local Knights of Columbus council, co-host of the Catholic Nerds Podcast, and the board of the Men of the Immaculata. Smith has served as a minister and teacher far and wide: from Angola, Louisiana's maximum-security prison, to the slums of Kibera, Kenya.

Smith's books include *Consecration to St. Joseph for Children & Families*, which he co-authored with Fr. Donald Calloway, *Pray the Rosary with St. Pope John Paul II*, *The Catholic ManBook*, *Lord of the Rings & the Eucharist,* among other titles. His fiction includes *The Seventh Word* and the *Cajun Zombie Chronicles*, horror novels set in New Roads, Louisiana.

Scott regularly contributes to his blog, "The Scott Smith Blog" at www.thescottsmithblog.com, winner of the Fisher's Net Award for Best Catholic Blog. Scott's other books can be found at the Holy Water Books website, holywaterbooks.com, as well as on Amazon.

ANOTHER COLLABORATION BETWEEN BRIAN J. COSTELLO & SCOTT L. SMITH, JR.:

BLESSED IS HE WHO ... MODELS OF CATHOLIC MANHOOD

BIOGRAPHIES OF CATHOLIC BLESSEDS

You are the average of the five people you spend the most time with, so spend more time with the Saints! Here are several men that you need to get to know whatever your age or station in life. These short biographies will give you an insight into how to live better, however you're living.

From Kings to computer nerds, old married couples to single teenagers, these men gave us extraordinary examples of holiness:

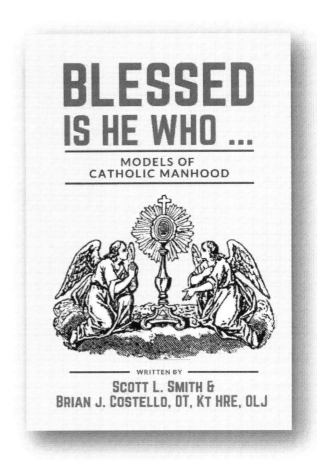

- Pier Giorgio Frassati & Carlo Acutis – Here are two extraordinary **young men**, an athlete and a computer nerd, living on either side of the 20th Century
- Two men of royal stock, Francesco II and Archduke Eu-gen, lived lives of holiness despite all the world conspiring against them.
- There's also the **simple husband and father**, Blessed Luigi. Though he wasn't a king, he can help all of us treat the women in our lives as queens.

Blessed Is He Who ... Models of Catholic Manhood explores the lives of six men who found their greatness in Christ and His Bride, the Church. In six succinct chapters, the authors, noted historian Brian J. Costello and theologian and attorney Scott L. Smith, share with you the uncommon lives of exceptional men who will one day be numbered among the Saints of Heaven, men who can bring all of us closer to sainthood.

CLASSIC CATHOLIC REPRINTS & NEW TRANSLATIONS

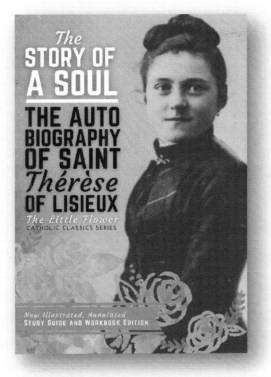

THE STORY OF A SOUL, THE AUTOBIOGRAPHY OF SAINT THERESE OF LISIEUX: NEW ILLUSTRATED, ANNOTATED STUDY GUIDE AND WORKBOOK EDITION

One of the most popular biographies, not just saint biographies, of ALL TIME. Saint Thérèse, one of the most beautiful souls of modern times, also gave us the most beautiful spiritualities of modern times: the "Little Way" of the "little flower" of Jesus.

Read this with your Catholic book group. This edition features additional sections with study questions to help your group dig into the spiritual wisdom of the Little Flower.

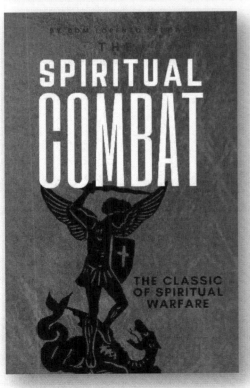

THE SPIRITUAL COMBAT: THE CLASSIC MANUAL ON SPIRITUAL WARFARE, BY DOM LORENZO SCUPOLI

St. Francis de Sales always carried this book in his pocket! The Spiritual Combat is the classic manual of spiritual warfare. Its wisdom has helped form the souls of the Church's greatest saints. Now this book can do the same thing for you. It's no longer fashionable to speak about the realities of the devil and demons, and so the world has become more vulnerable than ever before. The Christian life is a battle between God and the forces of darkness.

This is the *Art of War* for the Christian. Pick up your sword and fight! Here, Father Lorenzo Scupoli helps guide you through this spiritual battle, so that you can win - decisively - the war for your soul. Pick up the sword of prayer and conquer the evil which afflicts you, and through you, your family, your friends, and the world. Don't go into battle alone. Go with Christ and this classic combat manual.

THE SEVEN LAST WORDS SPOKEN FROM THE CROSS BY ST. ROBERT BELLARMINE S.J.

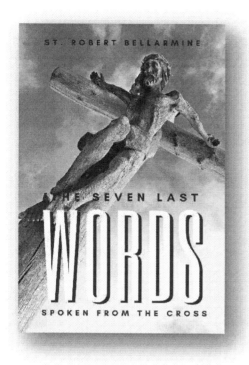

Come, sit at the foot of the Cross!

These seven words were the "last sermon" of the Savior of the World. Jesus' words from the Cross contain everything that the prophets foretold about His preaching, suffering, and miracles.

The Seven Last Words Spoken from the Cross is a powerful reflection on the final words of Jesus Christ. The author, St. Robert Bellarmine, was a major figure in the Catholic Counter-Reformation and his insights are as profound now as ever, perhaps more than ever.

Deepen the Way of the Cross! Use Bellarmine's contemplations of Christ's words to enrich your Lenten journey to Good Friday and Easter. The Seven Last Words Spoken from the Cross is a wealth of insights for the whole of the Christian life, which points always to Christ, who was lifted up on the Cross so "that everyone who believes in Him may have eternal life."

ST. LOUIS DE MONTFORT'S TOTAL CONSECRATION TO JESUS THROUGH MARY: NEW, DAY-BY-DAY, EASIER-TO-READ TRANSLATION

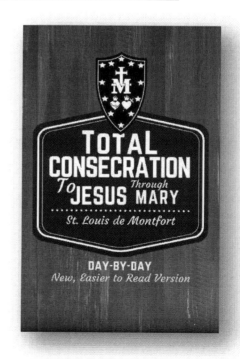

Featured on HALLOW, the #1 Catholic Prayer App and narrated by Sister Miriam Heidland!

Popes and Saints have called this single greatest book of Marian spirituality ever written. In a newly translated day-by-day format, follow St. Louis de Montfort's classic work on the spiritual way to Jesus Christ though the Blessed Virgin Mary.

Beloved by countless souls, this book sums up, not just the majesty of the Blessed Mother, but the entire Christian life. St. Louis de Montfort calls this the "short, easy, secure, and perfect" path to Christ. It is the way chosen by Jesus, Himself.

CATHOLIC PRAYER JOURNALS FROM HOLY WATER BOOKS

Holy Water Books has published a series of prayer journals, including *The Pray, Hope, & Don't Worry Prayer Journal to Overcome Stress and Anxiety.*

PRAY, HOPE, & DON'T WORRY: CATHOLIC PRAYER JOURNAL FOR WOMEN

Daily Bible verses and quotes from the Saints to reflect on. Use the prayer journal either as a 52-day or 52-week retreat to overcome stress and worry.

There is also a separate edition for women of other Christian faiths: *Pray, Hope, & Don't Worry Women's Prayer Journal For Overcoming Anxiety: A 52-week Guided Devotional of Prayers & Bible Verses to Conquer Stress & Fear.*

PRAYER JOURNAL FOR CATHOLIC HOMESCHOOLING MOMS: A 52-WEEK GUIDED DEVOTIONAL WITH SCRIPTURE, THE SAINTS, AND FELLOW CHRISTIANS TOWARDS PEACE, PURPOSE, AND CLARITY

Using a similar 52-day or 52-week format as the *Pray, Hope, and Don't Worry* Prayer Journal above, this journal was created by Mary Nadeau Reed specifically for Catholic homeschooling moms.

ROSARY DEVOTIONALS FROM HOLY WATER BOOKS:

PRAY THE ROSARY WITH ST. JOHN PAUL II

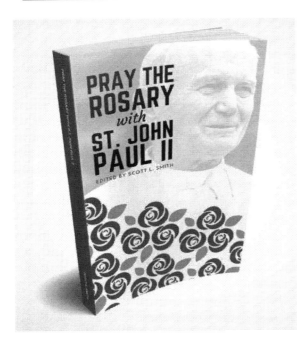

St. John Paul II said "the Rosary is my favorite prayer." So what could possibly make praying the Rosary even better? Praying the Rosary with St. John Paul II!

This book includes a reflection from John Paul II for every mystery of the Rosary. You will find John Paul II's biblical reflections on the twenty mysteries of the Rosary that provide practical insights to help you not only understand the twenty mysteries but also live them.

St. John Paul II said "The Rosary is my favorite prayer. A marvelous prayer! Marvelous in its simplicity and its depth. In the prayer we repeat many times the words that the Virgin Mary heard from the Archangel, and from her kinswoman Elizabeth."

St. John Paul II said "the Rosary is the storehouse of countless blessings." In this new book, he will help you dig even deeper into the treasures contained within the Rosary.

You will also learn St. John Paul II's spirituality of the Rosary: "To pray the Rosary is to hand over our burdens to the merciful hearts of Christ and His mother." "The Rosary, though clearly Marian in character, is at heart a Christ-centered prayer. It has all the depth of the gospel message in its entirety. It is an echo of the prayer of Mary, her perennial Magnificat for the work of the redemptive Incarnation which began in her virginal womb." **Take the Rosary to a whole new level with St. John Paul the Great! St. John Paul II,** *pray for us!*

PRAY THE ROSARY WITH BLESSED ANNE CATHERINE EMMERICH

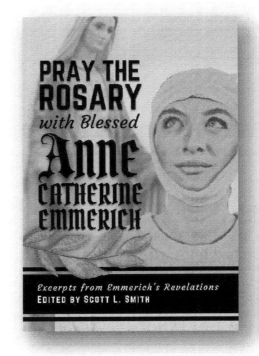

Pray the Rosary like never before! Enter into the mysteries of the Rosary through the eyes of the famous 19th-century Catholic mystic: Blessed Anne Catherine Emmerich.

Incredibly, God gave this nun the special privilege of beholding innumerable Biblical events from Creation to Christ's Passion and beyond. You may have already seen many of her visions, as depicted in the 2004 film The Passion of the Christ.

Never before have Emmerich's revelations been collected in a single volume to help you pray the Rosary. Emmerich was able to describe the events of the Rosary in intimate, exquisite detail. Adding depth and texture to the Gospel accounts, these passages will greatly enhance your experience of the meditations of the Rosary. Enjoy!

PRAYER LIKE A WARRIOR: SPIRITUAL COMBAT & WAR ROOM PRAYER GUIDE

Don't get caught unarmed! Develop your Prayer Room Strategy and Battle Plan.

An invisible war rages around you. Something or someone is attacking you, unseen, unheard, yet felt throughout every aspect of your life. An army of demons under the banner of Satan has a singular focus: your destruction and that of everyone you know and love.

You need to protect your soul, your heart, your mind, your marriage, your children, your relationships, your resolve, your dreams, and your destiny.

Do you want to be a Prayer Warrior, but don't know where to start? The Devil's battle plan depends on catching you unarmed and unaware. If you're tired of being pushed around and wrecked by sin and distraction, this book is for you.

Do you feel uncomfortable speaking to God? Do you struggle with distractions in the presence of Almighty God? Praying to God may feel foreign, tedious, or like a ritual, and is He really listening? What if He never hears, never responds? This book will show you that God always listens and always answers.

In this book, you will learn how to prayer effectively no matter where you are mentally, what your needs are, or how you are feeling:

- Prayers when angry or your heart is troubled
- Prayers for fear, stress, and hopelessness
- Prayers to overcome pride, unforgiveness, and bitterness
- Prayers for rescue and shelter

Or are you looking to upgrade your prayer life? This book is for you, too. You already know that a prayer war room is a powerful weapon in spiritual warfare. Prepare for God to pour out blessings on your life.

Our broken world and broken souls need the prayers and direction found in this book. Don't waste time fumbling through your prayer life. Pray more strategically when you have a War Room Battle Plan. Jesus showed His disciples how to pray and He wants to show you how to pray, too.

MATERIALS FOR THE CATHOLIC NERD IN ALL OF US:

CATHOLIC NERDS PODCAST

As you might have noticed, Scott is well-credentialed as a nerd. Check out Scott's podcast: the Catholic Nerds Podcast on iTunes, Spotify, Google Play, and wherever good podcasts are found!

THE THEOLOGY OF SCI-FI: THE CHRISTIAN'S COMPANION TO THE GALAXY

NOW ALSO AN AUDIOBOOK! Fold space using the spice mélange and travel from "a long time ago in a galaxy far, far away" to the planet Krypton, from Trantor to Terminus, and back to the scorched skies of earth.

Did you know there is a Virgin Birth at the core of *Star Wars*? A Jewish Messiah of *Dune*? A Holy Family in *Superman*? A Jesus and Judas in *The Matrix*? And the Catholic Church is Asimov's *Foundation*?

This book covers a lot of territory. It spans galaxies and universes. Nevertheless, the great expanse of human imagination will forever be captivated by the events of the little town of Bethlehem.

There is a reason that all of mankind's stories overlap, coincide, correlate, and copy. Like it or not, all mankind bears the same indelible stamp, the mark of Christ. Why should there be a singular story binding us all? Unless we are truly all bound as one human family. At the core of the Monomyth is not another myth, a neat coincidence, but a reality—the reality of Jesus Christ.

At the heart of the Monomyth is a man, a very real man. The God-Man. The source and summit of all hero stories and myths ever told, both before and after those short 33 years in First Century Israel.

LORD OF THE RINGS & THE EUCHARIST

NOW AN __AUDIOBOOK!__

What is "the one great thing to love on earth", according to J. R. R. Tolkien, the author of The Lord of the Rings? The Eucharist! Tolkien made sure his one great love was woven throughout his books. It's easy to find if you know where to look. In Smith's new book, find Tolkien's hidden Eucharist!

The Lord of the Rings can't be fully understood without understanding its hidden Eucharistic significance. What's more, perhaps: J. R. R. Tolkien can't be fully understood apart from his Catholic identity and his devotion to the Eucharist.

Are you ready to read Lord of the Rings like you never have before?

WHAT YOU NEED TO KNOW ABOUT MARY BUT WERE NEVER TAUGHT

NOW AN __AUDIOBOOK!__

Give a robust defense of the Blessed Mother using Scripture. Now, more than ever, every Catholic needs to learn how to defend their mother, the Blessed Mother. Because now, more than ever, the family is under attack and needs its Mother.

Discover the love story, hidden within the whole of Scripture, of the Father for his daughter, the Holy Spirit for his spouse, and the Son for his MOTHER.

This collection of essays and the All Saints University course made to accompany it will demonstrate through Scripture how the Immaculate Conception of Mary was prophesied in Genesis.

It will also show how the Virgin Mary is the New Eve, the New Ark, and the New Queen of Israel.

THE CATHOLIC MANBOOK

Do you want to reach Catholic Man LEVEL: EXPERT? *The Catholic ManBook* is your handbook to achieving Sainthood, manly Sainthood. Find the following resources inside, plus many others:

- Top Catholic Apps, Websites, and Blogs
- Everything you need to pray the Rosary
- The Most Effective Daily Prayers & Novenas, including the Emergency Novena
- Going to Confession and Eucharistic Adoration like a boss!
- Mastering the Catholic Liturgical Calendar

The Catholic ManBook contains the collective wisdom of The Men of the Immaculata, of saints, priests and laymen, fathers and sons, single and married. Holiness is at your fingertips. Get your copy today.

This edition also includes a revised and updated St. Louis de Montfort Marian consecration. Follow the prayers in a day-by-day format.

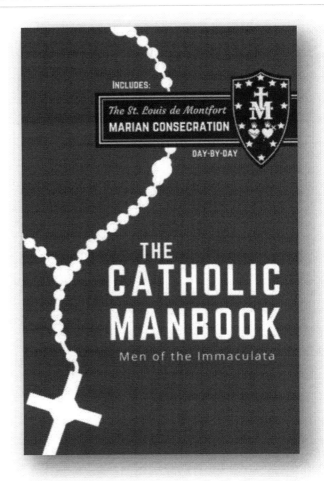

EVER HEARD OF CATHOLIC HORROR NOVELS?

It's time to evangelize *all* readers …

THE SEVENTH WORD

The FIRST Pro-Life Horror Novel!

Pro-Life hero, Abby Johnson, called it "legit scary … I don't like reading this as night! … It was good, it was so good … it was terrifying, but good."

The First Word came with Cain, who killed the first child of man. The Third Word was Pharaoh's instruction to the midwives. The Fifth Word was carried from Herod to Bethlehem. One of the Lost Words dwelt among the Aztecs and hungered after their children.

Evil hides behind starched white masks. The ancient Aztec demon now conducts his affairs in the sterile environment of corporate medical facilities. An insatiable hunger draws the demon to a sleepy Louisiana hamlet.

There, it contracts the services of a young attorney, Jim David, whose unborn child is the ultimate object of the demon's designs. Monsignor, a mysterious priest of unknown age and origin, labors unseen to save the soul of a small town hidden deep within Louisiana's plantation country, nearly forgotten in a bend of the Mississippi River. *You'll be gripped from start to heart-stopping finish in this page-turning thriller.* With roots in Bram Stoker's Dracula, this horror novel reads like Stephen King's classic stories of towns being slowly devoured by an unseen evil and the people who unite against it. The book is set in southern Louisiana, an area the author brings to life with compelling detail based on his local knowledge.

THE CAJUN ZOMBIE CHRONICLES
THE CATHOLIC ZOMBIE APOCALYPSE!

257

THANKS FOR READING!
TOTUS TUUS